Hiking Waterfalls Maine

Hiking Waterfalls Maine

A Guide to the State's Best Waterfall Hikes

Greg Westrich

FALCONGUIDES

GUILFORD, CONNECTICUT

An imprint of The Rowman & Littlefield Publishing Group, Inc.
4501 Forbes Blvd., Ste. 200
Lanham, MD 20706
www.rowman.com
Falcon and FalconGuides are registered trademarks and Make Adventure Your Story is a trademark of The Rowman & Littlefield Publishing Group, Inc.

Distributed by NATIONAL BOOK NETWORK

Photos by Greg Westrich unless otherwise noted
Maps by The Rowman & Littlefield Publishing Group, Inc.

British Library Cataloguing in Publication Information available

Library of Congress Cataloging-in-Publication Data available

ISBN 978-1-4930-4191-6 (paperback)
ISBN 978-1-4930-4192-3 (e-book)

∞™ The paper used in this publication meets the minimum requirements of American National Standard for Information Sciences—Permanence of Paper for Printed Library Materials, ANSI/NISO Z39.48-1992.

Contents

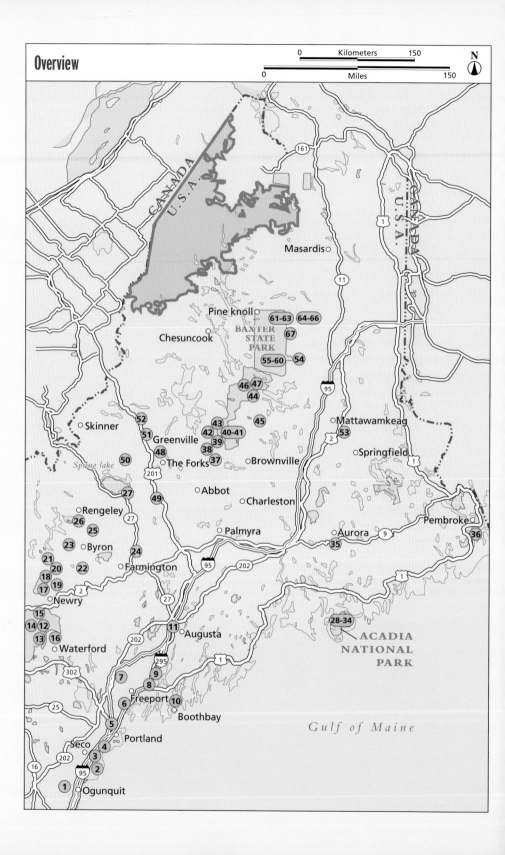

Introduction

Maine is famous for its rock-bound coast, granite peaks, endless forest, and moose—and you'll see plenty of those doing the hikes in this guide. But did you know that Maine is home to New England's highest waterfall? And the Appalachian Trail's highest. And the most remote waterfall east of the Mississippi River. There are waterfalls that are only spoken of in quiet tones, secrets that no one has laid eyes on in generations.

At the turn of the twentieth century, Josiah Maxey created the Sandy River and Rangeley Lakes Railroad (SR&RLRR). One line followed the Sandy River northwest from Strong to Eustis and beyond. It was built to haul lumber and later pulpwood. About halfway between Eustis and Strong was the small community of Redington, built around a mill. The town was on the south shore of Redington Pond. Almost directly across the pond, loggers discovered a high waterfall on a stream flowing into the pond. It was reputed to be more than 300 feet high. Sports on their way to Rangeley sometimes got off the train in Redington to stretch their legs and visit the falls.

The Great Depression killed SR&RLRR, and the tracks were pulled up and sold for scrap in 1936. Maps today of the region show a woods road following the route of the rail line, and the town of Redington is still in the *Maine Gazetteer*. No one has hiked to the falls for a long time, though. Whispers about its height and location turn up occasionally on the internet, but there's a problem: Redington Pond Falls is in the middle of a super-secret US Navy survival training facility. Unless you're a Navy SEAL, you're not going to see the waterfall.

Don't despair. There are more than one hundred waterfalls in this guide that you can hike to. The waterfalls come in all shapes and sizes. Many guides rate waterfalls on a one-to-five scale. But how can you compare a hundred-foot plunge with a horsetail that slides quietly into a clear pool? Rather than tell you what to think of each waterfall, I'll give you enough information so that you can decide for yourself. Every waterfall has its own character and

Baxter State Park's Green Falls is the most remote waterfall in the East.

1

The Little Androscoggin River pouring out of an arch at Snow Falls

charm. Beauty is truly in the eye of the beholder. There's something very compelling, almost hypnotic, about moving water. Maybe I should have just given them all a five.

People have always been drawn to water, and Maine's history bears that out. Many of the state's larger waterfalls have been reshaped by humans. In many cases the falls were dammed to regulate flow for industrial power. Towns sprung up around them, the streams lined with brick mills. One of the largest waterfalls in Maine is Pennacook Falls on the Androscoggin River in Rumford. The river drops almost 200 feet. Over the years, the Androscoggin was directed into canals leading to mills, and dams were built to maintain water flow throughout the year. Still, a stop at the park along US 2 to see the falls is worth it. In the spring the river surges over the black rock. You can almost ignore the man-made structures and power lines.

Even many of the wild waterfalls have been touched by humans. At the top of Cold Brook Falls, miles from the nearest paved road or human structure, the stream rushes toward the falls between a high cliff and a stone wall. Deep in Gulf Hagas, where the walls of the canyon almost touch, timbermen blasted the rock, widening the stream by about 10 feet. Between West Paris and South Paris on ME 26 is Snow Falls. This is a dramatic roadside waterfall. It looks completely wild, but as you explore the area around the falls, you realize it's not. A canal runs parallel to the Little Androscoggin River, and it has its own waterfall. There's lots of stonework above the falls as well.

More than humans, Maine's geology created the waterfalls you see. Less than a third of the state is underlain by granite, yet many of the highest and most spectacular waterfalls are in these areas. They include the southern half of Baxter State Park, Acadia National Park, and the mountains of western Maine. The Central Highlands are mostly underlain by slate, a black metamorphic rock. Numerous waterfalls in this guide are in slate gorges or fall over slate ledges.

While the bedrock affects the likelihood of waterfalls in a given landscape, Maine's hydrology was shaped by glaciers. Many of Maine's lakes and ponds were created by the retreating glaciers. The rivers and streams often follow the paths of features such as eskers created by melting glaciers. But the largest impact that the glaciers had on today's waterfalls isn't as apparent. The ice sheets scraped the mountains and highlands clean down to the bedrock. There have only been about 11,000 years to rebuild soils, and without deeper soils, most hills and mountains can't hold much water. As a result, the snowmelt drains away quickly and the waterfalls disappear or are greatly reduced by midsummer. Similarly, streams can rise dramatically after summer storms. I once saw Howe Brook (hike 62) rise more than a foot overnight because of an afternoon thunderstorm. The following day it was back down to its normal summer level.

Small purple-fringed orchis, one of Maine's wild orchids

On many hikes, half the fun is the process of reaching the destination. Along the trail to most waterfalls, you'll have opportunities to enjoy vistas, view wildlife, snap pictures of wildflowers, or just savor solitude in the Maine woods.

Wildlife

Many people come to Maine hoping to see a moose. You're most likely to see one along the road on the way to the trailhead, but I've seen moose on a number of the hikes included in this guide. The sound of a rushing stream can hide the sound of an approaching hiker, making a sighting more likely. I once came around a turn in the trail just upstream from Debsconeag Falls and almost walked into a young bull moose. He was hiking down the trail from Fifth Debsconeag Pond to Fourth, and I was hiking up the same trail. We were both quite surprised. The moose stood motionless for a moment, then crashed across the stream and up the embankment into the woods. As you hike watch for tracks and scat in the trail. Look for moose in shallow water eating aquatic vegetation. In summer cows, especially those with a calf, rarely stray far from waters where they feed. Bulls, however, tend to wander and can be found almost anywhere. Your best chance to see a moose on a hike is early in the morning.

By weight there are more salamanders in Maine than moose. Which is another way of saying that most wildlife is small. Hiking to a waterfall often offers opportunities to see frogs, toads, waterfowl, songbirds, ospreys, eagles, and, yes, salamanders. Don't rush from the trailhead to the waterfall. Take your time and see the woods you're hiking through. You might get lucky and see a porcupine napping in a pine

Moose with calf along Beaver Brook near Lily Pad Pond

Painted turtle on Otter Pond Road

tree, wood frogs congregating in a vernal pool to breed, or evidence that a bear passed through the night before.

Bugs

Blackflies are active during the day, especially between Mother's Day and Father's Day—prime waterfall viewing season. Mosquitoes love cool, damp places, like streams and ponds. Hiking to waterfalls, you're likely to get bit. Some hikers wear bug nets during early summer to ward off the biting hordes. Others dowse themselves with liberal doses of DEET. I prefer to just ignore the bugs or walk faster. You need to find your own comfort level and come prepared to deal with the bugs in your own way.

In the last few years, New Englanders have begun to really worry about ticks. You're most likely to have a problem where the trail passes through tall grass or thick ferns. Some experts suggest you wear long pants tucked into your socks. Personally, I wear shorts and check myself regularly for ticks on my shoes and legs. Since 2013 I've hiked several thousand miles in New England and pulled hundreds of ticks off myself. But I've never had one successfully attach itself to me. If you hike, you'll attract ticks. Avoid problems by stopping after passing through tick habitat and check for them on you. Once you get home, check your whole body. I make it part of my shower routine. Having said that, you'll run into very few ticks north of Bangor or above 1,000 feet of elevation.

Not all bugs are to be avoided. Maine is home to at least 120 species of butterflies. Many of the showiest are active in habitats you'll be hiking to.

Tiger swallowtail butterflies lapping up wet clay on the shoulder of Lower Enchanted Road

Plant Life

When the streams are running high in the spring and the waterfalls are at their peak, the woods are exploding with wildflowers. A succession of flowers bloom until the trees leaf out. The trail descriptions note especially good places to find wildflowers, particularly orchids. In the fall, when many streams are running at their lowest, mushrooms erupt beneath forests exploding with color.

Be Prepared

No matter when you hike in Maine, you need to be prepared for the weather to change. In general, wear layers and avoid cotton clothes. Never wear white; it attracts bugs and scares away birds. Keep snacks, water, a flashlight, and a first-aid kit in your pack. Always bring your raincoat. Even a short hike can turn epic if you don't dress and pack smart. With the right gear and clothes, even a dreary day can be a great one in the woods. If you choose to visit waterfalls in winter—which can be very reward-ing—make sure you have the right footwear and layers. Depending on the location and conditions, you may need snowshoes or spikes.

Nomenclature

Mainers have some unique ways to name bodies of water and landscape features. Within this guide, I've tried to be both consistent and true to local use. Let me explain. In Maine *pond* and *lake* are used pretty much interchangeably. In most of the country, lakes are large and ponds are small. Not here—many lakes are smaller than a lot of the ponds. People have tried to come up with rules to determine what's a pond and what's a lake, but let's be honest: In Maine it's truly random.

We're more consistent with flowing water. Rivers are large and usually flow into the ocean or at least into a major river. Streams are smaller rivers that flow into riv-ers. Especially in southern Maine, there are rivers that are smaller than some streams. Seems that flowing into the ocean trumps size. Usually, a stream is a body of water that was large enough to float logs down during the heyday of Maine river drives. A brook is a smaller flowing body of water. Creeks are tidal, usually filled with salt or brackish water. Knowing the size of the stream often helps you know the size of the waterfall and whether its flow reduces greatly in summer. But as with most things, there are exceptions. Often brooks that flow out of a large pond maintain good flow.

Most rivers and many streams have multiple branches. Mainers tend to think very locally and would never call a river East Branch Penobscot River, for example. It's just East Branch. In a statewide guide like this, that would create real confusion. I use complete names for both the rivers and the waterfalls.

A waterfall is a waterfall, right? Not in the Penobscot River drainage. There the features were named by nineteenth-century river drivers and timber cruisers. A waterfall is called a pitch. Most streams and rivers have a grand pitch—that's its largest waterfall. On these streams and rivers, a falls is a rapids that may have a small waterfall or waterfalls. The distinction between pitches and falls was important information. A canoe or bateau could run a falls but not a pitch. Similarly, falls presented little problem for the river drivers floating logs downstream to the mills in Old Town and Milford. A pitch, however, could cause problems. In western Maine and the Kennebec River drainage, there are no pitches, although there are a few grand falls.

Waterfalls come in several types. I've tried to be consistent in my usage to help you understand what you'll see with each hike. A horsetail is a waterfall that braids down a face in contact with the rock much of the time. A plunge is a waterfall that drops free into a pool or onto rocks. A cascade is something between a horsetail and a rapids. It's often a chain of small waterfalls. A slide is a waterfall where the stream flows down a smooth rock face. The water often flows along a joint or seam in the bedrock, sometimes within a flume. Of course, many of Maine's waterfalls are a combination of these types. That's what makes hiking to them so much fun. Every waterfall is unique, a complex dance between water and rock.

How to Use This Guide

Each hike begins with a summary that briefly describes the waterfall and the hike to it. Next you'll find the nitty-gritty details. **Start** lets you know where the trailhead is. Sometimes the trail is unmarked or confusing. This should clear things up. **Elevation gain** gives you a rough idea of how much work it'll be getting to the waterfall. For every hike, I use gross elevation gain. If a hike goes up 100 feet, down 50 feet, then up another 100 feet, the net gain is 150 feet, but you climbed 200 so that's the number I use. **Distance** tells you how far the entire hike is and whether it's an out-and-back, a loop, or a lollipop. **Hiking time** is my best guess as to how long the average person will take to complete the hike. This number is mostly for comparing hikes, not a judgment on how fast or slow you walk.

Difficulty lets you know how hard the hike is. For this guide, the scale is easier than for my other guides. Easy hikes have little climbing, are short, and require no route-finding skills. Moderate hikes are more than 4 miles, require some scrambling, or have short, steep climbs. Strenuous hikes are longer than 6 miles, require climbing or scrambling, or involve bushwhacking or using rough, unmarked trails. **Season** lets you know when it's best to see the waterfall. Sometimes access is limited and influences the season. Most waterfalls can be seen out of season, but are much diminished. Many of the waterfalls in this guide are accessible during winter. If you're prepared for the cold and snow, it can be a great adventure to see a waterfall with its winter coat on.

Trail surface lets you know what the path is going to be like. **Land status** lets you know who owns the property and whether it's a park or preserve. **Nearest town** is the closest community with a gas station and other services. **Other users** is included mostly to let you know whether hunting is allowed in the area of the hike. **Water availability** is a part of every hike, but it's not all good for drinking. Any water taken from a stream or pond should be treated or filtered. **Canine compatibility** lets you know if dogs are welcome and whether they need to be leashed. Even where there are no rules about dogs, please be respectful of other hikers. Not everyone likes dogs, and some people are afraid of them. They deserve to hike, too. **Fees and permits** lets you know if there are entrance, parking, or other fees to get to the hike and see the waterfall.

Other maps: Even though this guide includes an adequate map for each hike, some folks like more. I've listed the map number in DeLorme's *Maine Atlas & Gazetteer* and the USGS 1:24,000 topo for each hike. **Trail contact** information is included even though this guide should include everything you need to hike each waterfall. For folks interested in camping and other activities not included in this guide, it can be helpful to know where to find such information. **Finding the trailhead** gives specific mile-by-mile directions to the trailhead from a nearby town or highway junction. When the trailhead and parking are poorly marked—or not marked at all—it'll be noted in the directions. Getting to many of the trailheads requires driving on private logging roads. Conditions vary from season to season and year to year. I drove to most of these hikes in a Honda Fit and the rougher roads in a Honda CRV. If the road is a problem, I'll note that.

Short videos of most of the waterfalls are available on my Facebook page.

Trail Finder

Best hikes for high waterfalls

12. Bickford Slides
14. Mad River Falls
18. Screw Auger Falls
19. Step Falls
20. The Cataracts
21. Dunn Falls
23. Angel Falls
24. Mosher Hill Falls
25. Smalls Falls
27. Poplar Stream Falls

28. Hadlock Falls
31. The Sluiceway
38. Little Wilson Falls
42. Indian Falls
43. Gulf Hagas
44. Tumbledown Dick Falls
48. Moxie Falls
49. Houston Brook Falls
50. Grand Falls Dead River
56. Katahdin Stream Falls

Best hikes for solitude

14. Mad River Falls
15. Kees Falls
16. Kezar Falls
20. The Cataracts
21. Dunn Falls
24. Mosher Hill Falls
29. Canon Brook
31. The Sluiceway
35. Mariaville Falls
37. Tobey Falls
39. Slugundy Falls
40. West Chairback Falls
41. Hay Brook Falls
42. Indian Falls

46. Upper and Lower Pollywog Falls
47. Debsconeag Falls
51. Cold Stream Falls
52. Parlin Falls
54. Orin Falls
55. Blueberry Ledges
58. Big and Little Niagara Falls via Lily Pad Pond
60. Wassataquoik Stream
63. Grand Pitch Webster Stream
64. Sawtelle Falls
65. Shin Falls
66. Grand Pitch Seboeis River
67. East Branch Penobscot River

Best hikes for swimming

12. Bickford Slides
13. Rattlesnake Flume and Pool
14. Mad River Falls
17. Frenchman's Hole
18. Screw Auger Falls
19. Step Falls
20. The Cataracts
22. Swift River Falls and Coos Canyon
25. Smalls Falls
26. Cascade Stream Gorge

27. Poplar Stream Falls
39. Slugundy Falls
43. Gulf Hagas
45. Gauntlet Falls
54. Orin Falls
57. Little Abol Falls
60. Wassataquoik Stream
61. South Branch Falls
62. Howe Brook Falls

Best hikes for kids

1. Orris Falls
2. Tyler Brook Falls
3. Clifford Park
4. Cascade Falls
5. Jewell Falls
6. Royal River
7. Big Falls
8. Cathance River Preserve
9. Cathance River Falls
10. Josephine Newman Sanctuary
11. Vaughan Woods
13. Rattlesnake Flume and Pool
14. Mad River Falls
16. Kezar Falls
17. Frenchman's Hole
18. Screw Auger Falls
19. Step Falls
20. The Cataracts
22. Swift River Falls and Coos Canyon
23. Angel Falls
24. Mosher Hill Falls
25. Smalls Falls
26. Cascade Stream Gorge
27. Poplar Stream Falls
28. Hadlock Falls
29. Canon Brook
30. Man O' War Falls
31. The Sluiceway
32. Deer Brook Falls
33. The Gorge
34. Giant Slide Trail
35. Mariaville Falls
36. Pembroke Reversing Falls
37. Tobey Falls
38. Little Wilson Falls
39. Slugundy Falls
41. Hay Brook Falls
42. Indian Falls
45. Gauntlet Falls
47. Debsconeag Falls
48. Moxie Falls
49. Houston Brook Falls
50. Grand Falls Dead River
51. Cold Stream Falls
53. Mattawamkeag River
56. Katahdin Stream Falls
57. Little Abol Falls
59. Big and Little Niagara Falls via Appalachian Trail
61. South Branch Falls
62. Howe Brook Falls
64. Sawtelle Falls
65. Shin Falls
66. Grand Pitch Seboeis River

Best hikes for nature lovers

1. Orris Falls
2. Tyler Brook Falls
7. Big Falls
8. Cathance River Preserve
10. Josephine Newman Sanctuary
12. Bickford Slides
13. Rattlesnake Flume and Pool
14. Mad River Falls
15. Kees Falls
20. The Cataracts
21. Dunn Falls
24. Mosher Hill Falls
26. Cascade Stream Gorge
27. Poplar Stream Falls
28. Hadlock Falls
29. Canon Brook
30. Man O' War Falls
31. The Sluiceway
32. Deer Brook Falls
33. The Gorge
34. Giant Slide Trail
35. Mariaville Falls
36. Pembroke Reversing Falls
37. Tobey Falls

38. Little Wilson Falls
39. Slugundy Falls
40. West Chairback Falls
41. Hay Brook Falls
42. Indian Falls
43. Gulf Hagas
44. Tumbledown Dick Falls
45. Gauntlet Falls
46. Upper and Lower Pollywog Falls
47. Debsconeag Falls
48. Moxie Falls
50. Grand Falls Dead River
51. Cold Stream Falls
52. Parlin Falls
54. Orin Falls

55. Blueberry Ledges
56. Katahdin Stream Falls
57. Little Abol Falls
58. Big and Little Niagara Falls via Lily Pad Pond
59. Big and Little Niagara Falls via Appalachian Trail
60. Wassataquoik Stream
62. Howe Brook Falls
63. Grand Pitch Webster Stream
64. Sawtelle Falls
65. Shin Falls
66. Grand Pitch Seboeis River
67. East Branch Penobscot River

Best hikes for geology lovers

3. Clifford Park
4. Cascade Falls
10. Josephine Newman Sanctuary
12. Bickford Slides
13. Rattlesnake Flume and Pool
14. Mad River Falls
16. Kezar Falls
18. Screw Auger Falls
19. Step Falls
20. The Cataracts
22. Swift River Falls and Coos Canyon
23. Angel Falls
24. Mosher Hill Falls
25. Smalls Falls
26. Cascade Stream Gorge
29. Canon Brook
33. The Gorge
34. Giant Slide Trail
38. Little Wilson Falls
39. Slugundy Falls

42. Indian Falls
43. Gulf Hagas
44. Tumbledown Dick Falls
45. Gauntlet Falls
46. Upper and Lower Pollywog Falls
49. Houston Brook Falls
50. Grand Falls Dead River
52. Parlin Falls
53. Mattawamkeag River
55. Blueberry Ledges
56. Katahdin Stream Falls
57. Little Abol Falls
60. Wassataquoik Stream
61. South Branch Falls
62. Howe Brook Falls
63. Grand Pitch Webster Stream
64. Sawtelle Falls
65. Shin Falls
67. East Branch Penobscot River

Best hikes for history lovers

1. Orris Falls
3. Clifford Park
6. Royal River

9. Cathance River Falls
10. Josephine Newman Sanctuary
11. Vaughan Woods

Map Legend

Municipal

≡⟨5⟩≡ Interstate Highway

≡⟨101⟩≡ US Highway

≡⟨1⟩≡ State Road

──────── Local/County Road

= = = = Gravel Road

= = = = Unpaved Road

─ ⸱ ─ ⸱ ─ State Boundary

─ ─ ⸱ ─ County Boundary

•─•─•─• Power Line

Trails

- - - - - - Featured Trail

- - - - - Trail

──────── Paved Trail

Water Features

Body of Water

Marsh

River/Creek

Intermittent Stream

Spring

Waterfall

Symbols

⤬ Bridge

▪ Building/Point of Interest

▲ Campground

∧ Cave

🍴 Food

❗ Gate

🛏 Lodging

🅿 Parking

⤬ Pass

▲ Peak/Elevation

📞 Phone

🎪 Picnic Area

🚹 Ranger Station/Park Office

🚻 Restroom

🎐 Scenic View

🐴 Stables

○ Town

① Trailhead

❓ Visitor/Information Center

🚰 Water

♿ Wheelchair Accessible

Land Management

National Park/Forest

National Monument/Wilderness

State/County Park

Indian Reservation

1 Orris Falls

Orris Falls is a 15-foot plunge into a narrow, vertical gorge. The hike into the waterfall passes a balanced rock, ledges with views over surrounding forest, and substantial beaver ponds. It's a surprisingly high and wild waterfall for southern Maine.

Start: Emery's Bridge Road Trailhead
Elevation gain: 249 feet
Distance: 2.6 miles out and back
Hiking time: About 2 hours
Difficulty: Easy
Season: May to October
Trail surface: Woodland path
Land status: Orris Falls Conservation Area
Nearest town: North Berwick

Other users: None
Water availability: None
Canine compatibility: Dogs must be under control at all times.
Fees and permits: None
Other maps: *DeLorme: Maine Atlas & Gazetteer*, map 2; USGS Somersworth
Trail contact: Great Works Regional Land Trust, (207) 646-3604, www.gwrlt.org

Finding the trailhead: From the junction of ME 4 and ME 9 in North Berwick, follow ME 9 east. Drive 0.1 mile. Turn right onto Main Street. Drive 2.2 miles (the road's name changes to Boyd's Corner Road as you leave town). Pass Thurrell Road. Drive 1.4 miles. Turn right onto Emery's Bridge Road. Drive 0.5 mile. Parking is on the right at the preserve sign. GPS: N43 16.129' / W70 41.698'

The Hike

There are two trailheads for Orris Falls. The shorter hike is from Thurrell Road. This hike follows an old woods road most of the way. It's a nice walk through the woods, but much less interesting than our hike from Emery's Bridge Road.

The trail climbs gently to a short side trail that leads to Balancing Rock. The huge, irregular boulder sits in the woods atop a pedestal of smaller rocks. The rock seems to point due south. This has led to many legends as to how the erratic got here and why it's orientated the way it is. A bench is situated nearby so you can contemplate these mysteries.

The trail climbs gently to semi-open ledges. From Tatnic Ledges, you have views of the surrounding woods and rolling hills. The Tatnic Hills are part of an ancient volcanic caldera. You're standing on compacted ash.

The trail continues on to the first beaver pond. You walk along the southern edge of a series of connected ponds that have flooded much of the area. It's a good place to see wildlife, especially beavers, turtles, and waterbirds.

Orris Falls from the unofficial trail ▶

Orris Falls

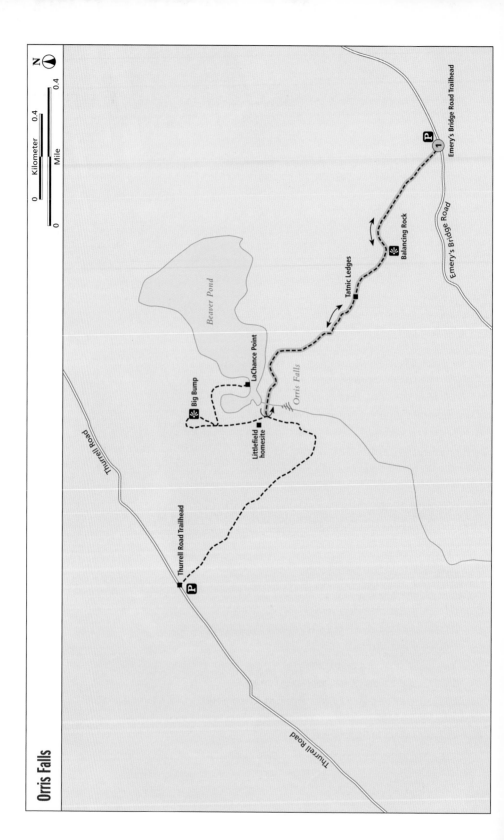

N

Kilometer
0   0.4   0.4

Mile
0   0.4

Thurrell Road

Thurrell Road Trailhead
P

Big Bump

LaChance Point

Beaver Pond

Littlefield homesite

Orris Falls

Tatnic Ledges

Balancing Rock

Emery's Bridge Road Trailhead
P   1

Emery's Bridge Road

Balancing Rock

Orris Brook flows out of the ponds where a natural bedrock dam holds the water back. The stream immediately begins dropping. In less than a tenth of a mile, it drops more than 100 feet into a deep, nearly vertical gorge. Cross the stream on a small bridge and follow a marked trail downstream, skirting the west edge of the gorge. You have several views of the waterfall, most partially blocked by trees.

An unmarked trail follows the stream on its eastern side. You can make your way to the bedrock at the top of Orris Falls and look straight down the waterfall. Farther downstream, you can reach a rocky hillside with a fine view of the waterfall.

Nearby, several trails come together at the Littlefield homesite. An information sign tells the settler history of these woods. You can follow the trail north around the beaver ponds and to the top of Big Bump. In spring the woods are a great place to find wildflowers.

Miles and Directions

0.0 Start from the Emery's Bridge Road Trailhead.

0.4 Pass a short side trail to Balancing Rock.

0.6 Pass Tatnic Ledges.

1.0 Arrive at the first beaver pond.

1.2 Cross the brook, then immediately turn left.

1.3 Arrive at the overlook above Orris Falls. To complete the hike, return the way you came to the trailhead.

2.6 Arrive back at the trailhead.

2 Tyler Brook Falls

Tyler Brook Falls is the smallest waterfall in this guide. It only drops 6 feet over a series of low ledges, but it's a picturesque waterfall in a quiet woods.

Start: Tyler Brook Trailhead
Elevation gain: 80 feet
Distance: 1.6-mile lollipop
Hiking time: About 1 hour
Difficulty: Easy
Season: May to October
Trail surface: Woodland path
Land status: Tyler Brook Preserve
Nearest town: Kennebunkport
Other users: None

Water availability: None
Canine compatibility: Dogs must be under control at all times.
Fees and permits: None
Other maps: *DeLorme: Maine Atlas & Gazetteer*, map 3; USGS Biddeford
Trail contact: Kennebunkport Conservation Trust, (207) 967-3465, www.kporttrust.org/tyler-brook

Finding the trailhead: From exit 25, follow ME 35 south toward Kennebunk. Drive 5.7 miles. Turn left onto ME 9. Drive 4 miles through Cape Porpoise. Turn left onto Tyler Brook Road. Drive 0.1 mile to the parking area at the end of the road. The trailhead is at the south end of the parking area. GPS: N43 23.435' / W70 26.825'

The Hike

Minutes from the tourist hubbub of Cape Porpoise, Tyler Brook wanders through a quiet hardwood forest. It drops down ledges and follows a sinuous course through a tidal marsh to the Batson River and the sea.

The hike passes through a marshy hardwood forest—a great place to find spring wildflowers. When you reach Tyler Brook, there's a bench on the bedrock next to Tyler Brook Falls. A footbridge crosses the brook above the falls. The stream only drops 6 feet over three ledges, but it's a pretty spot. The brook zigzags down the rounded bedrock along joints.

On the return hike, you follow Tyler Brook downstream as it winds through a tidal marsh. You can see where it flows into the Batson River, forming a larger tidal marsh that extends to the sea a short distance away. This intertidal zone is a great place to find wading birds.

This hike is part of a large group of connected trail systems that are part of Kennebunkport Conservation Trust preserves. There are other small waterfalls on the Batson River in Emmons Preserve and Round Swamps Brook in Smith Preserve.

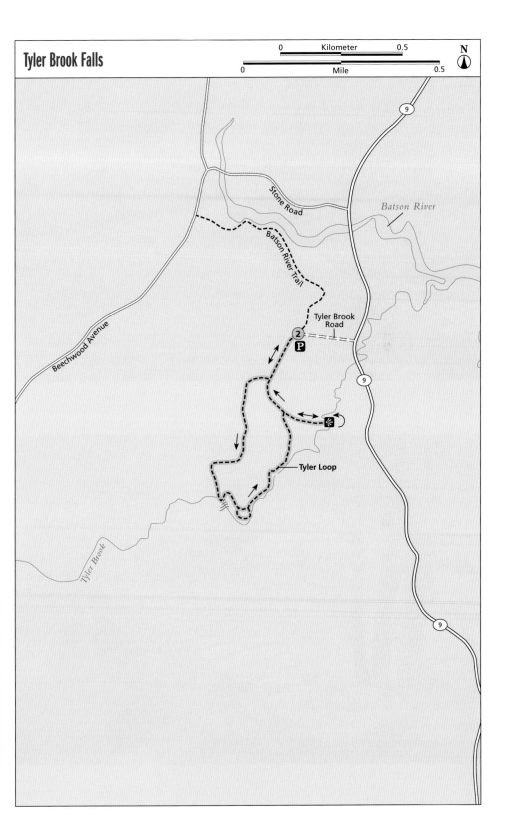

Tyler Brook Falls

0 Kilometer 0.5

0 Mile 0.5

N

Stone Road

Batson River

Batson River Trail

Beechwood Avenue

Tyler Brook Road

2 P

9

9

9

Tyler Loop

Tyler Brook

Looking up the falls to the bridge

The bridge over Tyler Brook

Miles and Directions

0.0 Start from the Tyler Brook Trailhead.

0.1 Hike southwest from the trailhead on the Batson River Trail down an old woods road. Turn right onto Tyler Loop.

0.6 Reach Tyler Brook Falls. To continue the hike, turn left, staying on Tyler Loop.

0.7 Turn right onto Blue Loop.

0.8 Pass overlook of Tyler Brook and arrive back at Tyler Loop. Turn right.

1.1 Turn right onto the trail to Tyler Brook Overlook.

1.2 Tyler Brook Overlook. To continue the hike, return to Tyler Loop.

1.3 Arrive back at Tyler Loop. Turn right.

1.5 Bear right back onto the Batson River Trail.

1.6 Arrive back at the trailhead.

3 Clifford Park

West Brook Falls is a picturesque cascade of 20 feet. The root-beer-colored stream bounces down an irregular staircase of bedrock into a large pool. A large rock outcropping rises above the falls, where hikers can get a nice view of the stream and falls.

Start: Clifford Park Trailhead
Elevation gain: 283 feet
Distance: 1.8-mile lollipop
Hiking time: About 2 hours
Difficulty: Easy
Season: May to June
Trail surface: Woodland path
Land status: Clifford Park, City of Biddeford
Nearest town: Biddeford
Other users: None

Water availability: Restrooms at parking area
Canine compatibility: Dogs should be leashed.
Fees and permits: None
Other maps: *DeLorme: Maine Atlas & Gazetteer*, map 3; USGS Biddeford
Trail contact: Biddeford Recreation, www.biddefordrec.com/info/facilities/details.aspx?FacilityID=12697

Finding the trailhead: From exit 36 on I-95, follow I-195 toward Saco. Drive 1.9 miles. Get off at exit 2A. Turn right on US 1. Drive 1 mile. Go straight onto ME 9. Drive 1.4 miles through downtown Saco and into Biddeford. Bear left onto Alfred Street, staying on ME 9. Drive 0.1 mile. Turn left at the light onto Pool Street, staying on ME 9. Drive 0.4 mile. Turn right into the Clifford Park parking area. The trailhead is at the southwest corner of the parking area. GPS: N43 29.276' / W70 26.893'

The Hike

The largest waterfall in Biddeford was the drop at head of tide on the Saco River, but it was dammed and surrounded by brick mills. Today, it's the bustling center of town. Not far away, Clifford Park is a quiet oasis of forest and rock domes. West Brook skirts along the southeast side of the park.

To get straight to the waterfall, follow the Black Trail to the Red Trail. The Red Trail leads directly to the falls, then follows West Brook upstream past a much smaller waterfall before looping back to the Black Trail. Supplement this short hike with some exploring. The Black Trail makes a complete loop around the park (in less than 2 miles). The Green Trail is not really one trail but a web of trails that covers the high, rocky center of the park. Along these trails you'll see lots of exposed bedrock and evidence of quarrying.

The geology of Biddeford is a complex mixture of rocks of different ages and types. It contains some of Maine's oldest and youngest bedrock. As you hike to the

Clifford Park falls from the outcropping ▶

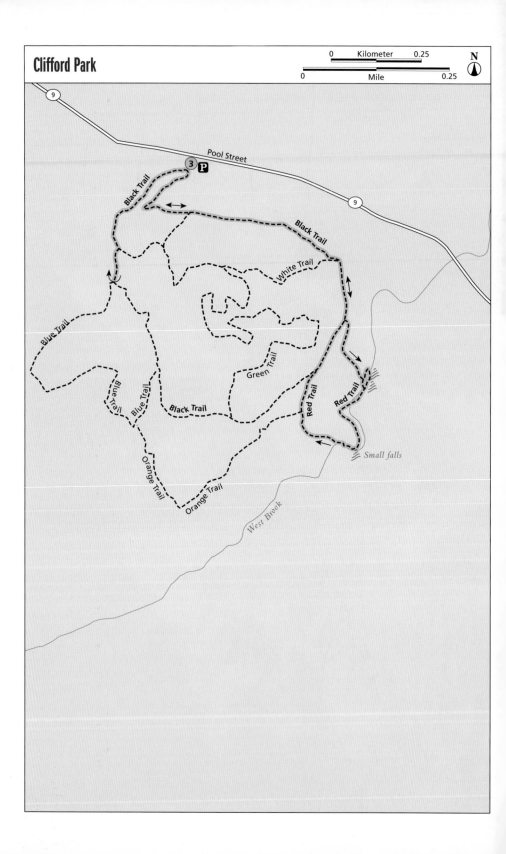

Clifford Park

Kilometer

0   0.25

Mile

0   0.25

N

9

Pool Street

3 P

Black Trail

Black Trail

9

White Trail

Blue Trail

Blue Trail

Blue Trail

Green Trail

Black Trail

Red Trail

Red Trail

Orange Trail

Orange Trail

Small falls

West Brook

Small waterfall on West Brook

waterfall, notice that you pass exposed rock of several kinds. The rock West Brook Falls tumbles over is different from the rock mounded up in the center of the park. Streams often follow the joints between different bedrock types. The harder rock at the center of the park remains, while the softer rock to the south becomes eroded and offers the stream a way from higher ground to the sea. At both waterfalls are quiet areas of forest for you to sit and enjoy the stream or contemplate the history of the bedrock that goes back hundreds of millions of years.

Miles and Directions

0.0 Start from the Clifford Park Trailhead.

0.1 Turn left onto the Black Trail.

0.2 Pass the Green Trail.

0.5 Pass the White Trail.

0.6 Turn left onto the Red Trail.

0.7 Reach West Brook Falls. To continue the hike, turn right.

0.8 Follow West Brook upstream to a small waterfall.

1.0 The Red Trail turns left away from West Brook. Pass the Orange Trail.

1.1 Arrive back at the Black Trail. To return to the trailhead, turn right.

1.8 Arrive back at the trailhead.

4 Cascade Falls

Minutes from US 1, Cascade Stream tumbles over black slate beneath hemlocks. Cascade Falls is a 20-foot horsetail waterfall. The very short hike leads to the base of the falls. The Pink Trail loops through the woods upstream from the falls and offers access to the top of Cascade Falls.

Start: Cascade Falls Park Trailhead
Elevation gain: 123 feet
Distance: 0.6-mile two-pronged out and back
Hiking time: About 1 hour
Difficulty: Easy
Season: May to October
Trail surface: Woodland path
Land status: Cascade Falls Park
Nearest town: Saco

Other users: None
Water availability: None
Canine compatibility: Dogs must be under control at all times.
Fees and permits: None
Other maps: *DeLorme: Maine Atlas & Gazetteer*, map 3; USGS Old Orchard Beach
Trail contact: Saco Bay Trails, www.sacobaytrails.org/trails

Finding the trailhead: From the junction of I-195 and US 1, follow US 1 north. Drive 2.8 miles. Turn right onto ME 98. Drive 0.4 mile. Turn left into Cascade Falls Park at the sign. The trailhead is at the north end of the parking area. GPS: N43 32.568' / W70 24.441'

The Hike

Cascade Falls looks a lot like the slate waterfalls more common in the Central Highlands. Cascade Brook drops 20 feet down an eruption of black slate. Notice that the bedding is different on the right and left sides of the waterfall. The slate outcropping is topped with large hemlocks. Little grows beneath them, opening the view.

From the trailhead, hike into the woods then turn right. When you reach a clearing, keep to the right. The trail to the left is the Pink Loop; you can follow it on your way back to enjoy a nice stroll through the woods upstream from the waterfall. The unmarked trail slightly to the right leads to the top of Cascade Falls. After visiting the top of the falls, return to the clearing and follow the main trail that descends to the base of the waterfall.

From the end of the trail, you can cross the muddy ground to the rocks at the base of the falls. In spring the falls are a wide horsetail covering most of the rock face. By summer it's a narrow horsetail only 2 feet wide down the center. As you stand watching the water cascade down the black bedrock, it's hard to believe you're less than a mile from Route 1 and all its tourist attractions and traffic.

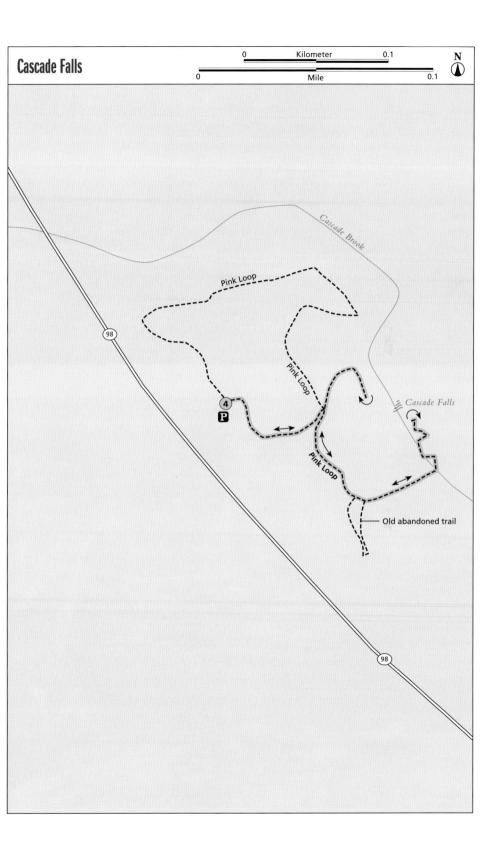

Cascade Falls

Kilometer
0   0.1

Mile
0   0.1

N

Cascade Brook

Pink Loop

98

Pink Loop

4

P

Cascade Falls

Pink Loop

Old abandoned trail

98

Cascade Falls from the end of the trail

Cascade Falls during low flow in August

Miles and Directions

0.0 Start from the Cascade Falls Park Trailhead. In 50 feet turn right at a T-intersection. In another 300 feet enter a clearing. Follow a rough trail slightly to the right.

0.1 Reach the top of Cascade Falls. To continue the hike, return the way you came back to the clearing. Cross the clearing on the main trail.

0.2 Bear left and descend.

0.3 Reach the base of Cascade Falls. To complete the hike, follow the main trail back to the trailhead.

0.6 Arrive back at the trailhead.

5 Jewell Falls

Jewell Falls is Portland's only waterfall. The Fore River drops 25 feet down a rock face in two separate horsetail slides. Below the falls, the narrow stream wanders through a productive estuary. A hillside of mature white pines overlooks the scene.

Start: Hillcrest Trailhead
Elevation gain: 235 feet
Distance: 0.4 mile out and back
Hiking time: About 1 hour
Difficulty: Easy
Season: May to June
Trail surface: Graded walking path
Land status: Fore River Sanctuary
Nearest town: Portland

Other users: None
Water availability: None
Canine compatibility: Dogs should be leashed.
Fees and permits: None
Other maps: *DeLorme: Maine Atlas & Gazetteer*, map 3; USGS Portland
Trail contact: Fore River Sanctuary, http://trails.org/our-trails/fore-river-sanctuary

Finding the trailhead: From exit 5 off I-295 in Portland, follow Congress Street west. Drive 0.6 mile. Turn right onto Stevens Avenue. Drive 0.2 mile. Turn left onto Capisic Street. Drive 1.3 miles. Turn hard left at light onto Hillcrest Street. Drive 0.1 mile. Park at the end of the street. The trailhead is at the end of the street. GPS: N43 40.313' / W70 19.005'

The Hike

The Fore River is a wide tidal ria separating Portland and South Portland, surrounded by city, industrial tank farms, and Portland's airport. Quickly it narrows to two streams: the Stroudwater River and the Fore River. The Fore River is a marshy estuary surrounded by quiet neighborhoods—not where you'd expect to find a beautiful waterfall.

Jewell Falls is reached by the trails in Fore River Sanctuary. A bridge crosses the stream just above the falls, offering a nice introductory view. The trail turns and descends beside the waterfall. The stream slides down exposed bedrock, catches its breath in a short flat, then drops again. The total drop is at least 25 feet. A stone bench next to the stream is a good place to sit and enjoy the view.

The hillside is covered with mature white pines. The trail continues beyond the waterfall up a small hill into a grove of the pines. Trails branch out and explore the estuarine stream and its sinuous course through reeds, cattails, and alders. You can come just to enjoy the waterfall or wander the preserve and do a little birdwatching—right in the middle of Maine's largest city.

Jewell Falls ▶

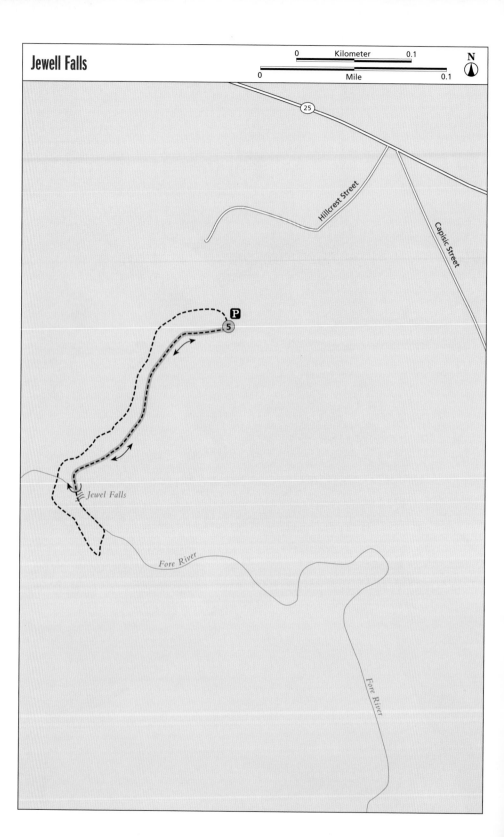

Jewell Falls

0   Kilometer   0.1

0   Mile   0.1

N

25

Hillcrest Street

Capisic Street

P

5

Jewel Falls

Fore River

Fore River

Bench beside Jewell Falls

Miles and Directions

0.0 Start from the Hillcrest Trailhead. In 250 feet bear left, staying on the main trail.

0.2 Reach the top of Jewell Falls. The trail continues to the bottom of the falls. To complete the hike, return the way you came.

0.4 Arrive back at the trailhead.

6 Royal River

In Yarmouth, there are four waterfalls on the Royal River. First Falls drops down what looks like a flight of stairs. Below the waterfall, the river is tidal. Upstream, Second Falls is another staircase with a dam at its head. Third Falls is a 10-foot plunge. The foundation of a mill that once spanned the river sticks up in several places in the river, diverting its flow. Fourth Falls is another staircase with a dam at its head. Second and Fourth Falls both have fish ladders.

Start: Grist Mill Park
Elevation gain: 144 feet
Distance: 1.7 miles out and back
Hiking time: About 2 hours
Difficulty: Easy
Season: May to November
Trail surface: Graded walking path
Land status: Grist Mill Park and Royal River Park
Nearest town: Yarmouth

Other users: None
Water availability: None
Canine compatibility: Dogs should be leashed.
Fees and permits: None
Other maps: DeLorme: Maine Atlas & Gazetteer, map 5; USGS Yarmouth
Trail contact: Royal River Conservation Trust, http://rrct.org/royal-river-water-trail/yarmouth-downtown

Finding the trailhead: From exit 17 off I-295 in Yarmouth, follow US 1 south. Drive 0.4 mile. Exit right onto East Main Street. Turn left from the exit ramp and pass over US 1. Drive 0.3 mile. Bear right, staying on East Main Street. Drive 0.2 mile. Turn right into Grist Mill Park just before the bridge over the Royal River. There's a viewing platform next to the parking area. GPS: N43 47.925' / W70 10.679'

To get to Royal River Park, return to US 1 south. Drive under East Main Street and continue another 0.7 mile. Exit right to School Street. Turn right off the exit into the school grounds. Parking is on the left and straight ahead. The trailhead is straight ahead at the kiosk next to the tennis courts. GPS: N43 48.167' / W70 11.219'

The Hike

The Royal River drops 45 feet in less than a mile from Fourth Falls to head of tide below First Falls. This drew settlers who wanted to harness that power. Yarmouth was first settled in 1636. A sawmill was built at First Falls in 1674, and the first gristmill was later built in the same location. Its foundation is the viewing platform where you stand to see the falls. As many as four mills occupied First Falls at the same time. Today, the river looks wild here even as it's flanked by old mill buildings and crossed by a bridge.

After enjoying First Falls and the river above it, drive up to the Royal River Trailhead to hike to Second Falls. The walk downstream along the Royal River passes through a piney woods. Second Falls is topped by a dam and flanked by a fish ladder.

First Falls from Grist Mill overlook

The mill building across the river dates back to the middle of the nineteenth century. The falls below the dam drop over a series of ledges. The water walks down a staircase and flows around the mill building in riffles.

Upstream from the trailhead, the trail enters a park. The river is wide here, almost a lake. Look for waterfowl and ospreys. Third Falls was the most industrialized of the waterfalls in Yarmouth. Today, all that remains are bits of foundation along the trail and the footers sticking out of the river that once supported a paper mill. Third Falls is the only one that is still an entirely natural waterfall. The river drops more than 10 feet down a steep rock face. In spring it surges and churns like an angry beast.

Fourth Falls, like Third Falls, was highly industrialized, with a tanning mill, a factory that manufactured machinery for other mills, and several other industries. Little remains of these but the walled-in brook that empties into the river below the falls. The river drops 8 feet over a dam and steps down over a series of ledges.

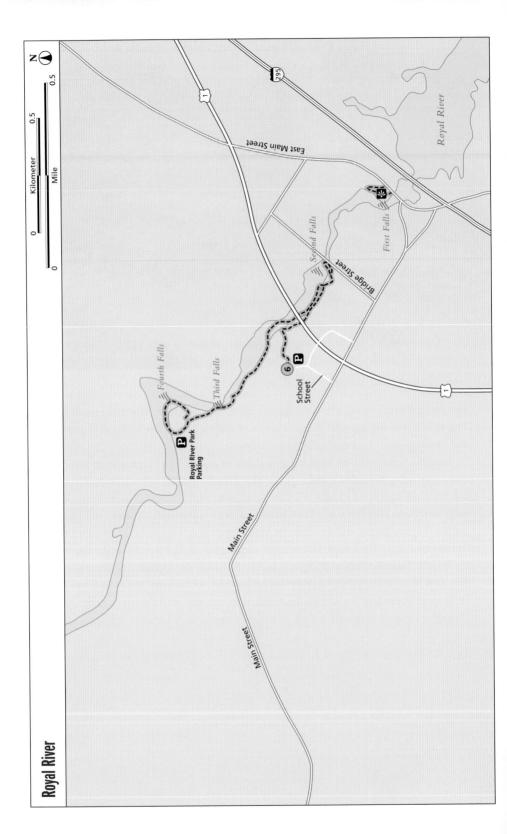

Royal River

Royal River

First Falls

Second Falls

Bridge Street

School Street

6

Royal River Park Parking

Third Falls

Fourth Falls

Main Street

Main Street

East Main Street

1

295

1

N

Kilometer

0   0.5

Mile

0   0.5

Foundation footer in Third Falls

Miles and Directions

0.0   Start from the overlook in Grist Mill Park. After viewing First Falls, drive up to the Royal River Trailhead.

0.1   Hike through tall pines. Turn right onto the River Trail.

0.3   Reach the top of Second Falls.

0.4   Reach Bridge Street, with a view of Second Falls. To continue the hike, hike back the way you came.

0.7   Pass the first junction.

0.9   Reach Third Falls.

1.1   Pass Royal River Park parking. Turn right along Elm Street.

1.2   Reach Fourth Falls. To complete the hike, retrace your steps to the trailhead.

1.7   Arrive back at the trailhead.

7 Big Falls

Meadow Brook drops 18 feet through a boulder field overhung with evergreens and hardwoods. The waterfall isn't dramatic, but it's very secluded and picturesque. The hike to the falls along rocky Meadow Brook through hemlocks is peaceful.

Start: Big Falls information kiosk
Elevation gain: 318 feet
Distance: 2.3 miles lollipop
Hiking time: About 2 hours
Difficulty: Easy
Season: May to June for best water level
Trail surface: Woods road and woodland path
Land status: Big Falls Preserve
Nearest town: New Gloucester

Other users: Hunters in season
Water availability: None
Canine compatibility: Dogs must be under control at all times.
Fees and permits: None
Other maps: *DeLorme: Maine Atlas & Gazetteer*, map 5; USGS North Pownal
Trail contact: Royal River Conservation Trust, (207) 847-8399, www.RRCT.org

Finding the trailhead: From exit 75 off I-95, follow US 202 west. Drive 3.6 miles toward New Gloucester. Turn left onto ME 231. Drive 3.2 miles. Turn left onto Woodman Road just across the railroad tracks. Drive 1.9 miles. Park on the right at the intersection where Woodman Road becomes private. The hike begins at the kiosk on the right side of the road. GPS: N43 58.486' / W70 14.501'

The Hike

Meadow Brook flows into the Royal River in a large wetland complex in New Gloucester surrounded by hay meadows and farms. It's a long way from the bustle of Yarmouth, where the Royal River empties into Casco Bay. The hike to Big Falls is through quiet woods along the babbling brook littered with rounded, mossy rocks.

Big Falls really isn't very big. Meadow Brook drops 18 feet over a ledge and through boulders. The main falls is about 6 feet high. Second-growth hardwoods lean out over the stream, while evergreens watch from the shore. Above the falls the stream ponds behind the natural dam created by the ledge. It's a quiet place to sit and watch the water tumble by.

On your hike back to the trailhead, make a short detour up the Stream Loop Trail. This trail follows a small stream up past two waterfalls to a chapel on Norumbega Green property. The first waterfall is a 10-foot slide down mossy black rock. The second is a steeper slide between rounded rocks. You walk up one side of the stream and return on the other.

Big Falls ▶

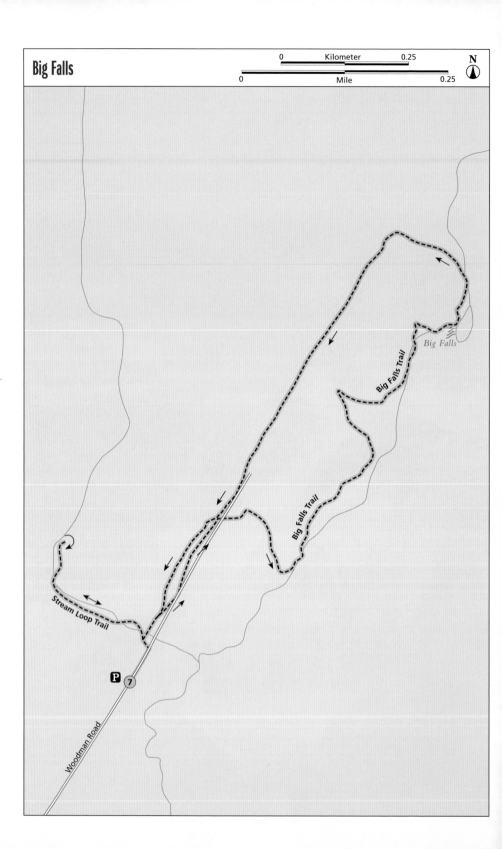

Big Falls

Big Falls Trail

Big Falls Trail

Big Falls

Stream Loop Trail

Woodman Road

P 7

Kilometer
0   0.25

Mile
0   0.25

N

Big Falls

Miles and Directions

0.0   Start at the Big Falls information kiosk.

0.2   Follow Woodman Road northeast. Turn right onto the Big Falls Trail.

0.9   Descend gently to Meadow Brook. Follow the brook upstream to Big Falls.

1.2   Above Big Falls, the trail bears left away from the stream. Reach Woodman Road. Turn left.

1.8   Just before arriving back at the trailhead, turn right onto the Stream Loop Trail.

2.0   Follow the small stream past two waterfalls to Yurt Field. Bear right toward the stream.

2.1   Cross the stream on a bridge and turn right, staying on the Stream Loop Trail.

2.2   Arrive back at Woodman Road. Turn right and walk 200 feet to the trailhead.

2.3   Arrive back at the trailhead.

8 Cathance River Preserve

After flowing under I-295, the Cathance River races through a deeply wooded ravine. There are multiple waterfalls and rapids along this pretty stretch of river. None of the falls is higher than 10 feet, but the bedrock crowds the stream, forcing it to twist and turn or race forward. The Cathance River Trail follows along the shore, with numerous side trail allowing you to create a loop hike to fit your needs.

Start: Ecology Center Trailhead
Elevation gain: 218 feet
Distance: 2.2-mile loop
Hiking time: About 2 hours
Difficulty: Easy
Season: Late April to June
Trail surface: Woodland path
Land status: Cathance River Preserve
Nearest town: Topsham
Other users: None

Water availability: None
Canine compatibility: Dogs are not allowed in the preserve.
Fees and permits: None
Other maps: DeLorme: Maine Atlas & Gazetteer, map 6; USGS Topsham
Trail contact: Brunswick-Topsham Land Trust, www.btlt.org/conserved-lands/cathance-river/cathance-river-nature-preserve

Finding the trailhead: From exit 31 off I-295, follow ME 196 toward Topsham and Brunswick. Drive 0.9 mile. Cross US 201, staying on ME 196. Drive 0.5 mile. Turn left at the light into the Highland Green retirement community onto Village Drive. Drive 0.7 mile. Continue straight onto Evergreen Circle. Drive 0.8 mile. Parking is on the left where the road makes a dip. GPS: N43 57.296' / W69 57.048'

The Hike

The Cathance River Trail winds along the shore from near I-295 to Head of Tide Park (hike 9). This hike makes use of the west end of the trail accessed through the Highland Green retirement community. A network of trails connect the Cathance River Trail to the CREA Ecology Center, the Heath, an abandoned feldspar mine, a large vernal pool, and the woods along the Cathance River. This hike makes a loop along the river, visiting all the rapids and waterfalls. Feel free to add to it to visit the other areas.

Along the entire hike, and especially around the Heath, look for pegmatic bedrock. This relative of granite is what was mined for feldspar in the area. It often has interesting textures and color patterns of black and white. Many of the water features along the Heath Loop Trail are actually flooded quarries where the mineral was mined.

From the parking area for the CREA Ecology Center, follow the Vernal Pool Trail past the eponymous pool to the Highland Trail. This trail wanders through the mixed forest to the river. As you follow the river downstream, you first reach a series

The Cathance River working around a ledge

Barnes Leap

Cathance River Preserve and Falls

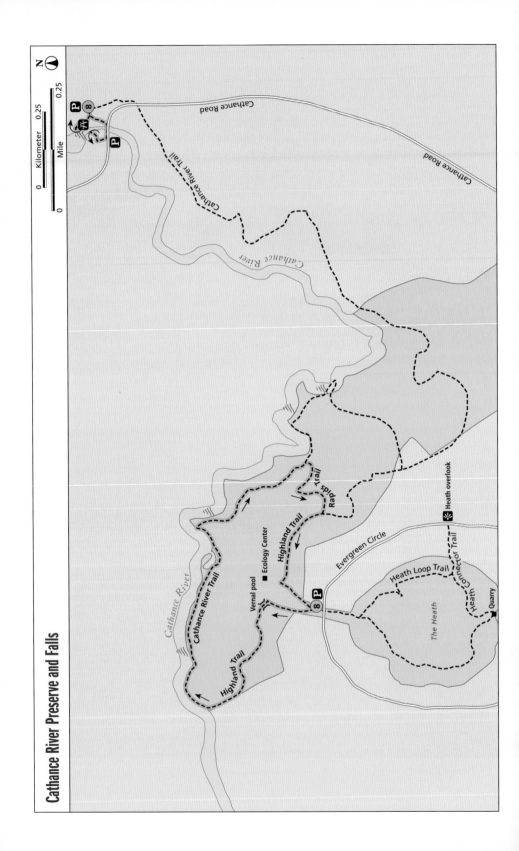

of rapids and a small waterfall. The river races between blocks of bedrock topped by evergreens, a formation known as Barnes Leap.

A short distance farther, you reach the first real waterfall. The river bends around a block of bedrock jutting out into the stream and slides over a ledge. Below the waterfall, the river slows and wanders around an island and among boulders for almost half a mile. Past the Rapids Trail, you reach the last waterfall. This is the largest. The river slides around a corner of bedrock and drops 10 feet. In spring it's a raging maelstrom; by summer, a gentle slide. From here you loop back to the trailhead on the Highland Trail.

Miles and Directions

0.0 Start from the Ecology Center Trailhead. Hike 150 feet, then turn left onto the Vernal Pool Trail.

0.1 Pass the vernal pool. Turn left onto the Highland Trail.

0.5 Reach the Cathance River. Turn right onto the Cathance River Trail.

0.7 Reach the first rapids at Barnes Leap.

0.8 Pass the Barnes Leap Trail.

1.0 Reach the first waterfall.

1.2 Pass the Beaver Trail.

1.5 Pass the Rapids Trail.

1.6 Reach a waterfall. To continue the hike, return to the junction with the Rapids Trail.

1.7 Turn left on the Rapids Trail.

1.8 Turn right onto the Highland Trail.

1.9 Pass the Beaver Trail.

2.1 Turn left onto the Ecology Center driveway (the center is within sight to the right).

2.2 Arrive back at the trailhead.

9 Cathance River Falls

Cathance Falls is a natural waterfall that has been altered slightly to accommodate a mill. Above the falls is a catchment that the tumbling river empties into. Below the falls is the tidal river, which is a narrow arm of Merrymeeting Bay. The waterfall drops 20 feet and is almost 100 feet wide. The park is on both sides of the river, with partial views of the falls from each. There's really no hiking involved, just walking around the park reading historical markers and finding the best views of the waterfall.

See map on p. 44.
Start: Head of Tide Park picnic area
Elevation gain: 27 feet
Distance: 0.3-mile two-pronged out and back
Hiking time: Less than 1 hour
Difficulty: Easy
Season: April to October
Trail surface: Graded path and gravel road
Land status: Head of Tide Park
Nearest town: Topsham

Other users: None
Water availability: None
Canine compatibility: Dogs should be leashed.
Fees and permits: None
Other maps: *DeLorme: Maine Atlas & Gazetteer*, map 6; USGS Topsham
Trail contact: Brunswick-Topsham Land Trust, www.btlt.org/conserved-lands/cathance-river/head-of-tide

Finding the trailhead: From exit 31 off I-295, follow ME 196 toward Topsham and Brunswick. Drive 0.9 mile. Cross US 201, staying on ME 196. Drive 1.3 miles. Turn left onto ME 24 at the light. Drive 0.1 mile. Turn left onto ME 24. Drive 1.7 miles. Turn right into Head of Tide Park (there is additional parking across the bridge on the left). The trailhead is at the back of the parking area. GPS: N43 57.754' / W69 55.781'

The Hike

The Cathance River is a small stream that rises in rural Bowdoin. The stream flows south through Bradley Pond. From there it races through a steep-sided valley in Topsham (hike 8) to Cathance Falls. Below the falls, the tidal river flows north to Bowdoinham, where it flows into Merrymeeting Bay—a total journey of less than 17 miles.

The falls are within Head of Tide Park. There are picnic areas and parking on both sides of the river. It's best to park on the south side of Cathance Road. From there you can walk down the stairs provided for canoeists. From the stairs, especially when the tide is out, you have a good view of the falls, looking across the length of the falls as the river tumbles over a rocky defile.

If you walk across the bridge over the Cathance River, you enter the other half of the park. You have a nice view from above the falls here, partially obscured by the brushy vegetation growing along the shore. There's a picnic area and signs explaining the natural history of the area and the feldspar mill that used the river's power. Only a few miles away, the head of tide falls on the Androscoggin River were dammed.

Cathance River Falls from picnic area

Mills sprung up along the shore to use the abundant power the river provided. The brick mill buildings now house offices, restaurants, and shops, and the dam produces electricity instead of waterpower. This pattern has been repeated across Maine. The mill building on the Cathance River was converted to apartments after the collapse of the feldspar industry but were eventually torn down.

Miles and Directions

0.0 Start at the Head of Tide Park picnic area. Walk through the picnic area on the path and down the steps to the river below the falls. To continue the hike, return to the trailhead.

0.1 Walk out the parking area to ME 24.

0.2 Turn right on the road and cross the bridge over the Cathance River into the park.

0.3 Arrive back at the trailhead.

10 Josephine Newman Sanctuary

The Josephine Newman Sanctuary is on a finger of land that bisects the southern reaches of Robinhood Cove. The sanctuary's trails loop through the woods past a waterfall, old stone walls, piney woods, low boggy ground, rocky ridges, and a mile of shoreline that includes a reversing falls in the narrowest section of Robinhood Cove.

Start: Trailhead at south end of parking area
Elevation gain: 370 feet
Distance: 2.4-mile loop
Hiking time: About 3 hours
Difficulty: Easy
Season: May to October
Trail surface: Woodland path
Land status: Josephine Newman Audubon Sanctuary
Nearest town: Georgetown

Other users: None
Water availability: None
Canine compatibility: No dogs allowed
Fees and permits: None
Other maps: *DeLorme: Maine Atlas & Gazetteer*, maps 6 and 7; USGS Phippsburg and Boothbay Harbor
Trail contact: Maine Audubon, (207) 781-2330, http://maineaudubon.org/visit/josephine-newman

Finding the trailhead: From exit 31A on I-295, take ME 196 through Topsham. Drive 3.2 miles. Merge onto US 1 North. Drive 8.1 miles to Woolrich. Exit onto ME 127 South. Drive 8.7 miles to Georgetown village. ME 127 turns left and drops down to a bridge over Robinhood Cove. Cross the bridge and drive 0.1 mile. Turn right onto the Josephine Newman Sanctuary driveway at the small—and hard to see—sign. If you come to a second bridge, you've gone too far. Drive 0.1 mile to the parking area at the end of the driveway. The trailhead is at the south end of the parking area. GPS: N43 48.037' / W69 45.049'

The Hike

This hike follows several of the sanctuary's trails. First, follow the Horseshoe Trail across a meadow and into the woods. The trail parallels Robinhood Cove, visible through the trees. Beyond the southern end of the cove, the trail follows a stream to a 10-foot waterfall at the head of a narrow valley. After the waterfall, the trail crosses to the east past several stone walls.

Next, follow the Rocky End Trail toward Robinhood Cove. Be sure not to take the blue-blazed trail that leads south into Berry Woods Preserve. The Rocky End Trail drops down a rocky hill beside a stone wall to the shore of Robinhood Cove. The trail turns north, following the shore. There is a short side trail that leads out onto a rocky spit of land with fine views of the cove.

The trail climbs away from the cove. Turn right onto the Geology Trail, which drops back down to Robinhood Cove. The trail passes a rock face of dark and white rock. As Robinhood Cove narrows, the bluff the trail follows rises. The forest is dominated by mature pines. Far below, at the narrowest point of the cove, is a small

Waterfall nestled in the woods

Robinhood Cove

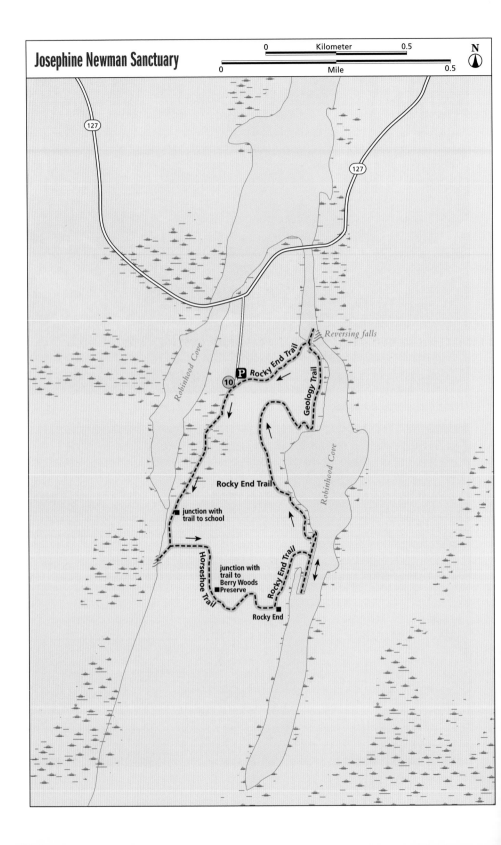

Josephine Newman Sanctuary

0   Kilometer   0.5

0   Mile   0.5

N

127

127

Robinhood Cove

Reversing falls

Rocky End Trail

Geology Trail

Robinhood Cove

P

10

Rocky End Trail

junction with
trail to school

Horseshoe Trail

junction with
trail to
Berry Woods
Preserve

Rocky End Trail

Rocky End

reversing falls. The waterfall is underwater when the tide is in, but it is visible when the tide is low. On the changing tide, the water appears to go up the waterfall.

The trail climbs back up toward the trailhead, passing a marshy area. Throughout the sanctuary are benches to sit on and contemplate the view or soak in the sounds and scents of the woods and shore. After enjoying the contemplative quiet of this hike, you may want to continue south on ME 127 to the nearby beaches at Reid State Park.

Miles And Directions:

0.0 Start from the trailhead at the south end of the parking area. In 400 feet you will come to a large sign with a map and other information. Bear left onto the Horseshoe Trail.

0.4 The Horseshoe Trail crosses a meadow and enters the woods along Robinhood Cove. Pass a side trail that leads west to Georgetown Elementary School.

0.5 A short side trail leads to a waterfall at the head of a narrow valley. The Horseshoe Trail turns east and follows an old stone wall.

0.6 Turn right onto the Rocky End Trail.

0.7 Turn left at the intersection. The trail that continues south connects with Berry Woods Preserve. This junction is unmarked and both trails are blazed blue.

0.9 The trail crosses over a hill following a stone wall to Robinhood Cove. The trail turns north along the cove.

1.1 A side trail leads 400 feet out a rocky point.

1.7 Turn right onto the Geology Trail.

2.1 A rough side trail leads down to a reversing falls in Robinhood Cove.

2.3 Turn right on the Horseshoe Trail to return to the trailhead.

2.4 Arrive back at the trailhead.

11 Vaughan Woods

There are three waterfalls in Vaughan Woods on Cascade Brook. First, the stream falls over the dam and cascades over a series of low ledges. Downstream is the famous Twelve Foot Falls, where the stream drops down a shale rock face. Farther along, the stream flows under a stone arch bridge and horsetails down a 20-foot rock amphitheater.

Start: Vaughan Woods Trailhead
Elevation gain: 154 feet
Distance: 1-mile loop
Hiking time: About 1 hour
Difficulty: Easy
Season: May to October
Trail surface: Woodland path
Land status: Vaughan Homestead
Nearest town: Hallowell

Other users: None
Water availability: None
Canine compatibility: Dogs should be leashed.
Fees and permits: None
Other maps: *DeLorme: Maine Atlas & Gazetteer*, map 12; USGS Augusta
Trail contact: Vaughan Homestead, https://vaughanhomestead.org

Finding the trailhead: From exit 109A on I-95, take US 202 toward Winthrop. Turn south onto Whitten Road just west of the bridge over I-95. (There's a median in the road that makes this turn impossible. You'll need to continue west past the shopping center and make a U-turn.) Drive 1.3 miles on Whitten Road. Turn left onto Winthrop Street. Cross I-95 and drive 1.1 miles. Turn right onto Middle Street about halfway down the hill to US 201. Drive 0.7 mile. Where Middle Street ends at Litchfield Road, the trailhead and parking are directly across Litchfield Road. GPS: N44 16.689' / W69 47.794'

The Hike

Cascade Brook tumbles through Vaughan Woods in Hallowell on its short journey to the Kennebec River. The town is named for Benjamin Hallowell, a well-connected Massachusetts businessman who bought the land in 1661. The woods are named for his grandsons who settled here and made their homestead a model farm. Luminaries such as Daniel Webster and John James Audubon came for a visit. In 1991 it became a preserve.

There are three waterfalls to visit. The Corniche Trail leads to a bridge over Cascade Brook just below the dam where it exits Cascade Pond. The stream pours over the dam looking like a waterfall, then falls over a series of low ledges.

You then follow the Twelve Foot Falls Trail downstream past the waterfall of that name. The brook stairsteps down a rock face into a small pool. The stream is surrounded by mature evergreens. Below Twelve Foot Falls, the ravine deepens and steepens.

Vaughan Woods

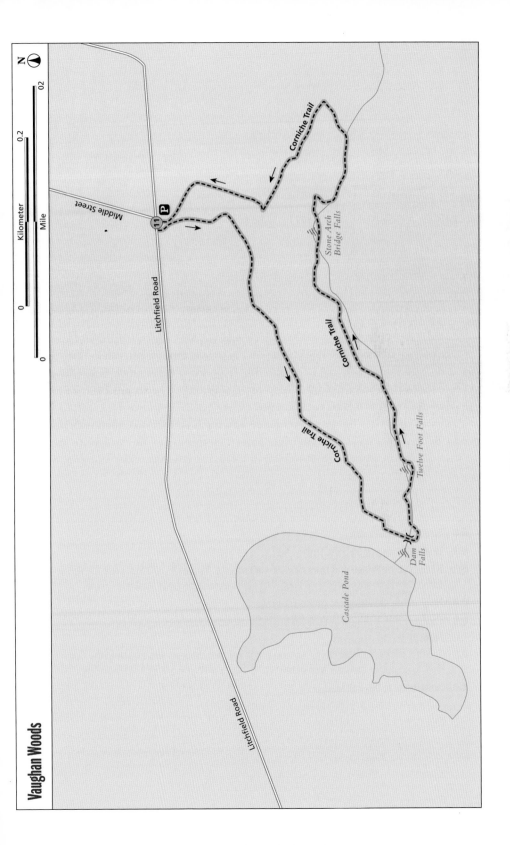

N

Kilometer
0   0.2
Mile
0   0.2

Middle Street

Litchfield Road

P
11

Corniche Trail

Stone Arch
Bridge Falls

Corniche Trail

Twelve Foot Falls

Corniche Trail

Dam
Falls

Cascade Pond

Litchfield Road

The bridge below the dam

The trail passes a stone arch bridge across the stream. From it you can look directly down on a 20-foot waterfall. The stream horsetails down a shale rock face. The rock curves toward the banks, making a kind of amphitheater. The arched bridge frames the downstream view in a picturesque way.

The trail then slabs up the steep hillside. You reach an overlook, then switchback and walk through a stand of huge white pines. The stream and the bridge are visible far below. Vaughan Woods is well-known to locals, but deserves wider attention than it gets.

Miles and Directions

0.0 Start from the Vaughan Woods Trailhead.

0.1 Bear right, staying on the Corniche Trail.

0.3 Reach Driving Bridge and Dam Falls. To continue the hike, walk 100 feet back the way you came. Turn right onto the Twelve Foot Falls Trail. Descend gently to Cascade Brook.

0.4 Hike beside the stream to Twelve Foot Falls.

0.6 Continue hiking beside the stream to the Stone Arch Bridge with a good-sized waterfall beneath it.

0.9 The trail climbs up away from Cascade Brook and switchbacks. Arrive back at the Corniche Trail. To complete the hike, turn right.

1.0 Arrive back at the trailhead.

12 Bickford Slides

Bickford Slides consists of three waterfalls on Bickford Brook. Upper and Middle Slides are a half mile apart on the stream. A narrow, vertical-sided gorge separates Middle and Upper Slides. Lower and Middle Slides are dramatic in different ways. Upper Slide is very picturesque. Each waterfall is between 40 and 50 feet high.

Start: Bickford Brook Trailhead
Elevation gain: 893 feet
Distance: 2.6-mile lollipop
Hiking time: About 3 hours
Difficulty: Strenuous. The hike isn't that difficult, but Bickford Slides Trail is poorly marked and hard to follow in places.
Season: Mid-May, when gate on ME 113 opens, to October
Trail surface: Woodland path
Land status: White Mountain National Forest
Nearest town: Fryeburg

Other users: None
Water availability: Bickford Brook
Canine compatibility: Dogs must be under control at all times.
Fees and permits: White Mountain National Forest parking fee
Other maps: *DeLorme: Maine Atlas & Gazetteer*, map 10; USGS Speckled Mountain
Trail contact: White Mountain National Forest, (603) 536-6100, www.fs.usda.gov/whitemountain

Finding the trailhead: From the junction of US 302 and ME 113 in Fryeburg, follow ME 113 north. Drive 20 miles. Pass the Basin Area and drive through the gate, then turn right into Brickett Place. The trailhead is at the east end of the parking area. GPS: N44 16.040' / W71 00.213'

The Hike

Bickford Brook tumbles down Speckled Mountain between Blueberry and Sugarloaf Mountains. The three Bickford Slides are separated by about three-quarters of a mile. Each waterfall is unique. Lower Slide is the highest at more than 50 feet. The stream is channeled through a narrow cleft in the bedrock, dropping to a plunge into a pool before dropping again. The Blueberry Ridge Trail crosses the stream where the stream begins its channeled drop. A marked trail leads to an overlook at the top of the plunge. A rough trail continues along the steep hillside to a viewpoint where you can see all three parts of Lower Slide.

The Bickford Slides Trail crosses the stream just upstream from the Blueberry Ridge Trail. You hike along the stream through an open hardwood forest. The trail then climbs steadily to an overlook of Middle Bickford Slide. The stream drops 40 feet down a steep rock face into a deep green pool. This pool would be great for swimming if the trail led to it. To get to the base of the falls, you have to bushwhack down the very steep hillside.

The trail climbs from the overlook, then slabs around the very steep hillside. This section of the trail is very hard to follow. Your best bet is to find a route you're

Middle Bickford Slide

Top of Lower Bickford Slide

Bickford Slides and Mad River Falls

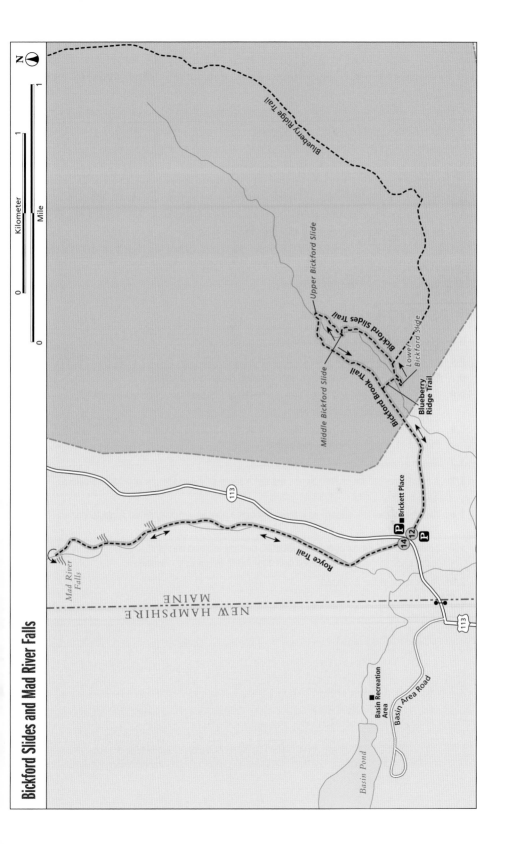

Mad River Falls

Royce Trail

NEW HAMPSHIRE
MAINE

113

Brickett Place

14
12

Bickford Brook Trail

Middle Bickford Slide

Upper Bickford Slide

Bickford Slides Trail

Lower Bickford Slide

Blueberry Ridge Trail

Blueberry Ridge Trail

Basin Recreation Area

Basin Area Road

Basin Pond

113

N

Kilometer
0   1
Mile
0   1

comfortable with and make your way to the boulders near the top of Middle Slide. The trail reappears in the boulders next to the waterfall. You climb to the top of the falls, where there's a good-sized pool and a smaller waterfall upstream.

The now-obvious trail follows the stream near the edge of a narrow, vertical gorge. The gorge is only about 20 feet deep, but as you hike the stream is out of sight within it. Soon, Upper Slide becomes visible through the trees. As you near it, you get fine views of the smallest of the three waterfalls.

The trail crosses Bickford Brook just upstream of Upper Slide. You climb through a boulder field along the bank. Where you reach level ground above the stream, an obvious but unmarked trail descends to the base of Lower Slide. The trail is rough but there are good viewpoints before the difficult section.

A short hike on level ground away from the stream leads you back to the Bickford Brook Trail. Turn left and descend easily back to the trailhead through mixed forest. This is a good area to see wildflowers.

Miles and Directions

0.0 Start from the Bickford Brook Trailhead.

0.6 Climb steadily. Turn right onto the Blueberry Ridge Trail.

0.7 Descend to Bickford Brook. Turn right onto the Bickford Slides Trail.

0.8 Descend on a rough trail to an overlook of Lower Bickford Slide. To continue the hike, return to the Blueberry Ridge Trail.

0.9 Cross the Blueberry Ridge Trail. Walk on bedrock along the stream for 50 feet. Cross Bickford Brook onto the Bickford Slides Trail.

1.2 Reach an overlook of Middle Bickford Slide.

1.3 A poorly marked rough trail climbs around a steep ravine to the top of Middle Bickford Slide below a series of small waterfalls.

1.5 The trail follows the stream as it flows through a narrow, vertically sided gorge to Upper Bickford Slide.

1.7 Cross Bickford Brook above the waterfall, bearing left and climbing away from the stream. Arrive back at the Bickford Brook Trail. Turn left to return to the trailhead.

2.6 Arrive back at the trailhead.

13 Rattlesnake Flume and Pool

Rattlesnake Flume is a 10-foot-wide gorge that is a couple of hundred yards long and about 10 feet deep. There's a waterfall at its head and a bedrock dome at the other end with nice views. A short distance upstream is Rattlesnake Pool. The brook slides down a fault in the bedrock, dropping 15 feet into the prettiest pool in Maine.

Start: Stone House Trailhead
Elevation gain: 347 feet
Distance: 2.4 miles out and back
Hiking time: About 3 hours
Difficulty: Easy
Season: Mid-May, when Stone House Road opens, to October
Trail surface: Woods road and woodland path
Land status: White Mountain National Forest
Nearest town: Fryeburg
Other users: None

Water availability: None
Canine compatibility: Dogs must be under control at all times.
Fees and permits: None
Other maps: *DeLorme: Maine Atlas & Gazetteer*, map 10; USGS Center Lovell and Speckled Mountain
Trail contact: White Mountain National Forest, (603) 536-6100, www.fs.usda.gov/whitemountain

Finding the trailhead: From the junction of US 302 and ME 113 in Fryeburg, follow ME 113 north. Drive 17.8 miles. Turn left onto Stone House Road. Drive 1.1 miles. Parking is on the right just before the gate across the road. The trailhead is at the gate. GPS: N44 15.121' / W70 59.449'

The Hike

An easy walk through a meadow and into the woods leads you to Rattlesnake Flume. A short bridge crosses this narrow gorge. Standing on the bridge and looking upstream, you see Rattlesnake Brook drop 10 feet into the gorge, then race between its walls. The gorge is a wide, straight joint in the granite bedrock.

Downstream from the bridge, the gorge opens up and deepens. A large dome of bedrock rises vertically from the water. By crossing the bridge, you have access to the top of the rock, with views of the stream as it curls around its base. The gray bedrock contrasts with the sandy stone in the streambed. It's a geologically fascinating spot.

The Stone House Trail continues upstream out of sight of Rattlesnake Brook. Another side trail leads down to Rattlesnake Pool. Here the brook slides down a 15-foot waterfall into a deep pool ringed with granite. The water appears turquoise where it's shallow, then deeper blue, then black where it's deepest. This is the most beautiful pool in Maine.

The stream slides over a natural stone dam then down a joint in the bedrock and away toward Rattlesnake Flume. The pool sits in a deep bowl against a steep hillside covered with tall evergreens. It's a cool refuge on a hot summer day, but can be very

Rattlesnake Flume and Pool

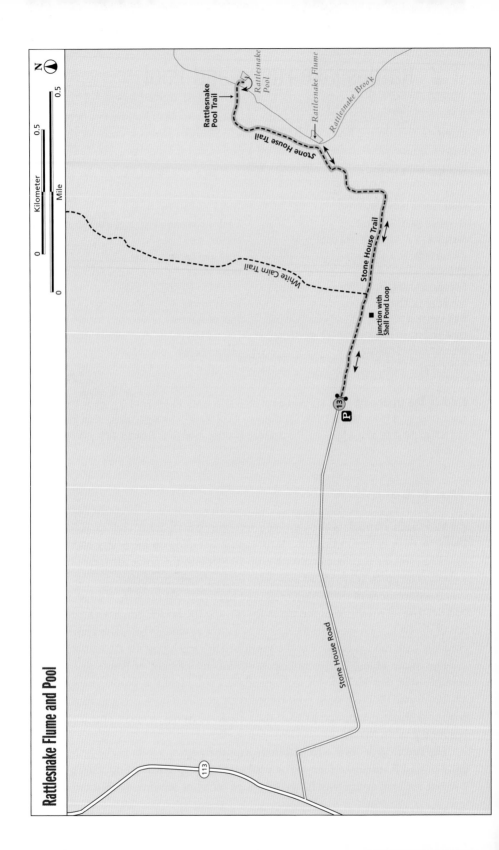

Rattlesnake Flume

buggy in spring. There are flat rocks around the pool where you can sit and dry off after a swim.

On your hike back to the trailhead, you have a fine view to the west of Baldface Mountain.

Rattlesnake Pool

Miles and Directions

0.0 Start at the trailhead at the gate across Stone House Road.

0.2 Walk up the road, passing the Shell Pond Loop.

0.3 Continue up the road, passing the White Cairn Trail.

0.5 Turn left off the road onto the Stone House Trail.

0.8 Turn right at the sign toward the gorge. Hike 100 feet to the bridge over Rattlesnake Brook with a view of the flume and falls at its head. Return to the Stone House Trail.

0.9 Turn right on the Stone House Trail.

1.1 Cross a small wooden bridge, then turn right onto the Rattlesnake Pool Trail.

1.2 Reach Rattlesnake Pool. To complete the hike, retrace your steps to the trailhead.

2.4 Arrive back at the trailhead.

14 Mad River Falls

The Royce Trail follows the Mad River upstream past several waterfalls and interesting rock formations. Where the stream splits into two forks, the trail climbs between them to an overlook of Mad River Falls. The stream drops well over 100 feet in two plunges.

See map on p. 57.
Start: Royce Trailhead
Elevation gain: 470 feet
Distance: 3.4 miles out and back
Hiking time: 2 to 3 hours
Difficulty: Easy
Season: Mid-May, when ME 113 through Evans Notch opens, to October
Trail surface: Woodland path
Land status: White Mountain National Forest
Nearest town: Gilead and Stow

Other users: None
Water availability: Mad River
Canine compatibility: Dogs must be under control at all times.
Fees and permits: National forest parking fee
Other maps: *DeLorme: Maine Atlas & Gazetteer*, map 10; USGS Wild River
Trail contact: White Mountain National Forest, (603) 536-6100, www.fs.usda.gov/whitemountain

Finding the trailhead: From the junction of US 302 and ME 113 in Fryeburg, follow ME 113 north. Drive 20 miles. Pass the Basin Area and drive through the gate, then turn right into Brickett Place. The Royce Trailhead is across ME 113 and a few steps north. GPS: N44 16.060' / W71 00.268'

The Hike

The Royce Trail descends gently on an abandoned roadbed to the Mad River. Most of the year the river isn't mad, but rather a babbling mountain stream with a cobble bed. The trail fords the stream. By late May, you should be able to cross without getting your feet wet.

The trail follows the bank upstream past small waterfalls and a cliff on the far bank. You ford the river again. Just upstream from the ford, you should be able to cross on stones. A short hike farther and you reach the first waterfalls. The stream drops through a series of deep pools and slides over a granite ledge across the river, a very picturesque swimming hole.

A few tenths of a mile more and you cross a side stream and reach another waterfall. You cross the stream on boulders below the deep pool in front of a 6-foot horsetail.

Just upstream two forks come together to create the Mad River. The trail crosses the western one and climbs a steep hill between the two streams. A marked side trail leads west to an overlook of Mad River Falls. The stream drops more than 100 feet in two closely linked plunges. (There's another waterfall above these that's hard to see.)

Mad River Falls

Falls on the Mad River

A deep pool is at the base of the falls, but from the overlook, there's no obvious way to descend to it. A rough trail to the right of the overlook descends to the clearest view of the waterfall, and you can see where others have downclimbed from there to reach the pool. Rather than make that risky climb, swim at one of the two smaller falls you passed.

Miles and Directions

0.0 Start from the Royce Trailhead.

0.2 Ford the Mad River.

0.7 Ford the Mad River again.

1.2 Pass the first set of waterfalls and pools.

1.4 Cross the Mad River just below a waterfall and pool.

1.5 Cross the South Branch Mad River.

1.7 Climb steadily to a junction with a side trail to Mad River Falls. Turn left and hike 200 feet to a waterfall overlook. To complete the hike, retrace your steps to the trailhead.

3.4 Arrive back at the trailhead.

15 Kees Falls

Kees Falls is a 30-foot plunge on Morrison Brook. The trail follows the brook past several smaller water features before reaching Kees Falls. It's an easy hike through a fine hardwood forest.

Start: Caribou Mountain Trailhead
Elevation gain: 690 feet
Distance: 3.8 miles out and back
Hiking time: About 3 hours
Difficulty: Moderate
Season: Mid-May, when ME 113 through Evans Notch opens, to October
Trail surface: Woodland path
Land status: White Mountain National Forest
Nearest town: Gilead

Other users: None
Water availability: Morrison Brook
Canine compatibility: Dogs must be under control at all times.
Fees and permits: None
Other maps: *DeLorme: Maine Atlas & Gazetteer*, map 10; USGS Speckled Mountain
Trail contact: White Mountain National Forest, (603) 536-6100, www.fs.usda.gov/whitemountain

Finding the trailhead: From the junction of US 2 and ME 113 in Gilead, take ME 113 south. Drive 4.9 miles. Turn left onto the short road to the parking area at the brown sign for the trailhead. The trailhead is at the north end of the parking area. GPS: N44 20.159 / W70 58.516

The Hike

The Caribou Trail heads north from the parking area parallel to ME 113. You cross Morrison Brook then turn east and follow the stream. The rest of the hike is along this picturesque brook. There are several small waterfalls and other features that you'll hike by on your way to Kees Falls.

Morrison Brook drains the west side of Gammon and Caribou Mountains. The stream flows into Evan Brook, which flows into the Wild River at Hastings. The trail climbs gently toward Gammon Notch through a hardwood forest. This is a great hike for spring wildflowers.

You cross the stream again then enter the Caribou-Speckled Mountain Wilderness. Kees Falls sneaks up on you. Unlike many other waterfalls, you don't hear it coming. Suddenly, there's a 30-foot plunge beside the trail. Morrison Brook falls down mossy bedrock into a deep, narrow pool.

If you're willing to do some scrambling on the rock, you can get a great picture from the base of the falls and enjoy a dip in the pool. Most hikers will settle for a great view from the side and then at the top of the falls, where the trail crosses Morrison Brook a third (and final) time. The Caribou Trail continues climbing past Kees Falls all the way to the large, open summit of Caribou Mountain, with great views and lots of blueberries.

Kees Falls

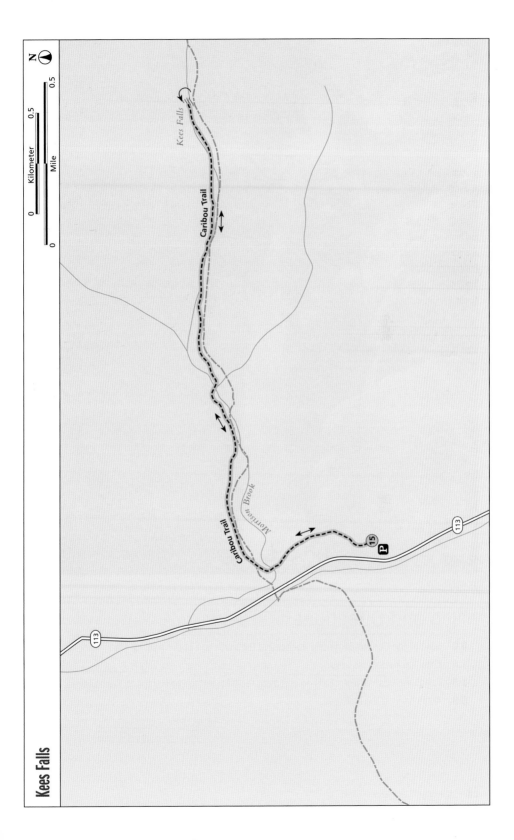

Kees Falls

Miles and Directions

0.0 Start at the Caribou Mountain Trailhead at the north end of the parking area.

1.5 Enter the wilderness area.

1.9 Reach the base of Kees Falls. To complete the hike, retrace your steps to the trailhead.

3.8 Arrive back at the trailhead.

16 Kezar Falls

Kezar Falls is one of the geologically more interesting waterfalls in Maine. The Kezar River flows out of Five Kezar Ponds and plunges 30 feet into a narrow gorge, winding through the sculpted bedrock into a large, dark pool.

Start: Kezar Falls turnout
Elevation gain: 60 feet
Distance: 0.2 mile loop
Hiking time: Less than 1 hour
Difficulty: Easy
Season: May to October
Trail surface: Woodland path
Land status: Unknown
Nearest town: Waterford

Other users: None
Water availability: None
Canine compatibility: Dogs must be under control at all times.
Fees and permits: None
Other maps: DeLorme: Maine Atlas & Gazetteer, map 10; USGS North Waterford
Trail contact: None

Finding the trailhead: From the junction of ME 26 and ME 117 in Norway, follow ME 117 west. Drive 13.4 miles. Turn left on ME 35 south. Drive 0.2 mile. Turn right onto Five Kezars Road. Drive 3.2 miles. Just after you drive up a small hill away from Five Kezar Ponds, turn right onto a rough turnout. The trailhead is on the right side of the turnout. GPS: N44 11.859' / W70 48.871'

The Hike

The Kezar River flows out of Five Kezar Ponds to Kezar Pond, but not nearby Kezar Lake. There are a lot of features named Kezar in and around Lovell. George Kezar was a well-known eighteenth-century trapper who worked the area.

Five Kezar Ponds is a complex shallow lake full of islands and hidden bays. It's a good place to find wildlife. Take your time as you drive to the waterfall to check it out. Kezar Falls is just south of the ponds in a piney woods.

The Kezar River flows out of the ponds and plunges 30 feet into a narrow granite gorge only 10 feet across. The bedrock is sculpted into sinuous curves and surprising overhangs. The gorge is only 50 feet long, but the river seems to flow twice that far within it.

The rough trail leads to the top of the gorge. You can walk along its edge and look down into its shadowy depths. Kezar Falls shines at its head. In spring the falls roar, the sound echoing through the gorge and into the woods. By summer the waterfall has diminished and taken on a more humble appearance.

From the pool where the river exits the gorge, you have a great view of the sculpted bedrock and the overhangs, but can't see the waterfall. The deep pool is dark with tannin, its bottom covered with rotting logs and needles that stir up when you swim. It's not the best swimming hole. This is a waterfall for observing and studying.

Gorge below Kezar Falls

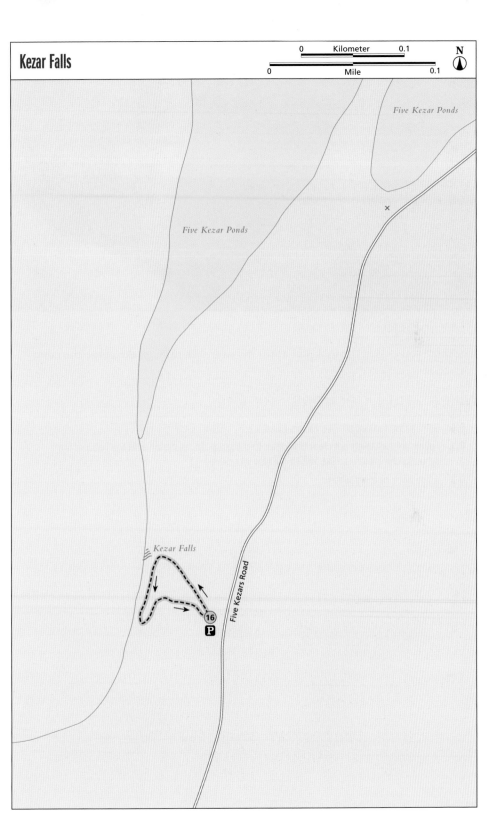

Kezar Falls

Five Kezar Ponds

Five Kezar Ponds

Kezar Falls

Five Kezars Road

16

Kezar Falls through the gorge

The more you look at the rock and watch the river slide through the gorge, the more you see.

Miles and Directions

0.0 Start at the turnout off Five Kezars Road.

0.1 Follow an unmarked but clear trail down to the gorge. The waterfall is at the head of the gorge. To complete the hike, return the way you came.

0.2 Arrive back at the trailhead.

17 Frenchman's Hole

Frenchman's Hole is a popular local swimming spot. Bull Branch creates a large pool behind a natural bedrock dam. The stream plunges over the center of the rock face, dropping 20 feet and creating a dramatic horseshoe falls. Downstream are more waterfalls, but there's no easy access to the gorge below Frenchman's Hole.

Start: Frenchman's Hole parking area (early in the season start at gate across Bull Branch Road)
Elevation gain: 40 feet (186 feet from gate)
Distance: 0.4 mile out and back (1.4 miles out and back from gate)
Hiking time: About 1 hour
Difficulty: Easy
Season: May to October
Trail surface: Woods road
Land status: Mahoosuc Public Reserved Land

Nearest town: Bethel
Other users: Hunters in season
Water availability: None
Canine compatibility: Dogs must be under control at all times.
Fees and permits: None
Other maps: *DeLorme: Maine Atlas & Gazetteer*, map 18; USGS Old Speck Mountain
Trail contact: Mahoosuc Public Lands, (207) 778-8231, www.maine.gov/cgi-bin/online/doc/parksearch/details.pl?park_id=58

Finding the trailhead: From the junction of ME 26 and US 2 in Bethel, follow the combined route north. Drive 2.8 miles. Turn left onto Sunday River Road at the sign for the ski resort. Drive 2.2 miles. Bear left at the entrance to the ski resort, staying on Sunday River Road. Drive 5.5 miles. Turn left and cross the Sunday River on Bull Branch Road. Across the bridge, bear right at the sign for Mahoosuc Public Reserved Land. Drive 0.2 mile. If the gate is closed, park here on the shoulder. GPS: N44 30.233' / W70 55.039'. If the gate is open, drive another 0.3 mile. Turn left and drive up the hill to the parking area. GPS: N44 30.576' W70 55.135'. Frenchman's Hole is across Bull Branch Road directly below the parking area.

The Hike

Bull Branch drains the south slope of Old Speck Mountain. One branch flows out of Speck Pond, drops through a steep valley, and empties into the Sunday River. Frenchman's Hole is a large, natural pool above a bedrock dam across the stream. It is a popular swimming hole, with a picnic area on the bank and steps down to the water.

There's no real hiking trail to Frenchman's Hole or the waterfall. With a little easy bushwhacking, you can see the waterfall from three angles. First, you can see its top from across Frenchman's Hole from the picnic area. Second, by walking down the road and descending a rough trail to the bedrock dam, you can walk out to the top of the waterfall. The bedrock arches across the stream, with a higher rock face on the far bank. The stream plunges 20 feet over the face into a good-sized pool.

By walking farther down the road, you can bushwhack down a rough trail to the pool. From here you have a fine view of the waterfall and the rock face it plunges

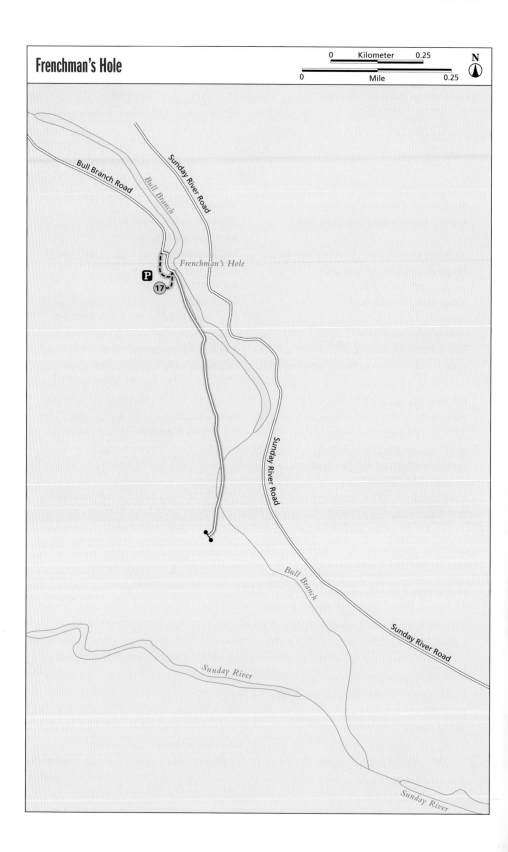

0   Kilometer   0.25

0   Mile   0.25

N

Bull Branch Road

Sunday River Road

Bull Branch

P

17

Frenchman's Hole

Sunday River Road

Bull Branch

Sunday River Road

Sunday River

Sunday River

The Frenchman's Hole waterfall

Top of the waterfall

over. Notice that Bull Branch is very rough heading downstream through a rocky gorge. There are waterfalls and other features within this gorge but no way to access them. You can bushwhack from the road but won't ever get a fine view. You'll have to be satisfied with Frenchman's Hole and its waterfall.

If you come in the spring to see the waterfall when Bull Branch is running high, you'll have to park on the shoulder of the road at the gate you passed on the way to the parking area. It adds about a mile overall to your hike. On your drive in, you pass another popular swimming hole on the Sunday River. Look for the paved and lined parking area along Sunday River Road. A trail descends to the river across from the parking area.

Miles and Directions

0.0 Start at the parking area on the hill above Bull Branch Road.

0.1 Walk back down the road and cross Bull Branch Road into the picnic area. From the bank of Frenchman's Hole, you have a view of the top of the waterfall. To continue the hike, walk down Bull Branch Road.

0.2 Turn left off the road and descend a rough, unmarked trail that leads to the natural bedrock dam. To continue the hike, return to Bull Branch Road.

0.3 Walk farther down Bull Branch Road to another rough, unmarked trail that descends to Bull Branch just below the pool at the base of the falls. To complete the hike, follow the road back to the parking area.

0.4 Arrive back at the parking area.

18 Screw Auger Falls

The Bear River drops onto a flat expanse of granite, then plunges 30 feet into a sinuous canyon. Through the canyon, the river drops another 30 feet before emerging. You can explore the granite atop the gorge on both sides of the river and peer deep into its sculpted depths.

Start: Screw Auger Falls Trailhead
Elevation gain: 62 feet
Distance: 0.2 mile out and back
Hiking time: Less than 1 hour
Difficulty: Easy
Season: May to October
Trail surface: Graded path and granite bedrock
Land status: Grafton Notch State Park
Nearest town: Newry
Other users: None
Water availability: None

Canine compatibility: Dogs should be leashed.
Fees and permits: Parking fee
Other maps: *DeLorme: Maine Atlas & Gazetteer*, map 18; USGS Old Speck Mountain
Trail contact: Grafton Notch State Park, (207) 824-2912, www.maine.gov/graftonnotch, and Mahoosuc Public Lands, (207) 778-8231, www.maine.gov/cgi-bin/online/doc/park-search/details.pl?park_id=58

Finding the trailhead: From the junction of US 2 and ME 26 in Newry, follow ME 26 north. Drive 9.6 miles. Turn left into the Screw Auger Falls parking area at the state park sign. The trailhead is at the south end of the parking area. GPS: N44 34.313' / W70 54.155'

The Hike

There are two Screw Auger Falls in Maine—one in Gulf Hagas and this one in Grafton Notch State Park. This is perhaps Maine's best known and most visited waterfall. The gorge created by the Bear River is a natural wonder.

From the parking area, you follow a gravel path to the river. Along the way, you can walk through a crack in a granite boulder in the woods. You emerge onto a flat granite ledge. The river drops down, creating a small waterfall, then slides across the rock. Where the rock rises up, the river found a joint and over time widened it.

The river plunges 30 from the ledge into a narrow canyon. The canyon is only about 10 feet wide, and the bedrock is sculpted into smooth curves. There's a fence along the lip of the gorge just below Screw Auger Falls that allows you to look down into the canyon and get a fine view of the waterfall. But to see all of the canyon and its smaller waterfalls, pots, and kettles, you have to explore a bit.

You can hike around on the granite ledges on both sides of the river and look down into the gorge at various places. You can also descend the ledge on the east side of the river (where the trail and overlook are) down to the river where it exits the gorge. The view into the gorge here is great. You can really see how the river dug

Screw Auger Falls

through the granite one grain at a time. The rock is carved in sinuous curves that appear to glow in the afternoon sun. In several places, round kettles have been formed by small rocks spun in place for years and years.

Screw Auger Falls

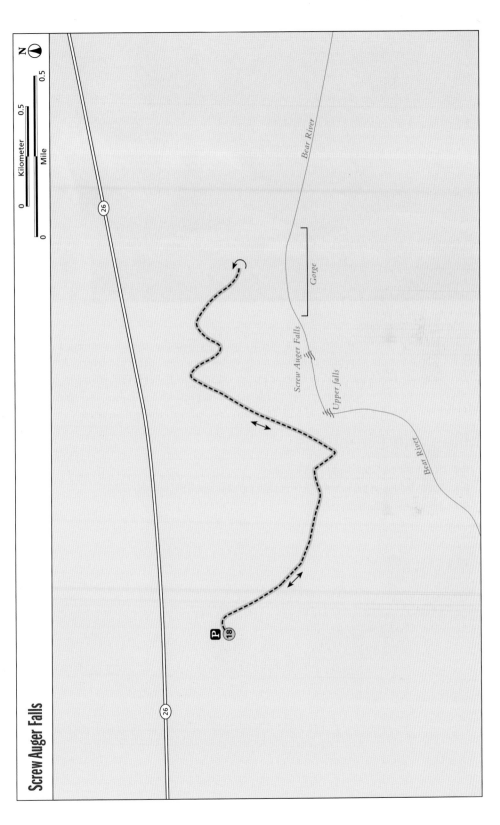

N

Kilometer
0   0.5

Mile
0   0.5

26

26

P
18

Bear River

Gorge

Screw Auger Falls

Upper falls

Bear River

Where the Bear River exits the gorge

Screw Auger Falls is more spectacular in spring when the river is running high, but you can do more exploring and see more of the geology when the river is lower. Whenever you visit, you need to stop at Puzzle Mountain Bakery. This roadside, self-service bakery is known by hikers across Maine for its pies, whoopie pies, and cookies. The bakery is on the west side of ME 26 south of Grafton Notch State Park.

Miles and Directions

0.0 Start from the Screw Auger Falls Trailhead.

0.1 Reach the top of the waterfall. To complete the hike, return the way you came.

0.2 Arrive back at the trailhead.

19 Step Falls

The trail climbs gently alongside Wight Brook to the top of Step Falls. The waterfall drops a total of more than 150 feet in a series of large and small falls over a wide expanse of exposed granite bedrock. The numerous large and small pools within the falls are popular swimming spots in the summer.

Start: Step Falls Trailhead
Elevation gain: 246 feet
Distance: 1.1 miles out and back
Hiking time: About 1 hour
Difficulty: Easy
Season: May to October. Step Falls is a popular swimming spot and is best visited during the week.
Trail surface: Woodland path
Land status: Mahoosuc Land Trust preserve, managed by the Nature Conservancy

Nearest town: Bethel
Other users: Most hikers are at Step Falls to swim.
Water availability: Wight Brook above the falls
Canine compatibility: Dogs are not permitted at Step Falls.
Fees and permits: None
Other maps: *DeLorme: Maine Atlas & Gazetteer*, map 18; USGS Puzzle Mountain
Trail contact: https://www.mahoosuc.org/hikes

Finding the trailhead: From the junction of US 2 and ME 26 in Newry, head north on ME 26 toward Grafton Notch State Park. Drive 4.7 miles to the trailhead parking for the Grafton Loop. Continue driving another 3.2 miles to Step Falls Preserve. The trailhead parking is on the right at a sign. Cars are often parked along the road on weekends. The trail begins at the north end of the parking area. GPS: N44 34.288' / W70 52.242'

The Hike

The trail is an easy walk through the woods alongside Wight Brook, climbing gently to the top of Step Falls. There are several side trails out onto the falls before the top. You can take the first of these and complete the hike to the top of the falls on the rock alongside the falls instead of the trail. From the top of the falls, you have a view of Sunday River Whitecap, across the Bear River valley, framed by Step Falls and the dense, green forest on its sides.

The falls drop more than 150 feet in total. Wight Brook slides over exposed granite bedrock and drops down several good-sized falls into deep pools, splitting and reforming as it makes its way down the wide expanse of rock in seemingly random fashion. Over time the stream has dug numerous small kettles in the bedrock below the smaller drops. Some of these are only a few feet across but 6 or more feet deep.

During the summer Step Falls is actually fifty or more falls. As is typical of many falls over granite in Maine, the stream flows into and expands natural seams and cracks in the bedrock, splitting off rounded blocks. The resulting falls is a series of bedrock pillows and slides that the water flows down. The exposed bedrock is 100 feet wide,

Step Falls

much of it water-free in the summer. Only during the spring freshet does the stream run high enough to cover all the rock as it drains the saddle between Puzzle Mountain and Mount Hittie.

On warm days the granite is busy with people who have come to swim. Children slide down small falls into deep pools, laughing and splashing. Braver folks slide down long expanses of slick rock on a ribbon of water into large, deep pools full of crystal-clear water. Hikers walk up the trail in swimsuits and flip-flops, a towel over their shoulder.

You can also drive 1.6 miles north up ME 26 into Grafton Notch State Park and visit Screw Auger Falls (hike 18). Those falls are also granite bedrock, but look very

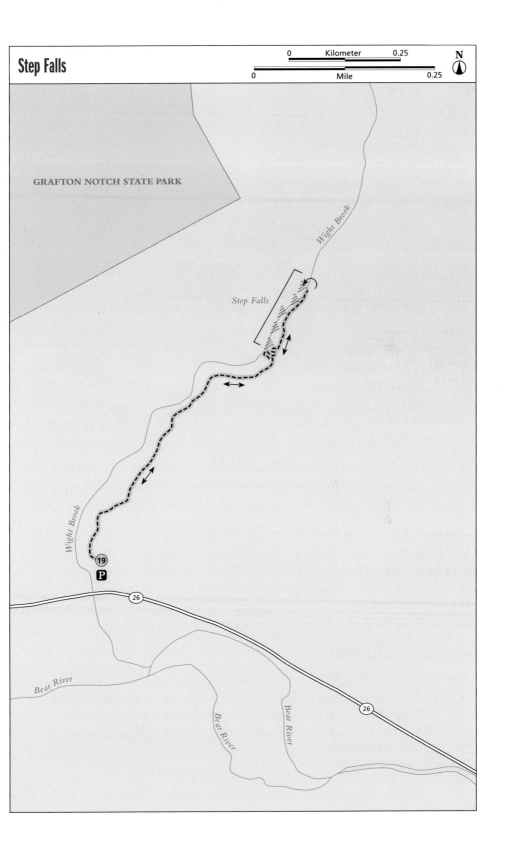

Step Falls

GRAFTON NOTCH STATE PARK

Wight Brook

Step Falls

Wight Brook

19

Bear River

Bear River

Bear River

26

26

Sunday River Whitecap across Step Falls

different. Step Falls is over granite on a steep slope, while Screw Auger Falls is on relatively flat granite. The falls are actually a narrow gorge that the Bear River has cut through the bedrock, zigzagging along seams in the granite, dropping down a falls, and creating kettles at the bottom of the gorge.

Farther up into Grafton Notch is Mother Walker Falls, a 1,000-foot-long gorge cut through the granite by the Bear River. The river drops about 100 feet through the gorge. Near the head of the gorge is an abandoned river channel cut in the rock and a natural bridge across the river, although you have to be standing in the stream to see the bridge. Above the falls you can see granite cliffs with interesting cracks on them. All around you rise the Mahoosuc Range of bare-summited mountains.

Miles and Directions

0.0 Start from the trailhead at the north end of the parking area.

0.4 The trail follows Wight Brook upstream to the bottom of the falls. You can continue to the top of the falls on the trail or scramble up the exposed bedrock that the falls drop down.

0.6 The trail ends at a private road just above the top of Step Falls. To complete the hike, return the way you came.

1.1 Arrive back at the trailhead.

20 The Cataracts

Frye Brook slides down bedrock into a pool, flows around a gentle bend, and then disappears. It drops 70 feet in two plunges into a narrow, deep gorge. The stream exits the gorge with a 15-foot waterfall. It's a rugged, wild ride. There are several pools to swim in and a picnic area near the upper falls.

Start: Cataracts Trailhead
Elevation gain: 318 feet
Distance: 1.2 miles out and back
Hiking time: About 1 hour
Difficulty: Easy
Season: May to October
Trail surface: Woodland path
Land status: Grafton Notch State Park
Nearest town: Andover
Other users: None
Water availability: Frye Brook

Canine compatibility: Dogs must be under control at all times.
Fees and permits: None
Other maps: *DeLorme: Maine Atlas & Gazetteer,* map 18; USGS Andover
Trail contact: Grafton Notch State Park, (207) 824-2912, www.maine.gov/graftonnotch, and Mahoosuc Public Lands, (207) 778-8231, www.maine.gov/cgi-bin/online/doc/park-search/details.pl?park_id=58

Finding the trailhead: From the junction of US 2 and ME 5 in Rumford Point, follow ME 5 north. Drive 10.9 miles into Andover village. Turn left onto Upton Road. Drive 5.4 miles. Parking is a gravel turnout on the right. The trailhead is across the road near the bridge over Frye Brook. GPS: N44 38.482' / W70 51.357'

The Hike

The Cataracts on Frye Brook is actually four waterfalls. As you hike up beside the stream from the Ellis River, you'll first come to a 15-foot waterfall where the brook emerges from a deep, narrow gorge. The brook leaps out of a cleft in the rock clogged with boulders. There's a nice pool at the base of the waterfall. Rough trails leave the hiking trail and descend to the base of this waterfall that locals call the Churn.

The trail climbs to the top of the gorge. You have partial views into the gorge and can see part of the two linked waterfalls within—these are the Cataracts. The total drop is 70 feet. There's a large, deep pool at their base within the gorge. The only way to get a good view of the Cataracts is to cross Frye Brook below the Churn. From there you can climb to an overlook. Enough other people have done this that the route is fairly clear, although it can be wet and slippery. In spring the first section is part of the stream. From the overlook you have a straight-on view of the Cataracts. You can downclimb from there to the pool fairly easily.

If you don't want to bushwhack, you can get an interesting view of the Cataracts from the top. As the trail crosses the top of the gorge, there's a fence to keep you away from the precipitous edge. Past the fence, you can step out onto the ledge the

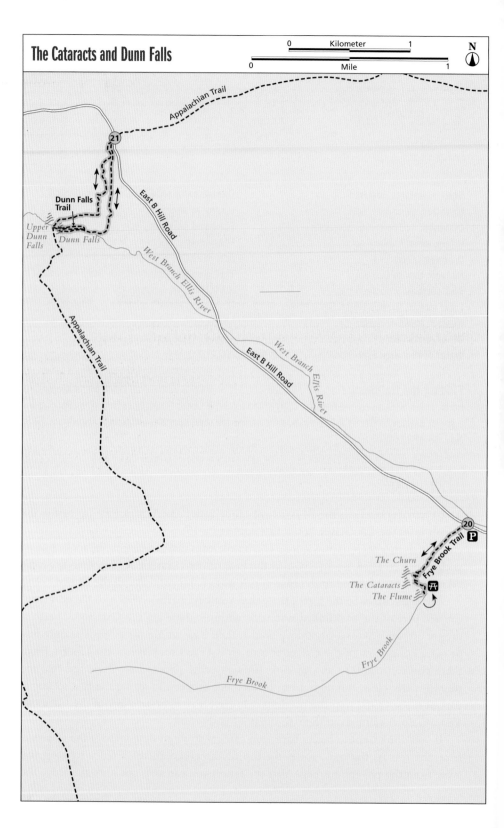

The Cataracts and Dunn Falls

0   Kilometer   1

0   Mile   1

N

Appalachian Trail

21

Dunn Falls Trail

East B Hill Road

Upper
Dunn
Falls

Dunn Falls

West Branch Ellis River

Appalachian Trail

East B Hill Road

West Branch Ellis River

20

P

The Churn

Frye Brook Trail

The Cataracts

The Flume

Frye Brook

Frye Brook

Left: The Cataracts; Right: The Churn

brook flows across before dropping into the gorge, and walk right up the lip where the water leaps into the air.

Farther upstream the trail passes through a picnic area. Just beyond that an unmarked side trail leads to the base of the upper falls that locals call the Flume. The stream slides down a joint in the bedrock into a deep pool. It's a very pretty waterfall.

Miles and Directions

0.0 Start from the Cataracts Trailhead.

0.3 Reach the base of the Cataracts.

0.4 Climb beside the falls to the top of the Cataracts.

0.5 Reach the picnic area.

0.6 Reach the upper falls. To complete the hike, return the way you came.

1.2 Arrive back at the trailhead.

21 Dunn Falls

This hike visits 80-foot Dunn Falls, 30-foot Upper Dunn Falls, and several waterfalls on a side stream—all in less than 2 miles. Dunn Falls plunges between vertical walls more than 100 feet high into a jumble of boulders.

See map on p. 86.
Start: Southbound Appalachian Trail at East B Hill Road
Elevation gain: 562 feet
Distance: 1.9-mile loop
Hiking time: About 3 hours
Difficulty: Moderate
Season: Late May to October
Trail surface: Woodland path
Land status: Appalachian Trail corridor

Nearest town: Andover
Other users: None
Water availability: West Branch Ellis River
Canine compatibility: Dogs must be under control at all times.
Fees and permits: None
Other maps: *DeLorme: Maine Atlas & Gazetteer*, map 18; USGS Andover
Trail contact: Maine Appalachian Trail Club, http://www.matc.org

Finding the trailhead: From the junction of US 2 and ME 5 in Rumford Point, follow ME 5 north. Drive 10.9 miles into Andover village. Turn left onto Upton Road, which becomes East B Hill Road when you leave Andover. Drive 8.3 miles, passing the Cataracts Trailhead along the way. Parking is a gravel lot on the right just past the trailhead, which is on the left. GPS: N44 40.063' / W70 53.580'

The Hike

Just below Dunn Notch, the West Branch Ellis River crosses the Appalachian Trail then drops 30 feet into a pool trapped between vertical rock walls. At the east end of the pool, the stream seems to disappear between the walls. From this vantage you can hear Dunn Falls, but you cannot see it. The stream drops more than 80 feet straight down between vertical walls more than 100 feet high. The hike crosses the top of the waterfall, but visits the base of Dunn Falls first.

The 1.9-mile loop hike to the falls begins on the southbound Appalachian Trail (AT) where it crosses East B Hill Road. You drop down to a small stream and turn left onto the Cascade Trail. This trail follows the stream down past numerous small and medium-sized waterfalls. These mossy falls, dropping over broken black rock, are worth the hike all by themselves. The trail then cuts through the woods to the West Branch Ellis River and follows it upstream.

After crossing the stream you come to a fork. The trail to the right leads to the base of Dunn Falls—the only place you can see the main drop. By scrambling out onto the rocks in the stream, you can stand at the pool at the base of the falls. Black cliffs rise vertically more than 100 feet over your head. In front of you Dunn Falls plunges 80 feet.

Dunn Falls

You then backtrack to the fork and take the left trail up to the AT, climbing beside the waterfall. Just before reaching the AT, you pass an overlook with a view of the upper falls. To complete the hike, turn right on the AT and follow it back to East B Hill Road.

Waterfall along the Cascade Trail

Miles and Directions

0.0 Start from the southbound Appalachian Trail at East B Hill Road. In 100 feet, cross a small stream and turn left onto the Cascade Trail.

0.4 Descend beside the stream, passing several waterfalls. Cross the stream.

0.6 Cross the West Branch Ellis River.

0.7 Bear right onto the Dunn Falls Trail.

0.8 Reach the base of Dunn Falls. To continue the hike, return to the Cascade Trail.

0.9 Turn right on the Cascade Trail.

1.1 Climb steadily to an overlook of Upper Dunn Falls.

1.2 Turn right onto the AT.

1.9 Arrive back at the trailhead.

22 Swift River Falls and Coos Canyon

Swift River Falls and Coos Canyon are two of Maine's most interesting roadside waterfalls. Swift River Falls drops about 10 feet, but what's noteworthy is the rock around the falls. The river has sculpted the bedrock into waves and edges, and there are numerous kettles in the bedrock beside the river as well. Just 6 mile upstream the Swift River flows through Coos Canyon, where it plunges 15 feet into a 30-foot canyon. The river is deep in the canyon, and you can jump into it from an overhang or just wade in.

Start: West side of ME 17 near USGS gaging station

Elevation gain: 34 feet

Distance: 0.2 mile (0.1-mile loop at Swift River Falls and 0.1-mile out and back at Coos Canyon)

Hiking time: About 1 hour

Difficulty: Easy

Season: Year-round

Trail surface: Sandy woods and bare bedrock

Land status: Unknown

Nearest town: Mexico

Other users: None

Water availability: None

Canine compatibility: Dogs must be under control at all times.

Fees and permits: None

Other maps: *DeLorme: Maine Atlas & Gazetteer,* map 18; USGS Roxbury

Trail contact: None

Finding the trailhead: From the junction of ME 17 and US 2 in Mexico, follow ME 17 north. Drive 6.9 miles. Park on the left shoulder near the USGS gaging station (it looks like a steel and concrete outhouse perched near the edge of the river). GPS: N44 38.575' / W70 35.305'. Coos Canyon is 6.6 miles farther north on ME 17. Park on the right at the state picnic area. GPS: N44 43.385' / W70 38.234'. The canyon is best viewed from the bridge over the Swift River on Dingle Hill Road.

The Hike

The Swift River flows from the same mountainous area as the Sandy River. Both rivers drop quickly into lowlands. Along the Swift River are two of Maine's most interesting roadside waterfalls: Swift River Falls and Coos Canyon.

Swift River Falls is only a 10-foot drop in three waterfalls. The reason to visit isn't the waterfall itself, it's the surrounding bedrock. The river has carved the rock into curves and fins and all manner of sculpted shapes. The relatively flat granite broke apart along its regular joints and then was shaped by the water. There are numerous large kettles in the bedrock where rocks have been trapped and spun by the water, digging themselves into the bedrock. This crazy section of river is more than 100 yards long.

There are nice pools within Swift River Falls, but the current makes them less than ideal for swimming. Save that for Coos Canyon. At Coos Canyon, the Swift

Swift River Falls

River drops 15 feet into a vertically walled canyon. You get the best view of the canyon from the bridge over the river on Dingle Hill Road, which is visible from the parking area.

There's an overhang on the canyon wall that swimmers often jump from. It's 20 feet to the water, but the river is very deep in the canyon. Right next to the overhang is a less-than-vertical section of the cliff that is easy to descend to the water. If you don't want to jump off the cliff, you can climb down to the water's edge.

The western Maine mountains are known for their tourmaline and gold. The Swift River is the gold center of Maine. In fact, there's a rock shop across ME 17 from Coos Canyon. The gold is placer gold, meaning that weathering removed it from quartz veins in granite bedrock far upstream. Because it's heavy, it settles in slow sections of the river. So while gold is panned nearby, especially on the East Branch Swift River up Dingle Hill Road, the bedrock in Coos Canyon isn't even granite—it is essentially metamorphosed mud. The rock does contain mica and garnets, though.

Swift River Falls and Coos Canyon

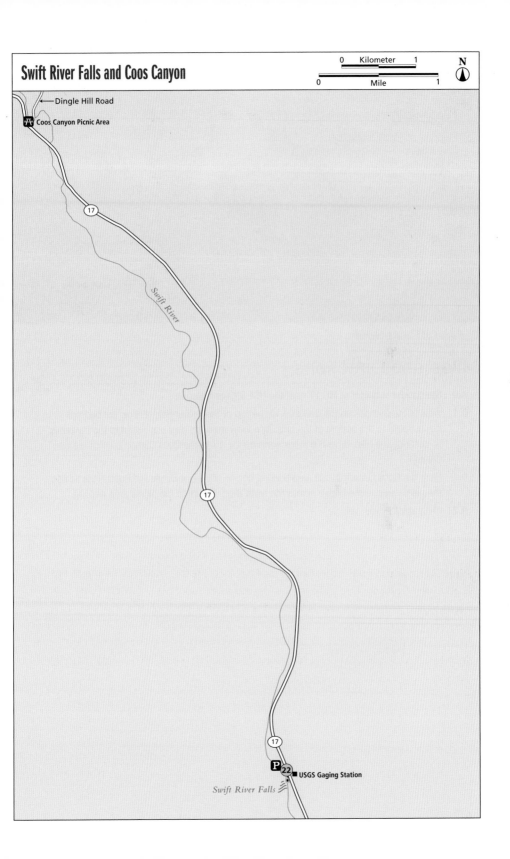

Dingle Hill Road

Coos Canyon Picnic Area

17

Swift River

17

17

P 22 ■ USGS Gaging Station

Swift River Falls

The head of Coos Canyon

Miles and Directions

0.0 Start at the shoulder of ME 17 near the USGS gaging station.

0.1 Walk out to bedrock on the riverbank at the top of Swift River Falls. Follow the bedrock downstream to the bottom of the falls. Turn away from the river and return to the trailhead. To continue the hike, drive 6.6 miles north on ME 17 to the Coos Canyon picnic area on the right.

0.1 From the Coos Canyon picnic area parking beside ME 17 at Dingle Hill Road, walk across the picnic area to the bridge across the Swift River. Return to the picnic area parking.

0.2 Arrive back at your vehicle.

23 Angel Falls

Mountain Brook drops over a cliff of tilted bedrock in one of the highest plunge falls in Maine. To see Angel Falls, you hike into a steep, narrow gorge to the base of the falls. Moss-covered quartzite boulders litter the gorge and surround the pool at the base of the falls. This is one of Maine's most dramatic waterfalls.

Start: Angel Falls Trailhead
Elevation gain: 376 feet
Distance: 1.4 miles out and back
Hiking time: About 1 hour
Difficulty: Moderate. The trail is steep and rocky with multiple stream crossings.
Season: Late May to October
Trail surface: Woods road, woodland path, rocky streambed
Land status: Private timberland

Nearest town: Mexico
Other users: Hunters in season
Water availability: Mountain Brook
Canine compatibility: Dogs must be under control at all times.
Fees and permits: None
Other maps: *DeLorme: Maine Atlas & Gazetteer*, map 18; USGS Houghton
Trail contact: None

Finding the trailhead: From the junction of ME 17 and US 2 in Mexico, follow ME 17 north. Drive 13.5 miles. Pass Coos Canyon in Byron. Continue north on ME 17 and drive another 4.2 miles. Turn left on an unmarked but prominent gravel road. Cross the Swift River and drive 0.3 mile. Turn right at the T-intersection onto Bemis Road. Drive 2.3 miles. Bear right at a fork in the road. Drive 1.1 miles. Turn left at the sign for Angel Falls onto a road that goes steeply downhill. Drive 0.2 mile to the parking area. The hike begins where the road continues south. GPS: N44 47.326' / W70 42.475'

The Hike

A debate has raged in Maine over the state's highest waterfall. Angel Falls and Moxie Falls (hike 48) are both 90 feet. It turns out that Katahdin Falls (not to be confused with Katahdin Stream Falls, hike 56) in Baxter State Park is much higher. There's no trail to Katahdin Falls, so we can say that Angel Falls is the highest waterfall you'll hike to.

Angel Falls drops from a gap in a quartzite cliff. One of the boulders at the base of the falls appears to fit neatly into the gap, maybe explaining how the waterfall formed. The cliffs rise above the falls on both sides, creating a narrow gorge that Mountain Brook tumbles through.

To get to the falls, you have to hike up the brook. The trail starts out as a woods road. After you ford Berdeen Stream (in summer you can step from stone to stone), the woods road peters out and you follow a trail to Mountain Brook. Once you reach the brook, you have to cross it three times. This can be hard to do without getting

Angel Falls

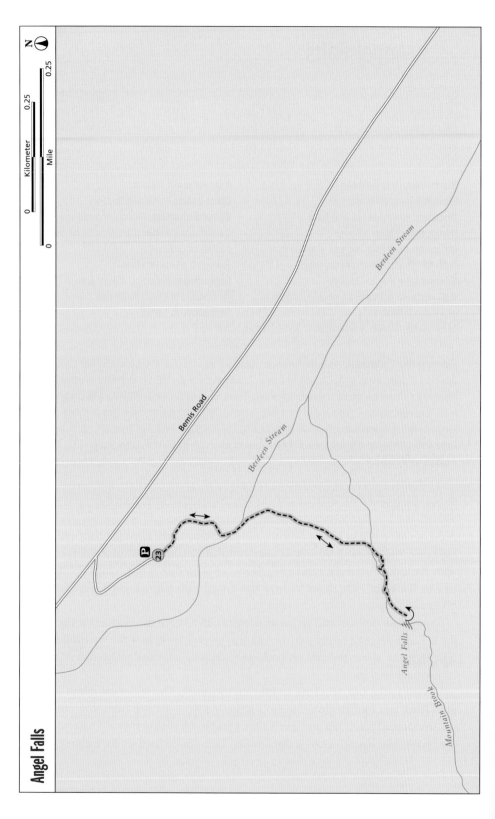

N

0   0.25   Kilometer   0.25
0   0.25
        Mile

Bemis Road

Berdeen Stream

Berdeen Stream

P 23

Angel Falls

Mountain Brook

Angel Falls

wet. The brook is narrow and steep, and its bouldery bed is hemmed in by nearly vertical walls of weeping rock.

After the third stream crossing, the trail climbs over some large boulders, shortcutting a bend in the brook. From the top of the boulders, you have a spectacular view of Angel Falls. The water plunges down the cliff, following the angled bedding of the rock. This creates a lacy screen of whitewater covering the dark bedrock.

It's possible to climb down the boulders from the viewpoint to and around the pool at the base of the falls. The climb isn't difficult, but the rock is always wet and slippery.

Miles and Directions

0.0 Start from the trailhead at the south end of the parking area.

0.1 Follow the woods road to a ford of Berdeen Stream.

0.4 Climb gently to Mountain Brook.

0.5 Cross Mountain Brook three times.

0.7 Climb beside Mountain Brook to the base of Angel Falls. To complete the hike, retrace your steps to the trailhead.

1.4 Arrive back at the trailhead.

24 Mosher Hill Falls

Mosher Hill Falls is one of the most spectacular waterfalls in Maine. Mosher Brook flows out of a pond, through a stand of pines down a smooth bedrock bed, and plunges 60 feet into a deep gorge. The hike visits the top of the falls and then goes up the gorge to the base of the falls.

Start: Trailhead at back of parking area
Elevation gain: 175 feet
Distance: 0.6 mile out and back
Hiking time: About 1 hour
Difficulty: Moderate. The hike to the base of the falls is on a rough, wet trail.
Season: May to July
Trail surface: Woodland path
Land status: Unknown

Nearest town: Farmington and New Vineyard
Other users: None
Water availability: None
Canine compatibility: Dogs must be under control at all times.
Fees and permits: None
Other maps: *DeLorme: Maine Atlas & Gazetteer*, map 20; USGS New Sharon
Trail contact: None

Finding the trailhead: From the junction of US 2 and ME 27/ME 4 in Farmington, follow ME 27/ME 4 toward downtown. Drive 3.1 miles. Turn right onto ME 27. Drive 4.3 miles. Turn right onto Ramsdell Road. Drive 0.5 mile. Turn left, staying on Ramsdell Road. Drive 1 mile. There's a small gravel parking area for two cars on the left at the bottom of a hill. The trailhead is at the back of the parking area. GPS: N44 44.729' / W70 06.747'

The Hike

The trail descends gently beside Mosher Brook beneath tall pines. The stream flows straight between low vertical banks over smooth bedrock. The trail reaches a rocky outcropping where the brook plunges 60 feet into a deep gorge. From the open rock you have a view of the waterfall and the head of the gorge. The viewpoint can be a bit vertigo-inducing—you're standing on broken bedrock looking straight down the waterfall.

To reach the base of Mosher Hill Falls and get that nice head-on view of the waterfall, look away from the falls for a rough trail that begins where you stepped up onto the outcropping. The trail descends along the gorge to the stream where it flows out of the gorge. Cross the stream and hike upstream on the far bank. There's no real trail, but the route is obvious. Mosher Brook fills almost the entire floor of the gorge. The walls rise 50 feet above you.

You can hike to the edge of the small, rock-filled pool at the base of the falls. Mosher Brook crashes down the rock face. To the left of the falls is the outcropping you stood on moments ago. To the right of the falls, the nearly vertical wall of the gorge curves around the base of the waterfall.

Mosher Hill Falls seen from within the gorge

Mosher Hill Falls

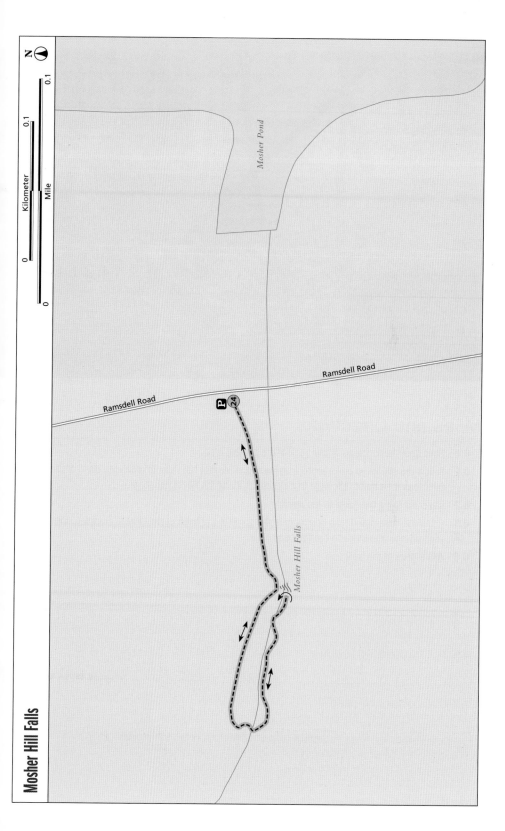

Mosher Pond

Ramsdell Road

Ramsdell Road

P (24)

Mosher Hill Falls

N

Kilometer
0   0.1

Mile
0   0.1

The gorge

Miles and Directions

0.0   Start from the trailhead at the back of the parking area.

0.1   Follow the stream to open bedrock at the top of Mosher Hill Falls. To reach the base of the falls, look for a trail to the right that descends along the rim of the gorge.

0.2   Descend along the gorge to the stream.

0.3   Cross the stream and hike upstream in the gorge to the base of the falls. To complete the hike, retrace your steps to the trailhead.

0.6   Arrive back at the trailhead.

25 Smalls Falls

You don't have to do much work to see Smalls Falls. It's a short stroll to the base of this 50-foot waterfall on the Sandy River. There are actually several waterfalls and deep pools among the weathered bedrock. You can easily explore all of them.

Start: Smalls Falls picnic area
Elevation gain: 76 feet
Distance: 0.6 mile out and back
Hiking time: Less than 1 hour
Difficulty: Easy
Season: May to October
Trail surface: Woodland path
Land status: State roadside picnic area
Nearest town: Phillips

Other users: None
Water availability: None
Canine compatibility: Dogs should be leashed.
Fees and permits: None
Other maps: *DeLorme: Maine Atlas & Gazetteer*, map 19; USGS Jackson Mountain
Trail contact: None

Finding the trailhead: From the junction of ME 4 and ME 142 in Phillips, follow ME 4 north. Drive 9.5 miles. Turn left into the state picnic area at the sign. Drive 0.2 mile through the picnic area to the waterfall parking area. The Smalls Falls picnic area is 2.5 miles south of where the Appalachian Trail crosses ME 4. GPS: N44 51.476' / W70 30.794'

The Hike

The Sandy River begins in a small chain of ponds in the notch between Saddleback and Beaver Mountains. Less than 2 miles downstream, the river drops through a bulge of granite bedrock in several drops. The largest and last waterfall is the 50-foot Smalls Falls, itself two linked waterfalls with a pool between them. The rock wall soars above the falls on the east side.

ME 4 passes within a few feet of the top of the waterfall chain, but you can't see it from the road. At the base of the falls is a state picnic area. To see the falls, walk through the picnic area to the bridge over the Sandy River.

From the bridge, you have a fine view of Smalls Falls across a large pool. The trail climbs in the woods next to the falls against the chain-link fence to its top and continues on past the upper falls and gorge. You have access to the bedrock atop and between the falls. There are several nice swimming pools where the river has dug deep holes in the bedrock. The large pool at the base of the falls is a good swimming hole as well.

In spring there's a kayak race through the gorge down the waterfall. When the water is high in the spring, only the pool at the base of the fall is safe to swim in. In summer people jump off the cliffs into the deep pools between waterfalls. The

Smalls Falls from the pool at its base

Jumping 30 feet into the pool between Smalls Falls' two main drops

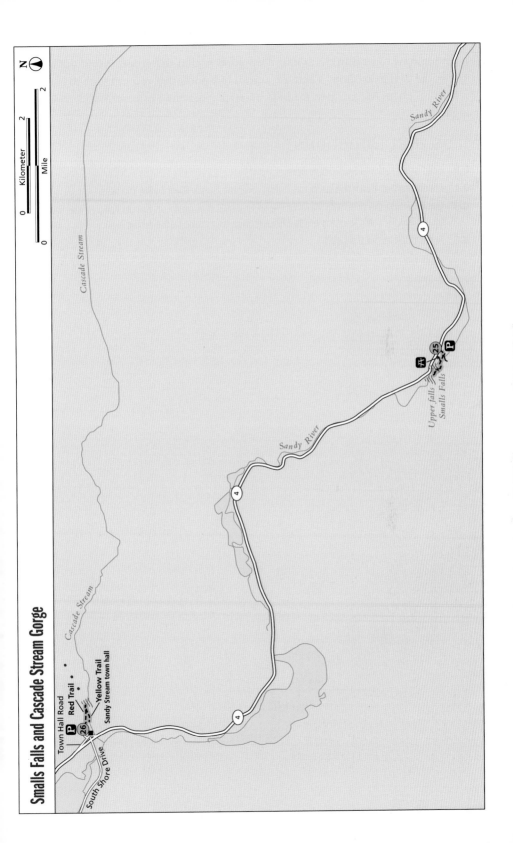

Smalls Falls and Cascade Stream Gorge

less adventurous can easily climb into deep pools within the gorge, except the one between the two main drops. There are at least five pools that you can walk to.

This is perhaps Maine's best roadside waterfall—certainly, its best roadside swimming hole.

Miles and Directions

0.0 Start at the Smalls Falls picnic area.

0.1 Follow the trail down the stairs to a bridge over the Sandy River below the falls.

0.3 Climb beside the river, with views of the several falls that make up Smalls Falls. Reach the top of Smalls Falls. To complete the hike, retrace your steps to the picnic area.

0.6 Arrive back at the trailhead.

26 Cascade Stream Gorge

Cascade Stream follows a crack in the granite bedrock to a 20-foot drop, then takes a sharp left and drops through the gorge. The gorge is as much as 60 feet deep and narrow enough to throw a rock across. Within the gorge are several small waterfalls.

See map on p. 105.
Start: Cascade Gorge Trailhead
Elevation gain: 104 feet
Distance: 0.6 mile out and back
Hiking time: About 1 hour
Difficulty: Easy
Season: May to October
Trail surface: Woodland path
Land status: Cascade Stream Gorge Preserve
Nearest town: Rangeley

Other users: None
Water availability: None
Canine compatibility: Dogs must be under control at all times.
Fees and permits: None
Other maps: *DeLorme: Maine Atlas & Gazetteer*, map 28; USGS Saddleback Mountain
Trail contact: Rangeley Lakes Heritage Trust, (207) 864-7311, www.rlht.org/lands-trails/item/cascade-stream-gorge-2

Finding the trailhead: From the junction of ME 4 and ME 142 in Phillips, follow ME 4 north. Drive 18.1 miles. Turn right onto Town Hall Road just past the sign for Rangeley Lake State Park and just before the left turn to the park. Drive 0.1 mile, passing the Sandy River town hall. Turn right at the sign for Cascade Stream Gorge Preserve. Drive 0.1 mile up a steep gravel drive to the parking area. GPS: N44 55.468' / W70 36.641'

The Hike

The steepest part of getting to Cascade Stream Gorge is the driveway to the parking area. The hike is fairly level, with a little up and down to get around in the gorge. After you hike under the power lines, turn right and follow a short trail to Cascade Stream at the mouth of the gorge. By clambering around and onto the boulders beside the stream, you get a fine view into the gorge. A small waterfall marks the stream's exit.

The second short side trail off the main trail leads to a flat slab of bedrock beside the stream where the gorge is at its deepest. Evergreens clutch the rock and hang out over the stream, leaving the gorge in cool shade. Upstream you can see the waterfall at the head of the gorge.

The trail continues to an overlook across the gorge from the waterfall. Bare rock rises to your left. Below you the stream drops between thick rock walls, then drops again. It's not the highest waterfall in Maine, but the setting is dramatic. You can climb around on the rocks, exploring the nooks and crannies within the gorge. In a few places you can get down to the water, but there's no swimming hole. The stream is too narrow and shallow.

Waterfall at the head of the gorge

Mouth of the gorge

Miles and Directions

0.0   Start from the Cascade Gorge Trailhead.

0.1   Pass under power lines on the Red Trail. Reenter the woods and turn right onto the first Yellow Trail, which leads 20 feet to the stream near the base of the gorge. Return to the Red Trail and turn right.

0.2   Reach the second Yellow Trail. Descend 50 feet to bedrock along the stream. Return to the Red Trail and turn right again.

0.3   Reach the end of the Red Trail, with a view of the waterfall at the head of the gorge. To complete the hike, follow the Red Trail back to the trailhead.

0.6   Arrive back at the trailhead.

27 Poplar Stream Falls

This scenic hike visits two waterfalls. The first is a 25-foot horsetail with a nice swimming hole at its base. The second is a 50-foot horsetail into a deep pool.

Start: Carrabassett Valley fire station
Elevation gain: 569 feet
Distance: 5-mile lollipop
Hiking time: 3 to 4 hours
Difficulty: Moderate
Season: May to October
Trail surface: Road, woodland path, cross-country ski trail
Land status: Maine Huts and Trails right-of-way on Penobscot Indian land

Nearest town: Carrabassett Valley
Other users: Skiers in season and residents of Carriage Road
Water availability: None
Canine compatibility: Dogs should be leashed.
Fees and permits: None
Other maps: *DeLorme: Maine Atlas & Gazetteer*, map 29; USGS Poplar Mountain
Trail contact: None

Finding the trailhead: On ME 27 5.9 miles south of the Sugarloaf ski resort entrance and 9.3 miles north of Kingfield, turn east onto Carriage Road. Drive 0.1 mile. Turn left toward the Carrabassett Valley fire department. Drive 0.1 mile around the east side of the fire station to the hiker parking area. GPS: N45 04.743' / W70 12.715'. Option: In summer the hut access road is open to within 0.1 mile of the bridge above the first waterfall.

The Hike

You begin the hike by walking up Carriage Road and through a gate. The hike continues up the road into Penobscot Indian land (the road is the access road to Maine Huts and Trails' Poplar Stream Falls Hut). Turn right off the road onto the Maine Huts and Trails ski trail toward the hut. In summer you can drive up the road almost all the way to the bridge over Poplar Stream. If you do that, you greatly shorten your hike but miss much of the stream.

Turn left off the ski trail onto Warren's Trail. This footpath follows Poplar Stream up to the first waterfall. The stream wanders through mixed forest, and there are many boulders along the way. It's a pleasant walk and loaded with wildflowers in the spring.

The trail reaches the pool beneath a 25-foot horsetail waterfall on Poplar Stream. This is a good-sized swimming hole. The stream crashes over a broken rock face, rests in the pool, then rushes downstream toward the Carrabassett River a few miles away. Just downstream is a very long, deep pool. All the pools on this hike are good for swimming even though the water is almost black with tannins.

The trail climbs up alongside the waterfall to the road. Turn right and cross a bridge over the stream just above the falls. Turn right onto Larry's Trail, which follows Poplar Stream across from Warren's Trail. In summer watch for small purple-fringed orchis.

Poplar Stream Falls

Waterfall along Warren's Trail

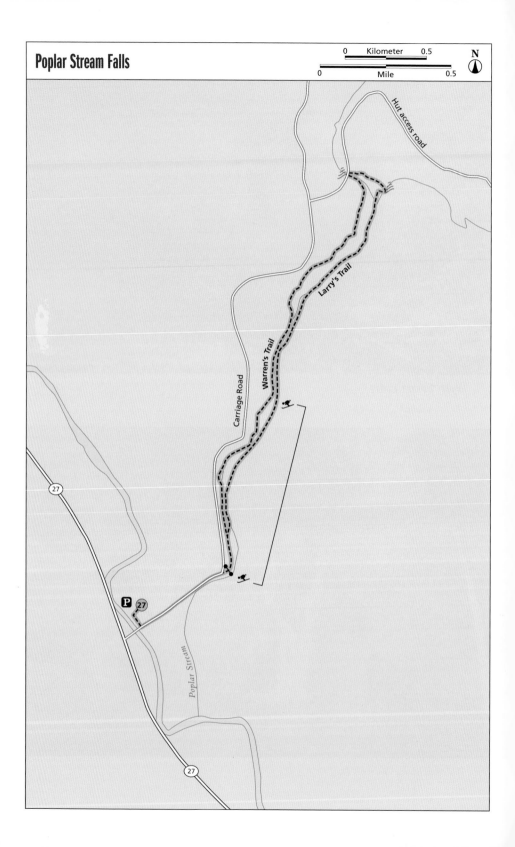

Hut access road

Larry's Trail

Warren's Trail

Carriage Road

27

P 27

Poplar Stream

27

0   Kilometer   0.5

0   Mile   0.5

N

A short side trail leads to a 50-foot horsetail on West Brook within sight of Poplar Stream. This is the waterfall called Poplar Stream Falls, even though it's not on Poplar Stream. The brook crashes down an irregular crack in the bedrock wall into a pool. It's a very picturesque drop and a quiet place for a swim.

Miles and Directions

0.0 Start at the parking lot east of the fire station. Walk back toward Carriage Road.

0.1 Turn left onto Carriage Road.

0.5 Walk up Carriage Road and past the gate. Carriage Road becomes the hut access road.

0.7 Turn right onto the ski trail.

0.9 Turn left onto Warren's Trail.

2.3 Follow Poplar Stream to a large pool at the base of the first waterfall.

2.4 Climb past the waterfall and turn right onto the hut access road. Cross the bridge over Poplar Stream, then immediately turn right onto Larry's Trail.

2.6 Turn right, staying on Larry's Trail.

2.7 A short side trail leads to the base of Poplar Stream Falls.

3.7 Turn right onto the ski trail.

4.1 Pass Warren's Trail.

4.3 Turn left onto Carriage Road.

5.0 Arrive back at the parking area.

28 Hadlock Falls

Hadlock Falls is the highest waterfall in Acadia National Park. Hadlock Brook drops 40 feet down a tiered granite face into a pool, then flows under Waterfall Bridge on the carriage road. It's a very dramatic waterfall that nearly dries up by mid-June.

Start: Hadlock Brook Trailhead
Elevation gain: 296 feet
Distance: 1.8 miles out and back
Hiking time: About 1 hour
Difficulty: Moderate
Season: May to June
Trail surface: Woodland path
Land status: Acadia National Park
Nearest town: Northeast Harbor

Other users: None
Water availability: None
Canine compatibility: Dogs must be leashed at all times.
Fees and permits: Acadia National Park fee
Other maps: *DeLorme: Maine Atlas & Gazetteer,* map 16; USGS Southwest Harbor
Trail contact: Acadia National Park, (207) 288-3338, www.nps.gov/acad

Finding the trailhead: Just onto Mount Desert Island, the road forks. The left-hand fork goes toward Bar Harbor, the right fork toward Southwest Harbor. Take the right fork, following ME 198. Drive 4.4 miles to a traffic light. Turn left, staying on ME 198. Drive 4.2 miles to the trailhead parking on the right. The trailhead is across the road from the parking area. GPS: N44 19.551' / W68 17.481'

The Hike

Hadlock Brook rises high in the notch between Sargent and Penobscot Mountains and empties into Upper Hadlock Pond. Hadlock Falls is about halfway down the mountain. It's the highest single-drop waterfall in Acadia National Park. You can hike directly to it, as described here, or combine it with the granite domes to the northeast—Bald and Gilmore Peaks and Parkman Mountain—as described in *Hiking Maine* (Falcon Guides).

The Hadlock Brook Trail crosses a low area that is often wet in spring, passing several trails. In winter this section is often continuous ice. After crossing a carriage road, the trail climbs to a ledge with fine views. You then continue climbing gently to Hadlock Brook. The trail follows the rushing brook through a steep valley. There are no waterfalls in this section, but lots of rapids and small pools.

The trail climbs to a carriage road a few feet west of Waterfall Bridge. You can see Hadlock Falls through the bridge. Many hikers scramble along the streambed under the bridge to the base of the falls. The hike climbs to the carriage road, where you have a great view from the bridge.

Hadlock Falls drops 40 feet down a face of granite. The wet rock shines orange against the dark green backdrop of hemlocks and cedars. In early spring the waterfall

Hadlock Falls from the bridge

is a solid 15 feet wide. By late spring it's a gentle horsetail bouncing from ledge to ledge into a good-sized pool, and by late June the stream is a mere trickle.

You can return the way you came or follow the carriage road northwest around Bald Peak to the Maple Spring Trail. North of the carriage road, the trail passes through a narrow, sheer-sided gorge with a spring-fed brook. There's no big waterfall, but it's very scenic. You can then descend the Maple Spring Trail rather than back-tracking to the Hadlock Brook Trail. This option is about the same length.

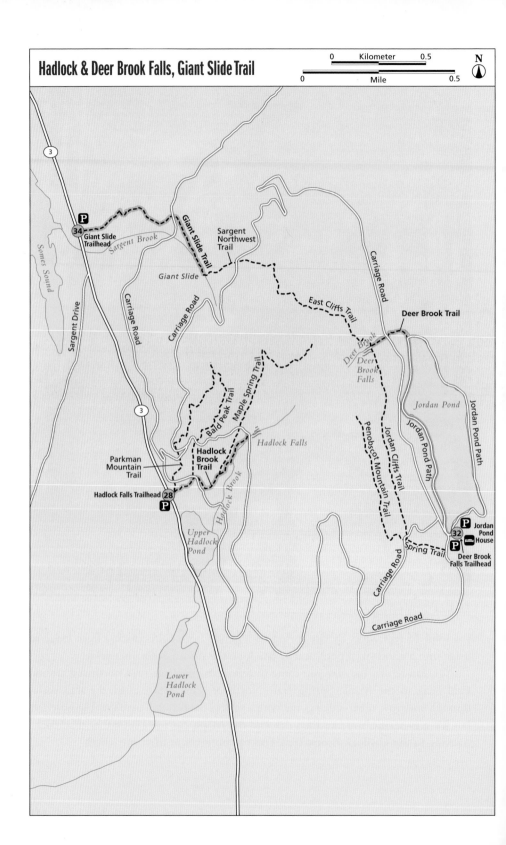

Hadlock & Deer Brook Falls, Giant Slide Trail

0   Kilometer   0.5

0   Mile   0.5

N

3

P **34** Giant Slide Trailhead

Somes Sound

Sargent Brook

Giant Slide Trail

Giant Slide

Sargent Northwest Trail

Carriage Road

East Cliffs Trail

Deer Brook Trail

Carriage Road

Deer Brook

Deer Brook Falls

Sargent Drive

Carriage Road

Carriage Road

Bald Peak Trail

Maple Spring Trail

Hadlock Falls

Jordan Pond

Jordan Pond Path

3

Penobscot Mountain Trail

Jordan Cliffs Trail

Jordan Pond Path

Jordan Pond Path

Hadlock Brook Trail

Parkman Mountain Trail

Hadlock Brook

Hadlock Falls Trailhead **28**
P

P **32** Jordan Pond House
P Deer Brook Falls Trailhead

Upper Hadlock Pond

Spring Trail

Carriage Road

Carriage Road

Lower Hadlock Pond

Hadlock Falls from under the bridge

Miles and Directions

0.0 Start from the Hadlock Brook Trailhead.

0.1 Pass the Parkman Mountain Trail.

0.2 Pass the Bald Peak Trail, then cross the carriage road.

0.4 Pass the Maple Spring Trail. Bear right, staying on the Hadlock Brook Trail.

0.9 Climb gently beside the stream to the carriage road. Hadlock Falls is viewed from the bridge over Hadlock Stream. To complete the hike, retrace your steps to the trailhead. ***Option:*** You can follow the carriage road 0.2 mile northwest to Hemlock Bridge. North of the bridge, the Maple Spring Trail passes through a narrow gorge with a beautiful spring-fed brook and small waterfalls. South of the bridge, the Maple Spring Trail junctions with the Hadlock Brook Trail in 0.3 mile.

1.8 Arrive back at the trailhead.

29 Canon Brook

Depending on how you count waterfalls, this hike passes between six and a hundred falls. The highlight is Canon Brook Falls, one of the most interesting in Maine. The stream slides down steep granite ledges and into a vertical-walled canyon 30 feet deep and 50 feet across. Before arriving at this waterfall you pass several others along Canon Brook and Otter Creek.

Start: Canon Brook Trailhead
Elevation gain: 1,116 feet
Distance: 4.2 miles out and back
Hiking time: About 4 hours
Difficulty: Moderate
Season: April to October
Trail surface: Woodland path
Land status: Acadia National Park
Nearest town: Bar Harbor
Other users: None

Water availability: Otter Creek and Canon Brook
Canine compatibility: Dogs must be leashed at all times.
Fees and permits: None
Other maps: *DeLorme: Maine Atlas & Gazetteer*, map 16; USGS Seal Harbor
Trail contact: Acadia National Park, (207) 288-3338, www.nps.gov/acad

Finding the trailhead: From the town square park in Bar Harbor, take ME 3 east toward Seal Harbor. Drive 3.1 miles, passing the Jackson Laboratory, the Sieur de Monts entrance to the park, and the Tarn. As the road begins to climb away from the Tarn, the trailhead parking is on the left. The trailhead is across the road from the parking lot. GPS: N44 20.887' / W68 12.140'

The Hike

The hike begins with a gentle descent to Tarn Brook. You cross the brook on a long, winding bridge that parallels a beaver dam. Across the bridge, you follow Tarn Brook downstream, then climb across the low shoulder of Dorr Mountain. The trail crosses a small stream where it drops off a 15-foot cliff and tumbles down to Otter Creek.

The trail parallels Otter Creek upstream to a long, shallow ledge falls. At the head of this waterfall, you cross the stream and begin climbing beside Canon Brook. In spring Canon Brook makes use of a dozen narrow channels on the steep mountainside, tumbling over, around, and under broken granite. As you climb, you cross the stream several times and see a number of waterfalls up to 20 feet high. By summer much of this section seems dry—the brook spends all its time beneath the rocks, out of sight.

Where the mountainside transitions from loose rock to steep ledges, you reach Canon Brook Falls. In spring the stream fills the floor of the canyon, water spilling over the entire length of the east side. By summer the stream is reduced to a picturesque waterfall at the upper end of the canyon.

Waterfall with a great pool on Canon Brook

The trail climbs up the west side of the canyon and continues up the ledges. There are more waterfall in this section—one is almost 20 feet and drops into a good-sized pool that makes a nice swimming spot. From the ledges you have fine views across Champlain Mountain of the Gulf of Maine.

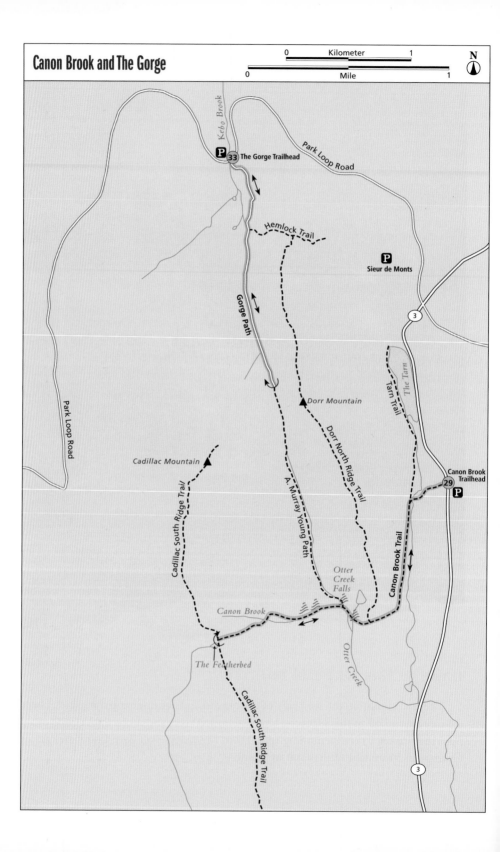

Canon Brook and The Gorge

0 Kilometer 1
0 Mile 1

N

Keho Brook

Park Loop Road

P 33 The Gorge Trailhead

Hemlock Trail

P Sieur de Monts

3

Gorge Path

The Tarn

Tarn Trail

Dorr Mountain

Dorr North Ridge Trail

Canon Brook Trailhead

P 29

Cadillac Mountain

A. Murray Young Path

Canon Brook Trail

Cadillac South Ridge Trail

Otter Creek Falls

Canon Brook

Otter Creek

The Featherbed

Cadillac South Ridge Trail

Park Loop Road

3

Canon Brook Falls

The trail continues climbing, finally entering the woods and reaching the Featherbed. In spring it's a pond perched atop Cadillac Mountain's south ridge; in summer it's a soft green meadow. This and a bog farther east on the shoulder of Cadillac Mountain are the sources of Canon Brook.

Miles and Directions

0.0 Start from the Canon Brook Trailhead.

0.3 Descend gently to a beaver pond. Cross the bridge over the dam and turn left, staying on the Canon Brook Trail.

1.0 Pass the Dorr Mountain South Ridge Trail.

1.1 Cross a small stream just below a waterfall.

1.2 Pass Otter Creek Falls. At the junction with the A. Murray Young Path, turn left and cross Otter Creek, staying on the Canon Brook Trail.

1.3 Climb steadily beside Canon Brook to the second waterfall.

1.5 Climb steadily past several small falls to Canon Brook Falls.

1.7 Climb up past Canon Brook Falls onto exposed bedrock with the stream and another waterfall.

2.1 Reenter the woods and arrive at the junction with the Cadillac Mountain South Ridge Trail at the Featherbed. To complete the hike, return the way you came to the trailhead.

4.2 Arrive back at the trailhead.

30 Man O' War Falls

This is one of the only waterfalls in Maine that drop directly into the ocean. Man O' War Brook tumbles down a steep slope through a cedar thicket then horsetails 25 feet into Somes Sound. The trail leads right to the base of the falls at the high tide line.

Start: Acadia Mountain Trailhead
Elevation gain: 217 feet
Distance: 2.5 miles out and back
Hiking time: About 2 hours
Difficulty: Easy
Season: May to November
Trail surface: Fire road and woodland path
Land status: Acadia National Park
Nearest town: Southwest Harbor

Other users: None
Water availability: None
Canine compatibility: Dogs must be leashed at all times.
Fees and permits: Acadia National Park fee
Other maps: *DeLorme: Maine Atlas & Gazetteer*, map 16; USGS Southwest Harbor
Trail contact: Acadia National Park, (207) 288-3338, www.nps.gov/acad

Finding the trailhead: From the junction of ME 3 and ME 102/198 at the head of Mount Desert Island, bear right onto ME 102/198. Drive 4.4 miles to a traffic light; ME 198 turns left and ME 102 goes straight. Go straight, staying on ME 102. Drive 3.5 miles to the trailhead parking area on the right. The trailhead is across ME 102 from the parking area. GPS: N44 19.300' / W68 19.964'

The Hike

In 1604 Samuel de Champlain explored and named Mount Desert Island. He sailed into Somes Sound—the only fjord on the Atlantic coast in the United States. His ship stopped at Man O' War Falls to restock their fresh water. This is how the brook got its name.

The place must have made an impression on the French because in 1613 the Jesuits established a mission nearby. St. Sauveur Mountain just south of the brook still bears its French name. That same year, the English burned the mission and took the Jesuits hostage. The Penobscots went back to living part of the year on the island as they had for generations.

The hike follows a fire road from near the trailhead almost all the way to Man O' War Falls. You hike beneath the almost vertical face of Acadia Mountain. Between you and the granite wall is a marshy area where the brook rises.

You can combine the hike directly into the falls with a climb of Acadia or St. Sauveur Mountain—or both. Acadia Mountain has a bare summit with fine views of

Man O' War Falls ▶

Man O'War Falls

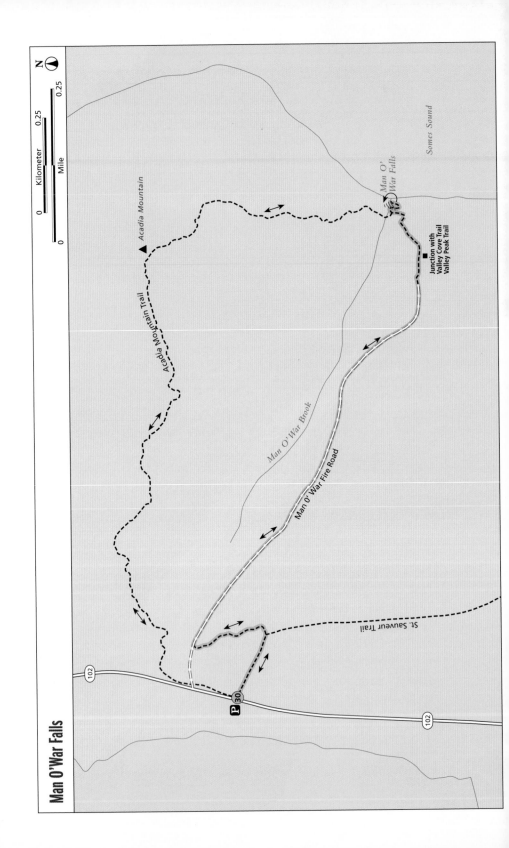

N

Kilometer
0   0.25

Mile
0   0.25

Acadia Mountain

Acadia Mountain Trail

Man O' War Brook

Man O' War Fire Road

St. Sauveur Trail

Man O'
War Falls

Somes Sound

Junction with
Valley Cove Trail
Valley Peak Trail

P 30

102

102

Man O'War Falls

Somes Sound and the Cranberry Islands. The face of St. Sauveur Mountain that faces Somes Sound is one of the highest cliffs in Acadia National Park. You can stand almost 600 feet directly above the water.

The fire road ends just before the trail junction that leads to the mountains and Man O'War Falls. A footbridge crosses the brook. Below the bridge the stream drops over exposed granite, tumbling through a cedar thicket. The trail descends beside the stream to the base of the waterfall, where it horsetails 25 feet down a granite face into Somes Sound.

Man O'War Falls is unique in Maine and not to be missed. It's not uncommon to see seals and eagles from the base of the falls.

Miles and Directions

0.0   Start from the Acadia Mountain Trailhead.

0.1   Climb the rocky trail to a junction. Turn left onto the St. Sauveur Trail.

0.3   Turn right onto the Man O' War fire road.

1.1   The fire road becomes a trail. In 200 feet turn left onto the Acadia Mountain Trail.

1.2   Descend gently to a junction. Turn right onto the Man O' War Falls Overlook Trail.

1.3   Descend to the base of the falls. To complete the hike, return to the Man O' War fire road.

2.3   Follow the fire road back to the junction with the St. Sauveur Trail. Go straight, staying on the fire road.

2.5   Arrive back at the trailhead.

31 The Sluiceway

The Sluiceway drops more than 400 feet down a boulder field in less than half a mile. The trail climbs beside the stream amid towering evergreens. It's a secret gem on Mount Desert Island's quiet side.

Start: Perpendicular Trailhead
Elevation gain: 901 feet
Distance: 3.2 miles out and back
Hiking time: About 3 hours
Difficulty: Moderate
Season: April to May
Trail surface: Woodland path
Land status: Acadia National Park
Nearest town: Southwest Harbor

Other users: None
Water availability: None
Canine compatibility: Dogs must be leashed at all times.
Fees and permits: None
Other maps: *DeLorme: Maine Atlas & Gazetteer,* map 16; USGS Southwest Harbor
Trail contact: Acadia National Park, (207) 288-3338, www.nps.gov/acad

Finding the trailhead: Follow ME 3 onto Mount Desert Island. Once on the island, go straight onto ME 102 where ME 3 bears left. Drive 10.3 miles into Southwest Harbor. Turn right onto Seal Cove Road. Drive 0.5 mile and turn right onto Long Pond Road. Drive 1.3 miles to the end of the road. Park to the east of the water pumphouse. The trailhead is to the west of the pumphouse. GPS: N44 18.004' / W68 21.033'

The Hike

The Sluiceway rises in Little Notch on Western Mountain near the summit of Bernard Mountain. The stream drops from the notch down the steep mountainside into the Reservoir. Almost the entire length of this short stream is a waterfall. Like most waterfalls in Acadia National Park, the Sluiceway is best seen in spring. By summer it's almost dry.

As you hike to the Sluiceway from the foot of Long Pond, you'll cross two parking areas (Gilley Field and Mill Field). You may wonder why you weren't directed to drive to one of these and complete a much shorter hike. Simple: By the time the gravel Western Mountain Road is open, the Sluiceway will be almost dry. To see this waterfall, you need to visit in late April or May as soon as the snow melts.

The Sluiceway crashes down the mountainside over a field of boulders. The stream drops more than 400 feet in less than half a mile. The steep trail stays close, often climbing stone steps. Tall pines tower over the streambed. It's a dramatic hike.

You can make the hike an out-and-back or combine it with one of the other trails on Western Mountain to make a loop. The summits on Western Mountain are

The Sluiceway

Descending beside the Sluiceway

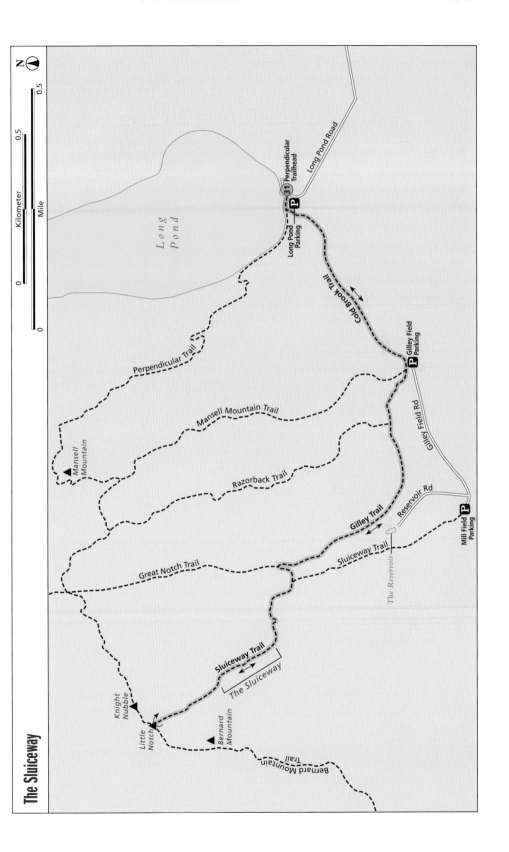

The Sluiceway

N

Long Pond

Perpendicular Trailhead

Long Pond Road

Long Pond Parking

Cold Brook Trail

Gilley Field Parking

Gilley Field Rd

Perpendicular Trail

Mansell Mountain

Mansell Mountain Trail

Razorback Trail

Great Notch Trail

Gilley Trail

Reservoir Rd

Sluiceway Trail

The Reservoir

Mill Field Parking

Sluiceway Trail

The Sluiceway

Knight Nubble

Little Notch

Bernard Mountain

Bernard Mountain Trail

Kilometer

Mile

all wooded, but the Razorback and Perpendicular Trails both offer fine views of the coast. However you complete the hike, be sure to visit the Reservoir. This small tarn-like pond is quite pretty.

Miles and Directions

0.0 Start from the Perpendicular Trailhead. In 150 feet, turn left onto the Cold Brook Trail.

0.4 Cross the Gilley Field parking area onto the Gilley Trail.

0.6 Pass the Razorback Trail.

0.8 Pass parking area at the Reservoir.

1.1 Turn left onto the Great Notch Trail.

1.2 Turn right onto the Sluiceway Trail.

1.6 Climb steeply at times beside the Sluiceway to Little Notch. To complete the hike, retrace your steps to the trailhead.

3.2 Arrive back at the trailhead.

32 Deer Brook Falls

Deer Brook Falls is as photogenic as it is ephemeral. Deer Brook descends from the notch between Sargent and Penobscot Mountains to Jordan Pond. Much of the stream's course is over bare granite bedrock. The highest waterfall is just above the bridge over the stream on the carriage road. By summer, the stream is completely dry.

See map on p. 116.
Start: Jordan Pond Path Trailhead at southwest corner of Jordan Pond
Elevation gain: 92 feet
Distance: 4.0 miles out and back
Hiking time: About 3 hours
Difficulty: Moderate
Season: May and early June
Trail surface: Woodland path
Land status: Acadia National Park

Nearest town: Seal Harbor
Other users: None
Water availability: Jordan Pond House
Canine compatibility: Dogs must be leashed at all times.
Fees and permits: Acadia National Park fee
Other maps: *DeLorme: Maine Atlas & Gazetteer*, map 16; USGS Southwest Harbor
Trail contact: Acadia National Park, (207) 288-3338, www.nps.gov/acad

Finding the trailhead: From the junction of ME 3 and ME 198 at the head of Mount Desert Island, bear left on ME 3 toward Bar Harbor. Drive 7.7 miles to the Hulls Cove entrance to Acadia National Park. Turn right into the park. Drive 0.1 mile to a stop sign. Turn left at the stop sign onto the Park Loop Road. Drive 3 miles to a T-intersection. Bear right at the T toward Cadillac Mountain and Jordan Pond. Drive 4.2 miles. Parking is on the right both before and at the Jordan Pond House. The trailhead is at the southwest corner of Jordan Pond in front of the Jordan Pond House. GPS: N44 19.202' / W68 15.235'

The Hike

The Jordan Pond Path hugs the west shore of the pond. You quickly leave the crowds at the Jordan Pond House behind, walking through quiet evergreens. As you approach the north end, the Jordan Cliffs drop nearly to the water. The trail crosses scree stacked along the shore. Across the pond, the Bubbles rise like two shaped domes of granite and Pemetic Mountain reaches into the sky.

Turn left onto the Deer Brook Trail just before the end of the pond. Deer Brook empties into the swampy area at the end of the pond, crossed by a bridge on the Jordan Pond Path. The Deer Brook Trail climbs steadily away from the pond through the woods. Soon Deer Brook Bridge on the Around Mountain Carriage Trail becomes visible above you. This beautiful stone arch rises almost 50 feet above Deer Brook and the trail. Through the arch, you can see the base of Deer Brook Falls.

The trail climbs to and crosses the carriage road, then becomes a staircase with railings beside the falls. Deer Brook slides down nearly vertical beds of orange granite, dropping 100 feet. Shortly after the snow melts, the waterfall is a torrent from rock

The dramatic approach to Deer Brook Falls. Notice Deer Brook is dry.

wall to rock wall. By mid-June, it's dry as a bone. Once the snowmelt is done rushing down to Jordan Pond, there's nothing left to feed the stream and it dries up.

On your return hike, you have lots of choices. You can return the way you came or follow the Jordan Pond Path around the east side of the pond for great views of Sargent and Penobscot Mountains. If you're feeling adventurous, you can climb Penobscot Mountain and descend the Penobscot Mountain Trail. If you're feeling *very* adventurous, you can descend the Jordan Cliffs Trail. This trail has some climbing, ladders, and exposure; it's usually closed in summer to protect nesting peregrine falcons.

Miles and Directions

0.0 Start from the Jordan Pond Path Trailhead at the southwest corner of Jordan Pond.

1.6 Hike around the west shore of Jordan Pond. Turn left onto the Deer Brook Trail.

1.8 Climb to the carriage road. Just before the carriage road, the lower falls is visible under the bridge over Deer Brook.

2.0 Cross the carriage road and continue climbing the Deer Brook Trail beside Deer Brook Falls. Turn back when the trail leaves the stream. To complete the hike, retrace your steps to the trailhead.

4.0 Arrive back at the trailhead.

Deer Brook Falls

33 The Gorge

If you hike the Gorge during the window in May when the stream is flowing, you'll be treated to numerous small waterfalls, sheer cliffs, and piles of granite boulders. Even when the stream is mostly dry, it's still a popular hike.

See map on p. 120.
Start: The Gorge Trailhead
Elevation gain: 901 feet
Distance: 2.8 miles out and back
Hiking time: About 2 hours
Difficulty: Moderate
Season: May, when the Park Loop Road opens, to June
Trail surface: Woodland path
Land status: Acadia National Park

Nearest town: Bar Harbor
Other users: None
Water availability: None
Canine compatibility: Dogs must be leashed at all times.
Fees and permits: Acadia National Park fee
Other maps: DeLorme: Maine Atlas & Gazetteer, map 16; USGS Seal Harbor
Trail contact: Acadia National Park, (207) 288-3338, www.nps.gov/acad

Finding the trailhead: From the junction of ME 3 and ME 198 at the head of Mount Desert Island, bear left on ME 3 toward Bar Harbor. Drive 7.7 miles to the Hulls Cove entrance to Acadia National Park. Turn right into the park. Drive 0.1 mile to a stop sign. Turn left at the stop sign onto the Park Loop Road. Drive 3 miles to a T-intersection and turn left toward Sand Beach. Drive 0.9 mile. Parking is on the right at the sign. GPS: N44 22.363' / W68 13.301'

The Hike

Kebo Brook drops from the notch between Cadillac and Dorr Mountains. It falls almost 1,000 feet through a narrow gorge with high cliffs. In some places the floor of the Gorge is piles of boulders; in others it's smooth granite bedrock. There are several small but beautiful waterfalls in the Gorge.

The challenge is that this is the most transient brook included in this guide. If you hike before the snow is completely melted, the top section is still frozen. Usually, the stream isn't really flowing until the first week in May. When flow is low, the upper section of the stream disappears beneath the boulders. You can hear water flowing, but the streambed and waterfalls are dry. If you wait until June to hike the Gorge, the brook will have become a trickle connecting small pools. It's still a great hike because of the cliffs and boulders, but it's no longer a waterfall hike.

The trail starts at the Park Loop Road where Kebo Brook flows under it. You hike upstream through dark hemlocks, climbing very little. After passing the Hemlock Trail, you begin to climb and the Gorge begins. You cross the small brook several

Waterfall in the Gorge in April

The Gorge

times on granite blocks. As you climb, the walls of the Gorge close in and grow higher. The cliffs are as high as 100 feet and smoothly vertical. In one place, the stream rushes down a chute hard against the base of a cliff. In another, the brook plunges off a granite block into a pool. The trail climbs an even higher block beside the stream, giving you a nice view down at the falls. Where the cliff is the highest, the stream burbles beside it over a bed of broken rocks. You can stand on the lip of the Gorge and see it far below you.

Before the Park Loop Road opens in the spring, you can access the Gorge via the Hemlock Trail from the Sieur de Monts entrance. In March and April, the walls of the Gorge are towers of ice. Any time, you can combine a visit to the Gorge with a climb of Dorr Mountain, making a nice loop hike.

Miles and Directions

0.0 Start from the Gorge Trailhead.

0.4 Pass the Hemlock Trail.

0.6 Reach the first waterfall.

1.0 Hike up the narrowing valley past small waterfalls into the Gorge.

1.1 The valley widens and Kebo Brook has mostly disappeared beneath boulders.

1.4 Reach the notch between Dorr and Cadillac Mountains. Retrace your steps to the trailhead.

2.8 Arrive back at the trailhead.

34 Giant Slide Trail

The Giant Slide Trail is the least used route up Sargent Mountain. The trail climbs a narrow gorge beside a stream with several waterfalls, slides, and pools. The hike includes a visit to Giant Slide.

See map on p. 116.
Start: Giant Slide Trailhead
Elevation gain: 501 feet
Distance: 2.4 miles out and back
Hiking time: About 2 hours
Difficulty: Moderate
Season: May to July
Trail surface: Woodland path
Land status: Acadia National Park
Nearest town: Northeast Harbor and Somesville

Other users: None
Water availability: None
Canine compatibility: Dogs must be leashed at all times.
Fees and permits: None
Other maps: *DeLorme: Maine Atlas & Gazetteer*, map 16; USGS Southwest Harbor
Trail contact: Acadia National Park, (207) 288-3338, www.nps.gov/acad

Finding the trailhead: From the junction of ME 3 and ME 198 at the head of Mount Desert Island, follow ME 198 toward Southwest Harbor. Drive 4.3 miles to a stoplight. Turn left, staying on ME 198. Drive 2.6 miles. Parking is a turnout on the right across the road from the trailhead. There's a trailhead signpost, but no large park sign. GPS: N44 21.013' / W68 18.114'

The Hike

The Giant Slide Trail climbs a semi-open ledge then wanders through the woods to a carriage road. Across the carriage road, you reach Sargent Brook. The rest of the hike climbs through a narrow gorge with the brook. In summer and fall Sargent Brook is little more than a series of pools with no flowing water. In winter and spring the stream slides down rock faces, leaps around and over boulders, and collects in deep, cold pools.

You hike beside the stream, climbing over and under large irregular boulders. Cliffs often rise beside the trail. Beech, maples, and especially white pines tower over the gorge. The north wall of the gorge is a 45-degree slope that is often bare bedrock. The south wall is mostly an irregular cliff of jumbled rocks. Boulders often choke the gorge, forcing the stream over and under. The trail hugs the south side, sometimes climbing high above the stream. In other sections you find yourself tiptoeing across granite boulders in the brook.

Eventually, the gorge widens. You reach an intersection. Straight ahead is the Giant Slide: a huge slab of granite that slid down and created a narrow cave the trail passes through. Beyond the slide the stream passes through a wide, swampy swale. You've

nearly reached its headwaters and hiked beyond any waterfalls. On the descent back down the gorge, the views look very different, almost like it's a new place.

Miles and Directions

0.0 Start from the Giant Slide Trailhead.

0.7 Cross the carriage road.

0.9 Reach Sargent Brook.

1.2 The trail climbs beside Sargent Brook past several waterfalls and slides to Giant Slide. To complete the hike, retrace your steps to the trailhead.

2.4 Arrive back at the trailhead.

Waterfall on Sargent Brook in March

The Giant Slide

35 Mariaville Falls

Mariaville Falls is a 6-foot plunge on the West Branch Union River in wild country north of Ellsworth. Above the falls is a large pool in a wide bend of the river. Below the falls are rapids before the river settles back into its sinuous course through the spruce forest.

Start: New Trail Trailhead
Elevation gain: 262 feet
Distance: 1.7-mile reverse lollipop
Hiking time: About 2 hours
Difficulty: Easy
Season: May to July
Trail surface: Woodland path
Land status: Mariaville Falls Preserve
Nearest town: Amherst
Other users: None

Water availability: None
Canine compatibility: Dogs must be under control at all times.
Fees and permits: None
Other maps: *DeLorme: Maine Atlas & Gazetteer*, map 24; USGS Hopkins Pond
Trail contact: Frenchman Bay Conservancy, (207) 422-2328, http://frenchmanbay.org/preserves-trails/mariaville-falls

Finding the trailhead: From the junction of ME 9 (The Airline) and ME 181 in Amherst, follow ME 181 south. Drive 3 miles. Turn right onto the Mariaville Falls access road at the sign. Drive 0.3 mile. Parking is at the end of the road. The trailhead is at the north end of the parking area. GPS: N44 47.828' / W68 23.170'. Note: Mariaville Falls is 18 miles north of US 1A in Ellsworth via ME 180 and ME 181.

The Hike

Northern Hancock County is wild country. There are several townships of unorganized territory and plenty of woods and bogs. The three branches of the Union River rise here and flow roughly south into the sea below Ellsworth west of Mount Desert Island. The West Branch Union River flows out of Great Pond, which has an elevation of 291 feet. That's not a lot of elevation loss in 34 miles of river. From Great Pond to Graham Lake the river drops about two-thirds of that elevation in 13 miles. The upper Union River is entirely wild. There are no dams, no towns, and few road crossings.

Mariaville (pronounced Muh-rye-uh-vil) Falls is in the middle of this section of the Union River. The river wanders through a mixed forest dominated by spruce between grassy banks. It makes a wide, slow turn through a stand of large pines, then drops 6 feet over a crumbling ledge of bedrock layers stood on end. Downstream, beyond a few rocky riffles, the Union River goes back to wandering through the spruce woods between its grassy banks.

The hike begins near an old borrow pit and follows a new trail built by the Frenchman's Bay Conservancy to the Fisherman's Trail along the bank of the river.

Mariaville Falls

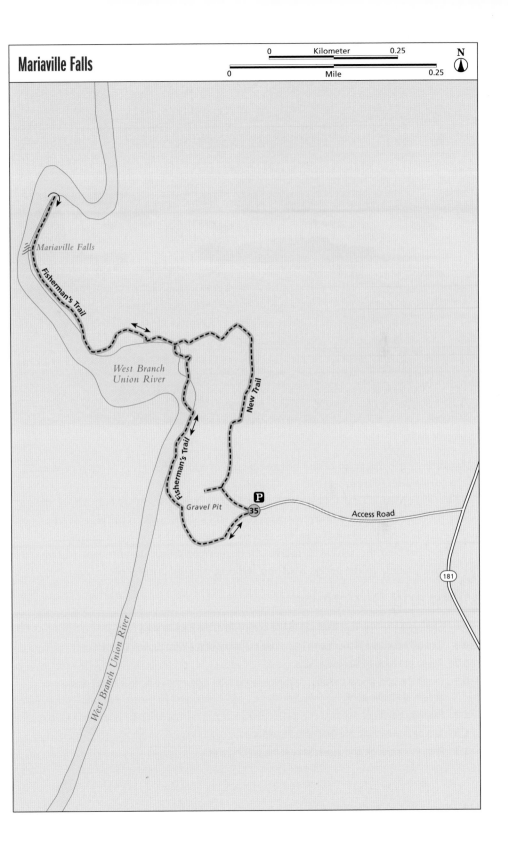

0   Kilometer   0.25

0   Mile   0.25

N

Mariaville Falls

Fisherman's Trail

West Branch
Union River

New Trail

Fisherman's Trail

Gravel Pit

P

35

Access Road

181

West Branch Union River

Mariaville Falls

You pass near the upper lip of the borrow pit, an overlook that gives you a nice view of the surrounding forest.

The Fisherman's Trail follows the river upstream past a low island. Above the island, the river is choppy and strewn with rocks. It's a short walk to the base of Mariaville Falls. The trail continues past the falls to the pool in the big bend upstream.

To get back to the trailhead, follow the Fisherman's Trail downstream past the New Trail, turning up the access road and walking past the borrow pit to your car.

Miles and Directions

0.0 Start from the New Trail Trailhead at the north end of the parking area.

0.4 Turn right onto the Fisherman's Trail along the shore of the West Branch Union River.

0.7 Reach the base of Mariaville Falls.

0.9 Reach the pool above the falls. To complete the hike, follow the Fisherman's Trail downstream along the bank.

1.3 Pass the New Trail.

1.5 Turn right away from the river onto the old road.

1.7 Pass the gravel pit and arrive back at the parking area.

36 Pembroke Reversing Falls

Pembroke Reversing Falls is the largest tidal falls in Maine. The 24-foot tide in Cobscook Bay struggles to create equilibrium among all the smaller bays and channels. In the channel between Mahar Point and Falls Island, seawater churns either up or down the ledges depending on which way the tide is running. It's a dramatic and powerful example of the forces of nature.

Start: Wide path at east end of parking area
Elevation gain: 188 feet
Distance: 1.4 miles out and back
Hiking time: 1 to 2 hours
Difficulty: Easy
Season: May to October
Trail surface: Woodland path
Land status: Downeast Coastal Conservancy Preserve and Pembroke town park
Nearest town: Pembroke

Other users: None
Water availability: None
Canine compatibility: Dogs must be on leash at all times.
Fees and permits: None
Other maps: *DeLorme: Maine Atlas & Gazetteer*, map 27; USGS Pembroke
Trail contact: Downeast Coastal Conservancy, (207) 255-4500, www.downeastcoastalconservancy.org

Finding the trailhead: From the junction of US 1 and ME 214 in Pembroke, drive south on US 1 0.3 mile. Turn left onto Old County Road. Drive 0.3 mile. Turn right onto Leighton Point Road. Drive 3.4 miles. Turn right onto Reversing Falls Road (there is no street sign). Drive 1.2 miles to a T-intersection. Turn left to stay on Reversing Falls Road, now gravel. Drive 1.6 miles to the end of the road. The trailhead is at the east end of the parking area. GPS: N44 52.976' / W67 07.817'

The Hike

There are numerous reversing falls in Downeast and Mid-Coast Maine. Some, like Goose Falls near Holbrook Island Sanctuary State Park in Brooksville, are where a stream flows into the ocean. At low tide there is a waterfall; at high tide the seawater rises above the falls and flows up the stream. In between, the waters can be chaotic, as if the outgoing freshwater and incoming seawater can't come to an agreement. Many reversing falls are of this type, including Blue Hills Falls on ME 175 south of Blue Hill, Bagaduce Falls on ME 175 in Brooksville, and the small falls on upper Robinhood Cove in the Josephine Newman Sanctuary (hike 10).

Others, like Sullivan Falls on the Taunton River in Hancock, are found at a point where a bay narrows and bedrock is near the surface. At low tide Sullivan Falls looks like a regular waterfall even though it's on a narrow bay, not a river—the name Taunton River is misleading. At high tide the falls are like riffles in the bay. Sipps Bay in Perry has several small waterfalls of this kind.

The largest reversing falls in Maine is Pembroke Reversing Falls. It is at a pinch point between Cobscook Bay and Whiting and Dennys Bays. The difference between

The falls on a falling tide are mostly riffles and whirlpools. Notice the falls beginning to emerge on the right.

high and low tides here is 24 feet—among the largest in the world. This huge difference adds to the power of Pembroke Reversing Falls. On a rising tide, as seawater is racing into Dennys and Whiting Bays, the falls are visible between Mahar Point and Falls Island and another spot to the west into Dennys Bay, where standing waves speak to the power involved. The water moves so forcefully around and over the ledges that it creates a whirlpool. On the falling tide, the falls reverse and push toward Cobscook Bay. *Cobscook* means "boiling water" in Passamaquoddy. You can see plenty of that here.

Mahar Point at the falls is a park managed jointly by the town of Pembroke and the Downeast Coastal Conservancy. From Mahar Point, you can walk right down to the water and see the falls from below or follow the hike and visit different viewpoints. The best view is from the end of the Spur Trail. You can see down the chute of the falls and into Dennys Bay. By turning your head east, you can see out into much larger Cobscook Bay. The channel connecting the two—where the waterfall is—is only 50 feet across.

The Reversing Falls Trail continues past the Spur Trail to a rocky prominence overlooking Cobscook Bay and the mouth of the channel. Out in Cobscook Bay, tidal forces like those that create Pembroke Reversing Falls create the world's largest whirlpool.

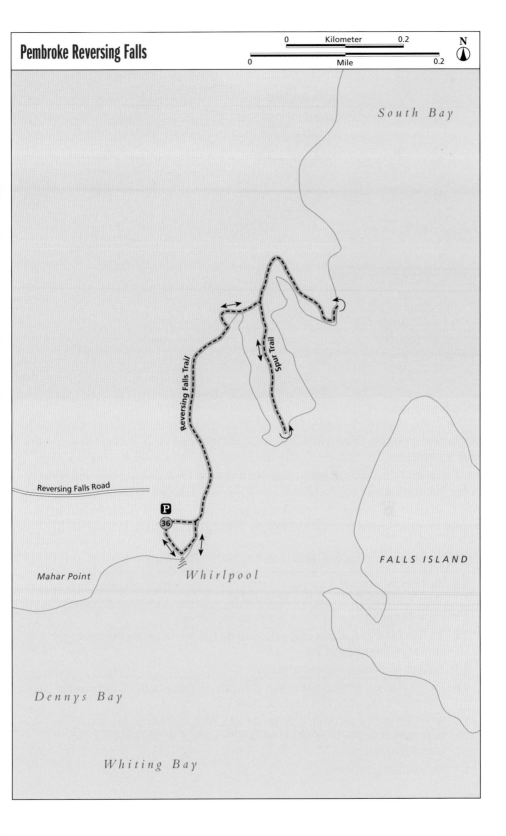

Pembroke Reversing Falls

0   Kilometer   0.2

0   Mile   0.2

N

South Bay

Reversing Falls Trail

Spur Trail

Reversing Falls Road

P

36

Mahar Point

Whirlpool

FALLS ISLAND

Dennys Bay

Whiting Bay

The falls from Mahar Point

To best appreciate Pembroke Reversing Falls, you need to see it multiple times or over several hours. The falls are most dramatic when the tide is out, but the channel is most dramatic when the tide is turning, when you can see standing waves and whirlpools. Remember, the tides at Pembroke Reversing Falls are delayed from normal tide chart times because of the complex geography of Cobscook Bay. Your best bet is to plan to spend several hours at the falls. Bring a lunch and make a day of it.

Miles and Directions

0.0   Start from the wide trail at the east end of the parking area. The trail descends 175 to the shore. Turn left and follow the Reversing Falls Trail.

0.3   The trail loops around a small cove to the Spur Trail. Turn right.

0.5   The Spur Trail ends at a rocky point overlooking the falls. To continue the hike, retrace your steps to the Reversing Falls Trail.

0.7   Turn right back onto the Reversing Falls Trail.

0.8   The trail ends at a rocky point with views of the falls and Cobscook Bay. To complete the hike, follow the Reversing Falls Trail back toward the trailhead.

1.3   Arrive back at the wide trail up to the parking area. Go straight 300 feet to a spot on the rocky shore with a view of the falls. To return to the trailhead, follow the trail that leads north to the parking area.

1.4   Arrive back at the trailhead.

37 Tobey Falls

Tobey Falls is the most impressive of the waterfalls on Big Wilson Stream. The river slides at a 45-degree angle down a slate rock face, dropping 15 feet. The banks are littered with broken boulders of weathered black rock.

Start: Boulders across logging road
Elevation gain: 57 feet
Distance: 0.6 mile out and back (1 mile if gate is closed)
Hiking time: About 1 hour
Difficulty: Easy
Season: May to October
Trail surface: Woods road
Land status: Private timberland
Nearest town: Guilford

Other users: Hunters in season
Water availability: None
Canine compatibility: Dogs must be under control at all times.
Fees and permits: None
Other maps: *DeLorme: Maine Atlas & Gazetteer*, map 31; USGS Monson East
Trail contact: American Forest Management, (207) 827-3700

Finding the trailhead: From the junction of ME 15 and ME 150 in Guilford, follow ME 150 north. Drive 8.8 miles. Bear left onto Elliotsville Road. Drive 1.5 miles. Turn left onto Tobey Falls Road (just past Titcomb Road). Drive 0.7 mile, passing a gravel pit. Drive through a gate and continue downhill 0.2 mile. Turn right into the parking area. The hike begins where boulders block the road. GPS: N45 18.760' / W69 24.978'

The Hike

Big Wilson Stream flows out of Lower Wilson Pond east of Greenville and drains into Sebec Lake. Several of Maine's best waterfalls are on side streams where they drop into Big Wilson's deep valley, including Little Wilson Falls (hike 38) and Indian Falls (hike 42). The stream flows over mostly slate bedrock. There are several waterfalls on Big Wilson Stream itself.

Big Wilson Falls is a roadside waterfall where Elliotsville Road crosses the stream near the Little Wilson Falls trailhead. Near Sebec Lake are two more roadside waterfalls along ME 150 at Earley Landing. You can park near the public boat landing to visit them. Tobey Falls is the most impressive waterfall on Big Wilson Stream and the least well-known.

Big Wilson Stream slides at a 45-degree angle down a face of black slate, dropping 15 feet. The falls are most impressive in spring when the waterfall covers the entire rock face. By summer it reduces to about 10 feet wide. Even at low flow, it's well worth visiting. The trail ends at a picnic area in the woods beside the waterfall. You can walk out to the edge of the top of the waterfall or out a ledge just downstream. From the top of the waterfall, you have a view of a smaller waterfall a couple of hundred yards upstream.

Tobey Falls

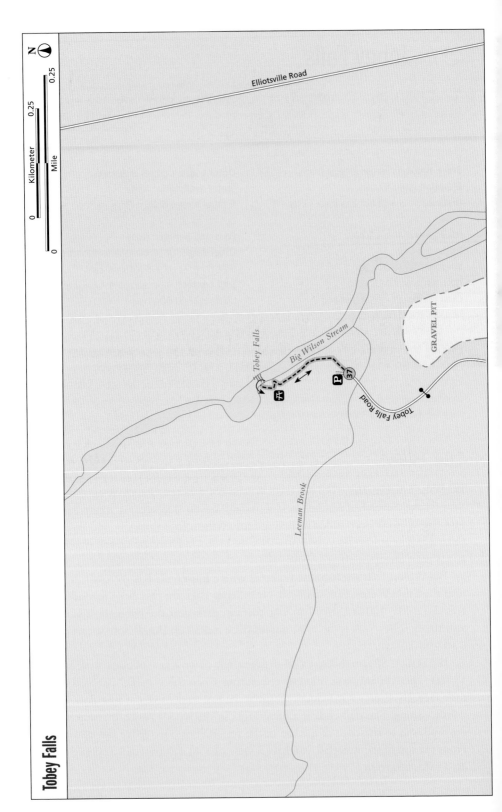

Elliotsville Road

Tobey Falls

Big Wilson Stream

Leeman Brook

37

Tobey Falls Road

GRAVEL PIT

N

0   0.25   Kilometer   0.25

0   0.25   Mile

Tobey Falls

Blocks of broken slate, some jagged and angular and others worn smooth, litter the banks. Big Wilson Stream disappears around a bend downstream. There's actually another waterfall almost as big as Tobey Falls around that bend. You could get to it by cutting through the gravel pit you drove by getting to the trailhead. The problem is that it's private property and used as a shooting range. Be content with the surprising beauty of Tobey Falls.

Miles and Directions

0.0 Start at the boulders across the road at the end of the parking area.

0.2 Follow the woods road north. Reach the picnic area at the base of the falls.

0.3 Reach the top of Tobey Falls. Another waterfall is visible upstream beyond an island. To complete the hike, retrace your steps to the trailhead.

0.6 Arrive back at the trailhead.

38 Little Wilson Falls

Little Wilson Falls, at 75 feet, is one of the highest in Maine. Little Wilson Stream drops from a calm pool into a narrow, black slate gorge overhung with dark cedars. Below the falls the stream cascades over a series of smaller waterfalls before flowing into Big Wilson Stream. The hike passes several of these falls and offers access to the rest.

Start: End of Little Wilson Falls Road
Elevation gain: 476 feet
Distance: 2.5 miles out and back
Hiking time: About 2 hours
Difficulty: Easy
Season: May to November are best, but during May and early June the falls have more water and are therefore more spectacular.
Trail surface: Woodland path with lots of roots and rocks
Land status: Elliotsville Plantation and Appalachian Trail

Nearest town: Monson
Other users: None
Water availability: Little Wilson Stream
Canine compatibility: Dogs must be under control at all times.
Fees and permits: None
Other maps: *DeLorme: Maine Atlas & Gazetteer*, map 41; USGS Barren Mountain West
Trail contact: Elliotsville Plantation, (207) 581-9462

Finding the trailhead: From the blinking light in Greenville, drive south on ME 15/6 13.8 miles. Turn left onto Elliotsville Road. There is a sign for Borestone Mountain just before the turn. Drive 7.6 miles on Elliotsville Road. Just before the bridge over Big Wilson Stream, there is an unmarked gravel road on the left. Turn down Little Wilson Falls Road and drive 0.5 mile to a fork in the road. At the fork go straight. Drive another 0.3 mile to the end of the road. The trail leaves the northwest corner of the parking area along the stream. At first the trail looks more like a small, gravelly streambed than a trail. GPS: N45 22.511' / W69 26.937'

The Hike

Monson is the center of Maine's slate industry. The black slabs of rock are harvested from several quarries around the town; in town you can see slate stacked, ready to be sold. Many of the streams in this part of Maine cut through slate gorges, drop over slate ledges, and have piles of broken slate along their banks. Nearby Big Wilson Falls is a good example. To the west in Blanchard, the Piscataquis River cuts through a shallow slate gorge below Abbott Road; at the head of the gorge is Barrow's Falls. Northeast of Little Wilson Falls is the most famous slate gorge, Gulf Hagas (hike 43).

In most of these cases, the sheets of slate are stood on end. Across Little Wilson Falls from the trail, the cliffs show this vertical bedding. Along the trail to the falls, there are several places where fins of slate stick out of the hillside. Near the falls, at the top of the gorge, several large fins of slate jut out into space. The blackness of the slate,

The author's dad lines up a photo of the top of Little Wilson Falls

the vertical bedding, and the forest closing over the gorge and falls all make Little Wilson Falls the most dramatic in Maine.

The trail begins at a no-longer-used state campsite. Originally, the trail was a shortcut used by locals to get to the falls. In the summer of 2013, the Appalachian Mountain Club improved and blazed the trail for Elliotsville Plantation, the land-owner. The trail begins along the stream at the large pool below a 15-foot waterfall and follows the stream up past another good-sized falls. Notice that the huge boulder sitting on the slate ledge across the stream is not the same kind of rock: It is an erratic dropped here by the retreating glaciers.

Beyond the second falls, the trail begins to gently climb the hillside, staying within earshot and often view of Little Wilson Stream. The trail turns away from the stream after it flattens out atop a ridge, and just before junctioning with the Appalachian Trail (AT).

To hike to Little Wilson Falls, turn left and hike southbound on the AT up a rocky and rooty climb beside the slate gorge. When you reach the sign-in box just before the falls, there is a place to climb out onto the rocks to see the falls from partway down. Remember as you climb around on the rock that slate is slippery when wet.

After exploring the falls, you may want to explore the slate gorge and the stream below the gorge. To do so, pass the Little Wilson Falls Trail and continue northbound on the AT as it drops down to Little Wilson Stream just below the gorge. To get the best view back up the gorge, you need to ford the stream or cross on the log that spans it. To explore a horseshoe bend and falls downstream, follow the rough trail on the west bank of Little Wilson Stream for 0.1 mile. When the water is low in late summer, you can cross and recross the stream on the slate at the falls. In the spring the water rushes over and around the rocks.

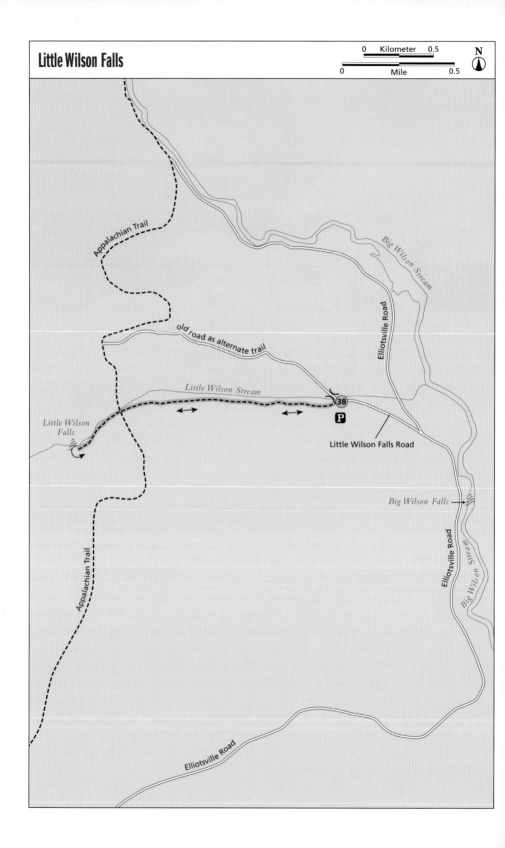

Little Wilson Falls

0　　　Kilometer　　0.5

0　　　　Mile　　　　0.5

N

Appalachian Trail

Big Wilson Stream

Elliotsville Road

old road as alternate trail

Little Wilson Stream

Little Wilson Falls

38

P

Little Wilson Falls Road

Big Wilson Falls

Appalachian Trail

Elliotsville Road

Big Wilson Stream

Elliotsville Road

Along Little Wilson Stream

After visiting Little Wilson Falls, stop at Big Wilson Falls. Across Elliotsville Road from Little Wilson Falls Road is a small parking area (with a porta-potty in summer). From the parking area, a short trail leads down to Big Wilson Falls. You can also see the falls from the bridge on Elliotsville Road over Big Wilson Stream.

Miles and Directions

0.0   Start at the northwest corner of the parking area. The unmarked trail looks like a small, rocky streambed that stays close to Little Wilson Stream.

1.1   The trail follows along the stream, passing several waterfalls, then begins to climb. The trail ends at the white-blazed Appalachian Trail. Turn left to hike toward Little Wilson Falls.

1.3   After hiking along the end of the gorge below the falls, you arrive at the top of the falls. When climbing around on the rocks, remember that slate is slippery when it's wet. To return to the trailhead, retrace your steps.

1.5   Arrive back at the Little Wilson Falls Trail. Turn right to return to the trailhead. ***Option:*** Hike straight ahead on the AT, descending to where the trail crosses the stream. This gives you a good view back up the dark gorge and, by bushwhacking downstream 100 yards, access to a horseshoe bend on Little Wilson Stream that is a great place for lunch or just to explore. If you take this option, you'll need to retrace your steps back up to the Little Wilson Falls Trail to get back to the trailhead.

2.5   Arrive back at the trailhead.

39 Slugundy Falls

Long Pond Stream drops more than 200 feet in the short stretch of stream this hike follows. There are no spectacular waterfalls, but a nice falls is at the head and tail of Slugundy Gorge. This slate gorge is more than 40 feet deep, with nearly vertical sides. Downstream from the gorge is nearly continuous whitewater with several small drops and pools.

Start: Obvious but unsigned trail at end of Otter Pond Road
Elevation gain: 870 feet
Distance: 3.2 miles out and back
Hiking time: About 3 hours
Difficulty: Moderate
Season: May to October
Trail surface: Woodland path
Land status: Private timberland and Appalachian Trail

Nearest town: Monson
Other users: Hunters in season
Water availability: Long Pond Stream
Canine compatibility: Dogs must be under control at all times.
Fees and permits: None
Other maps: *DeLorme: Maine Atlas & Gazetteer*, map 41; USGS West Barren Mountain
Trail contact: None

Finding the trailhead: From downtown Monson on ME 15/6, drive north. As you're leaving the village, turn right onto Elliotsville Road at the sign for Borestone Mountain. Drive 7.7 miles. Turn left onto Bodfish Valley Road just after the bridge over Big Wilson Stream. Drive 3 miles, passing the Borestone Mountain trailhead, to the bridge over Long Pond Stream. Drive another 0.5 mile. Turn left onto Otter Pond Road. Drive 0.8 mile to the end of the road. The trailhead is where the roadbed continues straight ahead into the woods. (The trail isn't the grassy lane to the left.) GPS: N45 24.821' / W69 25.020'

The Hike

Long Pond Stream flows from Long Pond nestled against the north side of the Barren–Chairback Range to Onawa Lake. The stream flows around the west end of the range, dropping 575 feet. About half that descent is in the short section of Long Pond Stream this hike visits. Slugundy Gorge is at the head of the steep section of river.

To get there, you drive past the entrance to Borestone Mountain Sanctuary and over the shoulder of the mountain into Bodfish Intervale. You cross Long Pond Stream in the middle of a meadow, then reenter the woods and turn onto Otter Pond Road. At a low spot near Otter Pond, you can park on the left across from an obvious trail that leads out to the pond. This pond is a great place to see wildlife. You also get a clear view of Barren Slides from the shore.

Slugundy Falls ▶

The trail is a continuation of the road. It's often wet even in summer, but a rough trail parallels the roadbed, allowing you to keep your feet dry. Past the wet area, the trail bears right and begins climbing. You can hear Long Pond Stream. It's only about 0.1 mile through the woods, but there's no trail to it. Climb along a hardwood ridge to the Appalachian Trail (AT). To the right are Barren Ledges and Barren Mountain itself. Turn right (make sure to note the spot since you'll have to find it on your return) and descend toward Long Pond Stream. You pass the side trail to the lean-to, visible through the pines.

The descent steepens and you reach a sharp turn in the trail. Straight ahead is an overlook, and below you is Slugundy Gorge with a waterfall at its head. It's possible to carefully descend to the stream from this spot, but remember the rock is slippery. Take great care. The stream slides between almost-sheer walls 30 feet high. Moss clings to everything. The dark water is more than a dozen feet deep.

The trail descends to Long Pond Stream where it exits the gorge. There's another waterfall here. For the next half mile, the AT parallels the river, which is almost continuous whitewater. There are many small falls and ledges. In several places the stream has created large pools, good for swimming.

The AT seems to just end at the stream. To continue southbound, you have to ford the knee-deep stream's swift current. There are several good swimming holes near the ford among the jumble of boulders in the streambed.

Lower Slugundy Falls

Slugundy Falls

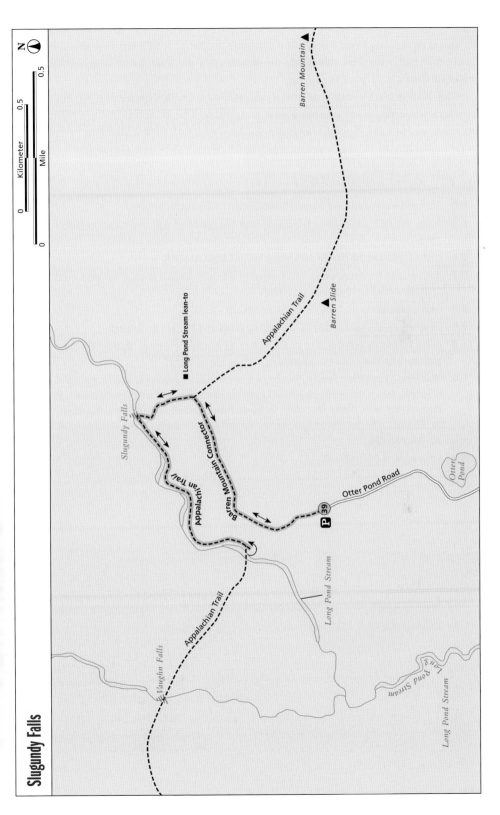

N

Kilometer
0   0.5   0.5

Mile
0   0.5

Barren Mountain

Appalachian Trail

Barren Slide

Long Pond Stream lean-to

Barren Mountain Connector

Slugundy Falls

Appalachian Trail

P 39

Otter Pond Road

Otter Pond

Long Pond Stream

Long Pond Stream

Long Pond Stream

Vaughn Falls

Appalachian Trail

If you cross Long Pond Stream and continue on the AT, you'll cross Vaughn Brook in another half mile. The trail fords the brook on a flat slate ledge atop a 20-foot waterfall with a nice pool at its base.

This hike doesn't visit a spectacular waterfall or a single wonderful pool, but the sum total of all the water features is just as satisfying. This is an especially good hike on a hot summer day. Cool air flows downstream with you as you hike. You can walk as far as you like or choose a swimming hole in or near Slugundy Gorge itself.

Miles and Directions

0.0 Start at the unmarked but obvious Barren Mountain Connector trailhead.

0.2 Follow the old roadbed through a marshy area. The trail bears right and begins to climb gently.

0.6 Climb steadily to the marshy area where the trail forks. Bear left.

0.7 Turn left onto the Appalachian Trail. Remember this spot. Since it is unsigned, you'll need to remember where to turn on your return.

0.8 Pass a side trail to the Long Pond Stream lean-to.

0.9 Descend steadily to an overlook of Slugundy Gorge and the falls at its head.

1.0 Descend steadily, passing another waterfall at the mouth of the gorge. ***Option:*** You can end your exploring here and retrace your steps to the trailhead.

1.6 Hike beside Long Pond Stream, passing almost continuous whitewater and several small waterfalls. Reach the point where the AT fords the knee-deep and swift-flowing stream. To complete the hike, retrace your steps to the trailhead. ***Option:*** Continue southbound on the AT. A half mile past Long Pond Stream, the trail crosses Vaughn Brook at the head of a 20-foot waterfall.

3.2 Arrive back at the trailhead.

40 West Chairback Falls

West Chairback Brook flows out of West Chairback Pond and tumbles off the mountain toward Long Pond. The Appalachian Trail crosses the stream in the middle of that tumble. Upstream from the crossing, the brook drops in an endless chain of very small falls in its bouldery bed. Downstream, the brook crashes down a rock face into a jumble of boulders. The total drop is about 50 feet.

Start: Third Mountain Trailhead
Elevation gain: 1,523 feet
Distance: 6.0 miles out and back
Hiking time: 4 to 5 hours
Difficulty: Strenuous
Season: Late May to October
Trail surface: Woodland path
Land status: AMC Maine Woods and Appalachian Trail
Nearest town: Brownville
Other users: None
Water availability: Trail follows stream in first half mile.

Canine compatibility: Dogs must be under control at all times.
Fees and permits: Katahdin Iron Works entrance fee
Other maps: *DeLorme: Maine Atlas & Gazetteer*, map 42; USGS Barren Mountain East
Trail contact: North Maine Woods, Inc., (207) 435-6213, www.northmainewoods.org, for road conditions; Appalachian Mountain Club, Greenville Office, (207) 695-3085, www.outdoors .org, for trail conditions

Finding the trailhead: From Brownville, drive north on ME 11 4.8 miles north from the bridge over the Pleasant River. Turn left onto K-I Road at the sign for Katahdin Iron Works and Gulf Hagas. Drive 6.5 miles to the gate, where you pay your fee. Cross the Pleasant River and turn right; drive 3.5 miles to a fork in the road. Take the left fork, following the signs to Gulf Hagas. Pass the Gulf Hagas parking area 2.9 miles beyond the fork. Continue driving another 1 mile. Turn left onto Long Pond Road at the sign for Gorham Lodge. Drive 2.1 miles, passing Gorman Lodge Road. The trailhead parking is on the left just past the trailhead. GPS: N45 27.250' / W69 18.937'

The Hike

West Chairback Pond is nestled into the saddle between Chairback and Third Mountains, surrounded by thick spruce. It's a picturesque lake popular with local fishermen. Its outlet stream flows through a marshy area, then drops quickly off the side of the mountain. The Appalachian Trail (AT) crosses the stream in the middle of its tumble.

To get there, you have to climb Third Mountain. The trail climbs gently through hardwoods. In spring this is a great place to see wildflowers. As the climb steepens, the trees transition to evergreens. A short, rocky climb with one ladder brings you to the AT. Turn left and hike toward Third Mountain.

A rocky climb brings you to the semi-open summit. There are partial views across the valley of the White Cap Range and the Lily Bay Mountains. This isn't the real

West Chairback Falls

view, though. Another quarter of a mile of hiking brings you to Monument Cliffs, where you get a wide-open panorama of the mountains to the north and west.

You descend off Third Mountain and reach West Chairback Falls. Upstream from the AT, the stream drops chaotically through its boulder-choked bed. It takes a breath at the AT crossing, then leaps off a rock face. Thirty feet down, you can see it flatten out and braid across the forest floor.

To get a good look at the falls from its base, you have to bushwhack down the hillside. The best spots are either about 100 feet west or east of the waterfall. The rocky hillside is somewhat overgrown, so even from the bottom you only get incomplete views. To really see the waterfall, you have boulder-hop around the stream near the base.

There's no pool for swimming, but you can take a dip in West Chairback Pond, which is 0.2 mile up a marked side trail.

West Chairback Falls

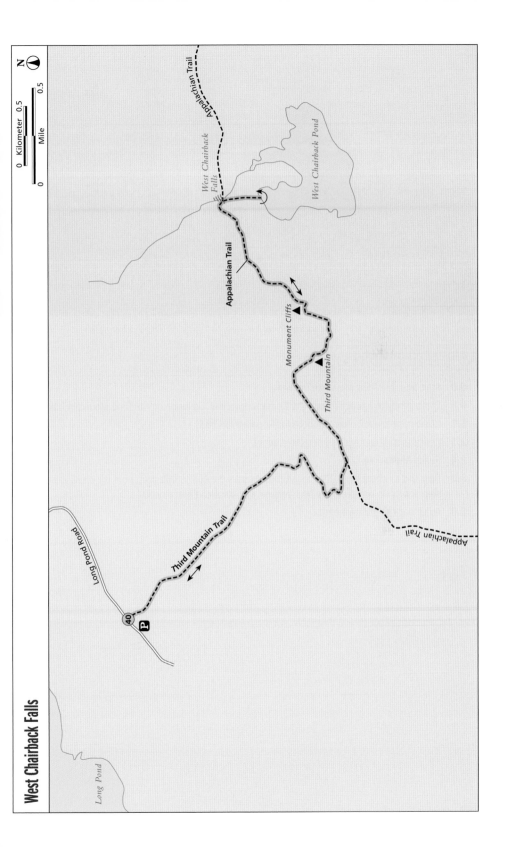

Long Pond

Long Pond Road

40
P

Third Mountain Trail

Monument Cliffs

Third Mountain

Appalachian Trail

Appalachian Trail

West Chairback Falls

West Chairback Pond

Appalachian Trail

N

0   Kilometer   0.5

0   0.5
Mile

Long Pond and the Lily Bay Mountains from Monument Cliffs on Third Mountain

Miles and Directions

0.0   Start from the Third Mountain Trailhead.

0.9   Climb gently to a junction with the Gorham Loop Trail. Continue on the Third Mountain Trail.

1.5   Climb more steadily. Turn left onto the Appalachian Trail.

2.1   Reach Third Mountain's semi-open summit.

2.4   Reach Monument Cliffs.

3.0   Descend to where West Chairback Brook crosses the AT. The falls drop from the rocks you step across. To complete the hike, retrace your steps to the trailhead.

6.0   Arrive back at the trailhead.

41 Hay Brook Falls

Hay Brook Falls is a 30-foot double drop on a stream that flows into the Pleasant River a few miles below Gulf Hagas. It's an easy walk to this little-visited gem.

Start: Gulf Hagas Trailhead
Elevation gain: 254 feet
Distance: 2.6 miles out and back
Hiking time: About 2 hours
Difficulty: Easy
Season: Late May to October
Trail surface: Woodland path
Land status: Katahdin Iron Works/Jo-Mary Multiple-Use Forest
Nearest town: Brownville
Other users: None

Water availability: Pleasant River and Hay Brook
Canine compatibility: Dogs must be under control at all times.
Fees and permits: Entrance fee paid at Katahdin Iron Works gate
Other maps: *DeLorme: Maine Atlas & Gazetteer*, map 42; USGS Barren Mountain East
Trail contact: North Maine Woods, Inc., (207) 435-6213, www.northmainewoods.org

Finding the trailhead: From the bridge over the Pleasant River in Brownville, follow ME 11 north. Drive 4.8 miles. Turn left onto K-I Road at the sign for Katahdin Iron Works and Gulf Hagas. Drive 6.5 miles to the gate, where you pay your fee. Cross the Pleasant River and turn right. Drive 3.5 miles to a fork in the road. Take the left fork, following the signs to Gulf Hagas. Drive 2.9 miles. The parking area is on the right at the sign for Gulf Hagas. GPS: N45 28.667' / W69 17.122'

The Hike

Most sources give directions to Hay Brook Falls via High Bridge and the three campsites along Hay Brook just below the falls. The problem is that the road is almost impassable and recently has been closed. As a result, most people miss out on this gem of a waterfall. But there's another route to the falls via the Gulf Hagas Trailhead.

From the Gulf Hagas Trailhead, ford the Pleasant River. The river is 100 feet across and usually around shin deep. The streambed is slippery, round rocks. It's best to bring water shoes for the crossing.

Across the river, follow the Appalachian Trail (AT) north as it loops around the Hermitage—a grove of old-growth white pines. You'll come to a T-intersection. The sign gives no indication what's to the right. Hay Brook Falls is. Turn right and follow a wide, flat trail along the river past several backcountry campsites.

The trail bends away from the river and reaches Hay Brook. You need to cross the stream. Either ford it or look for a spot just upstream where you can cross on rocks. Across the stream, turn left and hike through three campsites. An unmarked but obvious trail leads upstream beyond the campsites. In no time you can see Hay Brook Falls upstream. The trail passes several places where you can step out onto rocks along the stream for a view as it climbs to the top of the waterfall.

Hay Brook Falls and Gulf Hagas

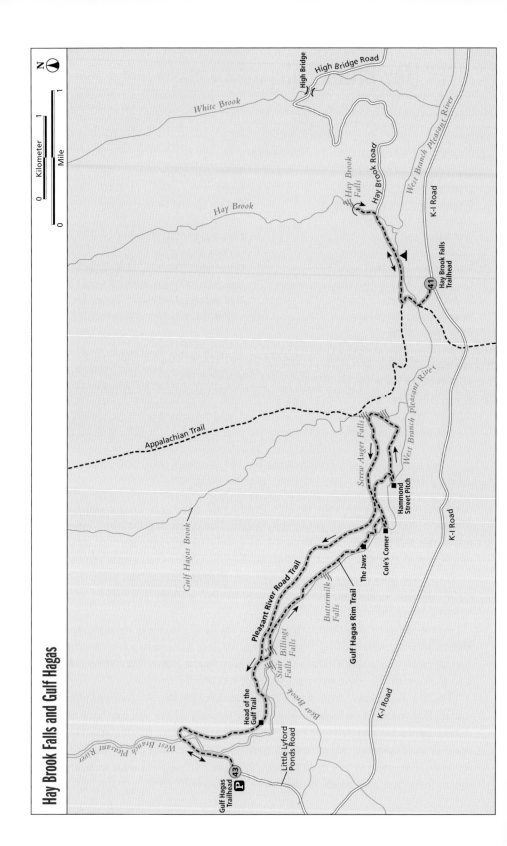

Hay Brook Falls

Hay Brook drops into a pool cupped in the cliff face, makes a turn, then drops 20 more feet into a good-sized pool. The pool is surrounded by flat slate boulders, making this a great swimming hole. The rock face around the pool is smooth black slate that gets very mossy as it blends into the hillside.

Miles and Directions

0.0   Start from the Gulf Hagas Trailhead.

0.2   Follow the Gulf Hagas Connector Trail to the Appalachian Trail and the Pleasant River. Ford the river.

0.4   Follow the AT northbound to a T-intersection. Turn right off the AT.

0.6   Pass Pugwash Pond and Pleasant River campsite 10.

1.1   Pass campsites 7–9. Reach Hay Brook and cross the stream. Turn left and pass through Hay Brook campsites 1–3.

1.2   Follow the obvious but unmarked trail from campsite 3 upstream to an overlook of Hay Brook Falls.

1.3   The trail continues past the base of the falls to the top of the falls. To complete the hike, retrace your steps to the trailhead.

2.6   Arrive back at the trailhead.

42 Indian Falls

Indian Falls is only a few miles from Little Wilson Falls as the crow flies. Both waterfalls are significant drops where small streams enter Big Wilson Stream's steep-sided slate valley. Indian Falls is reached by following an abandoned roadbed to a short trail that leads to the base of the falls. The falls drop over black slate, surrounded by towering evergreens—one of the most scenic in Maine.

Start: Where Indian Falls Road ends at railroad tracks
Elevation gain: 320 feet
Distance: 1.9 miles out and back
Hiking time: About 2 hours
Difficulty: Easy
Season: May to October
Trail surface: Woodland path and abandoned road
Land status: Commercial timberland

Nearest town: Greenville
Other users: Hunters in season
Water availability: Indian Stream
Canine compatibility: Dogs must be under control at all times.
Fees and permits: None
Other maps: *DeLorme: Maine Atlas & Gazetteer*, map 41; USGS Barren Mountain West
Trail contact: None

Finding the trailhead: From the blinking light in Greenville, drive north on Lily Bay Road 0.1 mile. Turn right onto Pleasant Street. Drive 2.1 miles to where the pavement ends, and continue driving another 1.6 miles. The road crosses Big Wilson Stream and changes names to K-I Road. Drive another 2.5 miles. Turn right onto Morkill Road. Drive 2.8 miles. Turn right onto Indian Falls Road, a small narrow road. You can park at the top and walk down to the trailhead or drive 0.3 mile to the end of the road. The road ends at the railroad tracks. The hike follows the route of the road across the tracks. GPS: N45 25.147' / W69 28.423'

The Hike

Full disclosure: My family and I spent the better part of a morning driving around on logging roads looking for the Indian Falls trailhead. You can avoid having an adventure like ours by carefully following the directions. Because of the number of logging roads and the dearth of road signs, this hike requires that you keep track of the mileage between turns on your way from Greenville to the trailhead.

As we were driving around, my wife suggested that Indian Falls shouldn't be in this guide—it was too hard to find. When we walked past the trail to the falls and followed the roadbed too far down toward Big Wilson Stream, she adamantly repeated her opinion.

But when we made it to the base of the falls, she changed her mind. Indian Falls drops 60 feet down a black slate face, following seams in the bedrock in several horsetails. The water crashes off joints in the rock, creating a chaotic pattern of dancing mist that dampens the surrounding forest and hikers gaping at the falls.

Indian Falls

Find a flat rock to bask on like a lizard, soaking up the warm summer sun and the white noise of water beating on slate. Or explore the rock face around the falls, viewing it from different angles. The stream above the falls is worth a look. It pools among jumbled boulders, slides down water-smoothed bedrock, and jumps into the air, sparkling with kinetic energy.

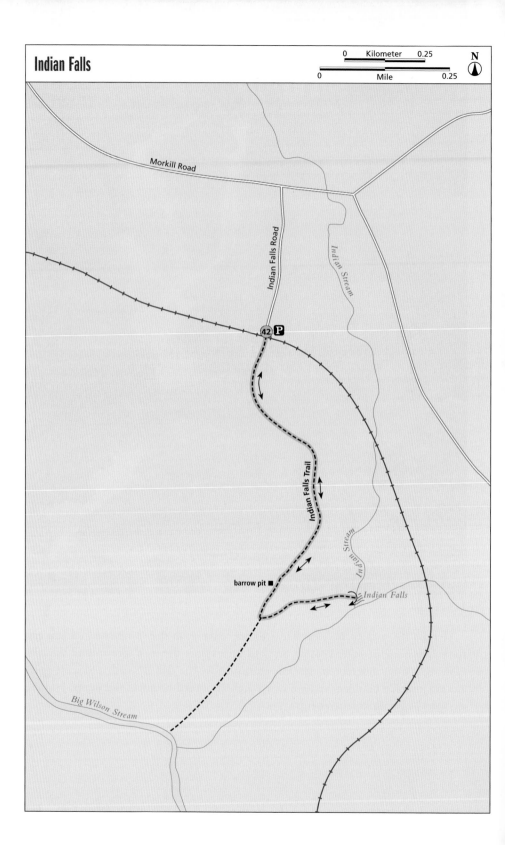

Indian Falls

0   Kilometer   0.25

0   Mile   0.25

N

Morkill Road

Indian Falls Road

Indian Stream

42 P

Indian Falls Trail

Indian Stream

barrow pit ■

Indian Falls

Big Wilson Stream

Indian Falls

Miles and Directions

0.0 Start by crossing the railroad tracks and following the old roadbed through an alder thicket.

0.1 Bear to the left and climb a gentle rise. Follow the red flagging all the way to the waterfall.

0.5 Descend off the rise and pass a barrow pit.

0.6 Turn left at a cairn onto the Indian Falls Trail, following the red flagging. (The roadbed continues downhill all the way to Big Wilson Stream.)

0.9 Arrive at Indian Falls. You can easily reach both the top and base of the falls. To complete the hike, return the way you came.

1.8 Arrive back at the trailhead.

43 Gulf Hagas

Gulf Hagas is one of Maine's deepest canyons. The hike follows the West Branch Pleasant River as it drops 400 feet in 4 miles through the Gulf. There are numerous waterfalls and rapids. The walls of the Gulf rise vertically at times as much as 140 feet. Below Gulf Hagas, the hike follows Gulf Hagas Stream up past numerous waterfalls, including Screw Auger Falls—the highest on the whole hike.

See map on p. 164.
Start: Head of the Gulf Trailhead, next to large information sign across road from parking area
Elevation gain: 1,696 feet
Distance: 10.2-mile lollipop
Hiking time: 5 to 8 hours
Difficulty: Strenuous due to distance
Season: Mid-May to October is best, especially after heavy rains when river levels are highest
Trail surface: Woodland path
Land status: Appalachian Mountain Club's North Woods Recreation and Conservation Area and Appalachian Trail corridor
Nearest towns: Greenville and Brownville
Other users: None

Water availability: West Branch Pleasant River at miles 0.5 and 2.0; Gulf Hagas Stream at miles 5.8 and 6.1 miles
Canine compatibility: Dogs must be under control at all times.
Fees and permits: Fee paid at Hedgehog gate
Other maps: *DeLorme: Maine Atlas & Gazetteer*, maps 41 and 42; USGS Barren Mountain East
Trail contact: Appalachian Mountain Club, Greenville Office, (207) 695-3085, www .outdoors.org; Maine Appalachian Trail Club, www.matc.org; KI Jo-Mary Multiple-Use Forest, (207) 435-6213, www.northmainewoods.org

Finding the trailhead: From Brownville, drive north on ME 11 4.8 miles north from the bridge over the Pleasant River. Turn left onto K-I Road at the sign for Katahdin Iron Works and Gulf Hagas. Drive 6.5 miles to the gate, where you pay your fee. Cross the Pleasant River and turn right. Drive 3.5 miles to a fork in the road. Take the left fork, following the signs to Gulf Hagas. Pass the Gulf Hagas parking area 2.9 miles beyond the fork and the Appalachian Trail 3.5 miles beyond the fork. Turn right onto Little Lyford Pond Road 7.3 miles past the fork (10.8 miles from the K-I gate). Drive 0.9 mile to the Head of the Gulf parking area on the left just past the trailhead. GPS: N45 29.908' / W69 21.418'

From Greenville, at the blinking light, drive north on Lily Bay Road. Almost immediately turn right onto Pleasant Street. As you leave Greenville the road becomes East Road. At the airport, the pavement ends. At Lower Wilson Pond, the road becomes K-I Road. There are numerous side roads, which change from year to year with the needs of the logging companies. The Appalachian Mountain Club has put up signs directing you to their lodges at most side roads. Follow the signs to the lodges, staying on K-I Road. At 12.1 miles from the blinking light in Greenville, you get to the Hedgehog checkpoint, where you need to pay the fee. Past the checkpoint, drive 2.9 miles, then turn left onto Little Lyford Ponds Road. Drive 0.9 mile to the Head of the Gulf parking area on the left just past the trailhead. GPS: N45 29.908' / W69 21.418'

The Hike

No one is sure of the origin of the name Gulf Hagas. It has been suggested that it is a corruption of an Abanaki word or phrase, but the Penobscot name for Gulf Hagas is *Mahkonlahgok*, which doesn't seem to lend itself to being corrupted to "Gulf Hagas" by the nineteenth-century loggers who named it. In the White Mountains there are several "gulfs"—a word associated with oceans—used in the names of cirques to describe the large empty space created by glaciers. Gulf Hagas is Maine's best known and deepest canyon, so *gulf* makes a certain amount of sense. But *hagas*, because it is a homophone with *haggis*, sounds Gaelic. *Haggis* does mean "chopped," so maybe there is a connection there. It seems as reasonable an explanation as falling back on the reliable corruption of an Abanaki term. Whatever the origin of its name, Gulf Hagas is one of Maine's natural wonders.

Billings Falls

The West Branch Pleasant River flows through the 4-mile-long canyon, dropping almost 400 feet. The walls of the Gulf are slate that at times rise vertically from the river for more than 100 feet. In places the canyon is less than 20 feet across. At the Jaws it was less than 8 feet wide until loggers blasted away rock, making it more than 20 feet wide. They widened it so the logs floated down the river in the spring freshet to Katahdin Iron Works wouldn't get jammed up at the Jaws. This was a dangerous stretch of river for the loggers; at least one river driver is known to have been killed in Gulf Hagas.

The hike begins at the west end of the Gulf along the river, which runs deep and silent above the Head of the Gulf. The advantage of beginning the hike here rather than at the Gulf Hagas trailhead you passed on your drive in is that you avoid both of the river fords. Coming in from the east requires fording the West Branch Pleasant River below the Gulf. The crossing is more than 100 feet across and the river bottom is slippery, round rocks. The water is usually cold enough to numb your calves and feet. Only in the driest times can the ford be done by hopping from rock to rock. When the river is that low, the falls in the Gulf are much less dramatic. You also have to ford Gulf Hagas Brook above Screw Auger Falls. This crossing is only 20 feet, but the water is deeper. The west end of the Gulf is generally less crowded, too. Many folks that hike in from the east don't make it much past Screw Auger Falls.

At the Head of the Gulf, the West Branch Pleasant River and Bear Brook come together and separately drop into a large pool, then the river drops twice in quick succession as it makes a sharp bend to the east. This is Stair Falls. There are several side trails off the Rim Trail that allow you to climb around on the rock along the river. Below Stair Falls the Gulf begins to get deeper and deeper. The steep, at times, sheer sides of the canyon are overhung with spruce and cedar trees, the river churning over rocks on its way to Billings Falls.

There is a short side trail out to the top of Billings Falls. You can stand on the uneven rock and look straight down on the river as it plunges into a large pool. Farther along the Rim Trail is an overlook from across that pool. After following along the Gulf for another mile, the canyon varying from 50 to 140 feet deep with the river rapid after rapid, you come to Buttermilk Falls. As at Billings Falls, there is an overlook above the falls and another looking back at it.

Below Buttermilk Falls, the walls of the Gulf narrow and are more vertical. Along this section are the two narrow pinches known as the Jaws. Past the Jaws a side trail leads down to the river at Cole's Corner, where you can look back upstream through the narrowest part of the canyon. There is an area of quiet water here that is often used as a swimming hole in summer.

After Cole's Corner, the Rim Trail climbs up and away from the Gulf. The forest changes from evergreens to hardwoods. The canyon is at its deepest, but the sides are somewhat less vertical. A side trail leads to an overlook above Hammond Street Pitch, named for the street in Bangor.

Screw Auger Falls

The Rim Trail leaves the Pleasant River and follows Gulf Hagas Stream up past several waterfalls. There are side trails to the lower falls and to Screw Auger Falls. In the 0.3 mile the trail follows Gulf Hagas Stream, the stream drops 150 feet. Above Screw Auger Falls, the Rim Trail ends. To the right, across the stream, is the Appalachian Trail that leads to the Gulf Hagas trailhead. To the left, 4 miles west on the Pleasant River Road Trail, is the Head of the Gulf trailhead where you started.

Looking down the Pleasant River from Stair Falls

Miles and Directions

0.0 Begin at the Head of the Gulf Trailhead across the road from the parking area.

0.5 Follow the Head of the Gulf Trail to a gravel road. Turn right and cross the West Branch Pleasant River.

0.6 At a cairn and a sign, the trail turns right and leaves the road.

1.0 The trail skirts around the west and south shore of Lloyd Pond; there is a 100-foot-long side trail to the pond.

1.9 The Head of the Gulf Trail ends at the junction with the Pleasant River Road Trail and the Gulf Hagas Rim Trail. Turn right onto the Gulf Hagas Rim Trail.

2.0 Reach the Head of the Gulf. There is a short side trail out onto the rocks at the top of Stair Falls. All signs for side trails on the Gulf Hagas Rim Trail face away from you as you hike. Most side trails have an upstream and downstream connection to the Rim Trail, with the sign near the downstream side trail. On this hike, you will mostly use the upstream, unmarked side trails.

2.1 A side trail leads out onto the rocks below Stair Falls.

2.2 A short side trail leads to a cliff top directly above Billings Falls.

2.3 A 150-foot side trail leads to an overlook with a view upstream to Billings Falls.

3.3 After Billings Falls numerous unmarked side trails lead to overlooks and cliff tops, all worth exploring. Arrive at a cliff-top overlook of Buttermilk Falls.

3.4 Arrive at a junction with a cutoff trail that leads in 0.6 mile to the Pleasant River Road Trail. You can shorten the hike to 6.7 miles by taking this cutoff and then turning left onto the Pleasant River Road Trail. To continue the hike, go straight on the Rim Trail.

3.7 After the cutoff trail, the Rim Trail passes several short side trails to overlooks. This section of the Gulf is particularly deep and narrow. The last of these is just upstream from the Jaws.

4.0 A 0.1-mile side trail leads down to the river, where there is a view upstream of the Jaws. At the Jaws the opposite walls of the canyon are only 18 feet apart.

4.8 Arrive at a junction with a second cutoff trail to the Pleasant River Road Trail. You can take the cutoff and make the hike 8.4 miles. To continue the hike, stay on the Rim Trail.

5.0 A 0.1-mile side trail leads to an overlook of Hammond Street Pitch. This is the deepest section of the Gulf. The trail appears to continue up and away from the cliff, but it peters out above a rocky area.

5.7 Past Hammond Street Pitch, the Rim Trail turns away from the rim of the Gulf and passes through a hardwood forest to a side trail that leads 0.1 mile to the lower falls on Gulf Hagas Brook.

5.9 A short side trail leads to an overlook of Screw Auger Falls. You can climb down from the overlook to the pool between the two falls.

6.0 The trail passes along the rocks at the top of Screw Auger Falls.

6.1 The Gulf Hagas Rim Trail ends at the junction of the Pleasant River Road Trail and the trail across Gulf Hagas Stream that leads to the Appalachian Trail and the main Gulf Hagas trailhead. Turn left onto the Pleasant River Road Trail.

6.7 Pass the second cutoff trail.

7.5 Cross the first cutoff trail.

8.3 Arrive back at the Head of the Gulf Trail. Go straight and retrace your steps to the trailhead.

10.2 Arrive back at the trailhead.

44 Tumbledown Dick Falls

The hike to Tumbledown Dick Falls passes two remote ponds, follows Tumbledown Dick Stream as it, well, tumbles down into the Penobscot River valley, and ends at one of the most scenic waterfalls in Maine. The trail passes right next to the rock-choked head of the falls, where it plunges more than 60 feet into a pool. A side trail leads down a steep slope to the base of the falls.

Start: Turtle Ridge East parking area
Elevation gain: 1,161 feet
Distance: 7.9 miles out and back
Hiking time: 3 to 5 hours
Difficulty: Strenuous due to distance
Season: May to October
Trail surface: Woodland path
Land status: Nahmakanta Public Reserved Land
Nearest town: Greenville
Other users: Hunters in season

Water availability: Leavitt and Tumbledown Dick Ponds, Tumbledown Dick Stream
Canine compatibility: Dogs must be under control at all times.
Fees and permits: Access fee paid at gate near ME 11
Other maps: DeLorme: Maine Atlas & Gazetteer, map 42; USGS Nahmakanta Stream
Trail contact: Nahmakanta Public Reserved Land, (207) 941-4412, www.maine.gov/nahmakanta

Finding the trailhead: From the bridge over the Pleasant River in Brownville on ME 11, drive north 15.7 miles. Turn left onto Jo-Mary Road at the Jo-Mary Campground sign. The gate where you pay the fee is 0.1 mile from ME 11. From the gate, drive 5.9 miles to a fork in the road. Bear right onto Wadleigh Pond Road. At 11.4 miles from the gate, you will cross a stream and the Appalachian Trail. At 14.1 miles from the gate, you will pass another gate that is remotely controlled from the gate where you paid your fee. At 15.8 miles from the first gate, and 2.7 miles past the second gate, you reach the trailhead parking on the left. The trailhead is 275 feet farther up the road on the opposite side from the parking area. GPS: N45 41.100' / W69 06.189'

The Hike

Tumbledown Dick was a nickname for Richard Cromwell, who ruled Great Britain for nine months in 1658–59. He was given the nickname because he fell from power so quickly after becoming Lord Protector upon his father's death. What Cromwell's failed monarchy has to do with a waterfall in northern Maine is a mystery.

The Tumbledown Dick Trail descends through a mostly hardwood forest to Leavitt Pond. A side trail leads through a campsite to the shore of the pond. You can often find ducks or loons bobbing in the water here. Many days, the only people you'll see on this hike are fishermen out in Leavitt Pond.

From Leavitt Pond the trail wanders through a broken landscape of bedrock ridges and old overgrown cuts. You walk in and out of dry, scratchy pine stands and aromatic hardwood lowlands, through blueberries and knee-high ferns and squishy bogs.

Tumbledown Dick Falls

The trail drops off a final granite ledge and follows a cliff down through scattered boulders to Tumbledown Dick Pond. A side trail leads out to the pond near the rock- and deadfall-choked north end, where Tumbledown Dick Stream begins its tumultuous run to Nahmakanta Stream.

The trail follows the stream, which is usually out of sight through the thick underbrush but always within earshot. Eventually, the trail doglegs right and climbs a gentle sidehill. The stream drops away. From the west, Dead Brook flows into Tumbledown Dick Steam, almost doubling its flow.

Tumbledown Dick Stream above the falls

The trail descends off the sidehill to the stream and ends at a logging road. Turn left and cross the stream on the road—a beautiful deadwater is visible around a rocky bend downstream. Across the bridge, the trail continues downstream along the deadwater.

The trail crosses a series of exposed bedrock slabs, several of which jut out into the stream. The trail then passes through a boulder choke at the head of the falls. Standing on the boulders, you can see the stream—choked down to only a few feet across—leap out over the rocks and drop almost 70 feet. A dark pool nestled against high black cliffs catches the water.

The trail turns away from the stream and descends to a junction. Straight ahead leads to the Appalachian Trail. The side trail to the right descends a wide chimney to the base of the waterfall. You can take time to explore the small meadow, trying to find the best view of Tumbledown Dick Falls and the cliffs.

One day, when I was doing just that, I almost stepped on a beaver chewing on a downed birch tree at the edge of the pool. We both froze, looking into each other's eyes. Then the beaver turned and slipped into the water. A few seconds later it surfaced and slapped its tail, letting me know what it thought of my intrusion into its peaceful world.

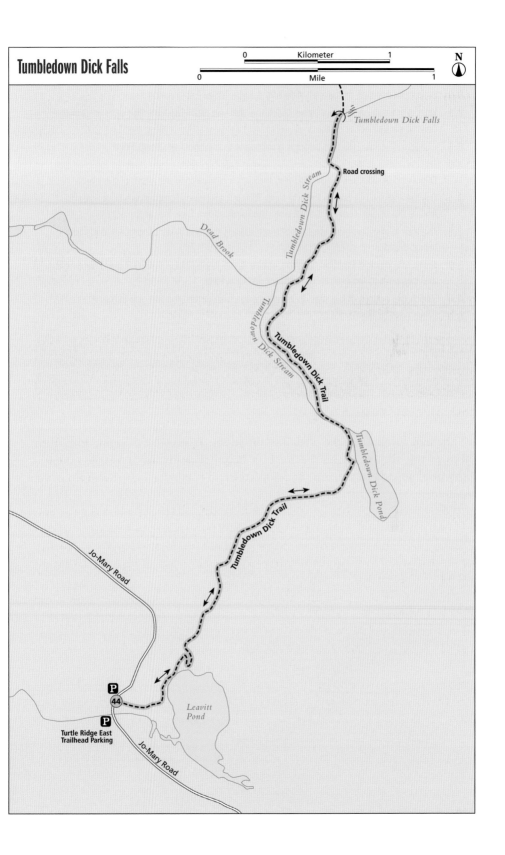

Tumbledown Dick Falls

Tumbledown Dick Falls

Road crossing

Tumbledown Dick Stream

Dead Brook

Tumbledown Dick Stream

Tumbledown Dick Trail

Tumbledown Dick Pond

Tumbledown Dick Trail

Jo-Mary Road

P
44
P

Turtle Ridge East
Trailhead Parking

Leavitt
Pond

Jo-Mary Road

Miles and Directions

0.0 Start from the sign at the east side of the Turtle Ridge East parking area.

0.1 Walk northeast on Jo-Mary Road (back the way you drove in). Turn right onto the Tumbledown Dick Trail at the sign.

0.6 A side trail leads 100 feet through a campsite to the shore of Leavitt Pond.

2.0 The trail crosses several rocky ridges and old cuts before dropping down to Tumbledown Dick Pond. A side trail leads 200 feet through a campsite to the shore of the pond.

3.6 The trail comes out onto a logging road. Turn left and cross Tumbledown Dick Stream. Across the bridge, turn right back onto the Tumbledown Dick Trail at the sign.

3.8 The trail follows Tumbledown Dick Stream toward the falls. A very short trail leads to the top of the falls.

3.9 Arrive at a marked junction. Straight ahead is the Appalachian Trail (0.3 mile). Turn right and descend to the bottom of Tumbledown Dick Falls.

4.0 Reach the bottom of the falls. To complete the hike, return the way you came.

8.0 Arrive back at the trailhead.

45 Gauntlet Falls

The East Branch Pleasant River drops 15 feet into a narrow slot between two huge slabs of slate. Below the falls is a large, deep pool. The streambed and shore are littered with huge blocks of black stone for the next 1,000 yards. In the middle of this jumble of rock is a 10-foot slide waterfall with a deep pool at its base. This may be the best swimming hole in Maine.

Start: Gauntlet Falls Trailhead
Elevation gain: 70 feet
Distance: 0.2 mile out and back (0.4 mile with bushwhack to lower falls)
Hiking time: About 1 hour
Difficulty: Easy (moderate with bushwhack)
Season: Late May to October
Trail surface: Woodland path, slate bedrock, rocky shore
Land status: Katahdin Iron Works/Jo-Mary Multiple Use Forest

Nearest town: Brownville
Other users: Anglers and hunters in season
Water availability: None
Canine compatibility: Dogs must be under control at all times.
Fees and permits: Entrance fee paid at gate on Jo-Mary Road
Other maps: DeLorme: Maine Atlas & Gazetteer, map 42; USGS Jo-Mary Mountain
Trail contact: North Maine Woods, Inc., (207) 435-6213, www.northmainewoods.org

Finding the trailhead: From the bridge over the Pleasant River in Brownville on ME 11, drive north 15.7 miles. Turn left onto Jo-Mary Road at the Jo-Mary Campground sign. The gate where you pay the fee is 0.1 mile from ME 11. From the gate, drive 5.9 miles to a fork in the road. Go straight at the fork onto Johnson Pond Road. Drive 2.7 miles. Turn left onto B Pond Road at the large snowplow. Drive 1.3 miles, passing Jo-Mary Pond. Turn right onto East Branch Pleasant River Road. Drive 1.5 miles. Bear right at the fork (East Branch campsite 2 is on the right). Drive 0.1 mile to the day-use parking area at the end of the road. The trailhead is on the west side of the parking area. GPS: N45 32.463' / W69 02.198'

The Hike

The West Branch Pleasant River has Gulf Hagas. The East Branch has Gauntlet Falls. Both features are defined by black slate. At Gauntlet Falls the river drops 15 feet into a crack between two huge blocks of slate. On the far shore, the bedrock is a jumble of angles and weathered slabs that nearly block the river. On the near side, the slate rises smooth and straight 20 feet above the river. You can stand atop this formation and look straight down at Gauntlet Falls. The bedrock angles down next to the river at a manageable 30 degrees. Below the falls is a deep, dark pool. The water is full of tannin picked up from spruce roots. The pool is at least 20 feet deep in the middle.

The large bedrock slab next to the falls is covered with graffiti. Most is recent and done with spray paint, but there are many older name and dates. The earliest is from 1881. Please don't add to it.

Gauntlet Falls

Below the pool, the river goes around a gravel island. The best views are from the island. You can easily cross to it without getting your feet wet by late June. This is a great swimming spot, with deep, cool water and lots of flat, smooth slate to relax on.

You can return to the trailhead by walking up the angled slate either the way you came down or farther east. Better yet, bushwhack down the shore. You can walk in the shallows along the shore or scramble over and around the boulders. About a tenth of a mile downstream, you'll come to a large bedrock eruption that crosses the river. A slot in it allows the river to slide down the sculpted rock, dropping 10 feet into a very deep pool. This is the best swimming spot at Gauntlet Falls.

If you're feeling really adventurous, you can continue down the stream another 0.2 mile. Mud Gauntlet Brook flows into the river from the west. Just upstream on that brook is the 15-foot-high Mud Gauntlet Falls. There's no trail to this waterfall.

Gauntlet Falls

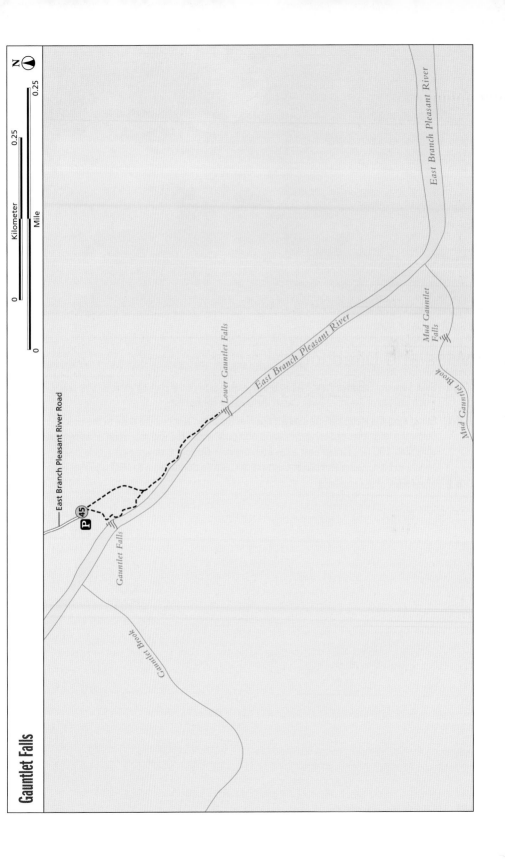

N

0   Kilometer   0.25

0   Mile   0.25

East Branch Pleasant River Road

Gauntlet Brook

Gauntlet Falls

P 45

Lower Gauntlet Falls

East Branch Pleasant River

Mud Gauntlet Brook

Mud Gauntlet Falls

East Branch Pleasant River

Lower Gauntlet Falls

Miles and Directions

0.0 Start from the Gauntlet Falls Trailhead at the west side of the parking area. In 100 feet you reach the top of Gauntlet Falls. Climb the bedrock to your left.

0.1 Stand atop the slate, looking straight down at the falls. Descend the slate to the river below the falls. After exploring the island and pool, return the way you came or ascend the slate slab 100 feet farther east away from the river. ***Option:*** Bushwhack 0.1 mile downstream to Lower Gauntlet Falls or bushwhack 0.3 mile downstream to Mud Gauntlet Falls.

0.2 Arrive back at the trailhead.

46 Upper and Lower Pollywog Falls

The north woods you hike through to get to the waterfalls is gorgeous. You hike around Crescent Pond and over a small spruce-covered hill. Upper Pollywog Falls is within sight of Pollywog Pond. It's a 20-foot drop down a seam in the granite bedrock. Lower Pollywog Falls drops 20 feet down a granite dam across the river into a large pool. A slab of granite overhangs the falls.

Start: Northbound Appalachian Trail from crossing on Wadleigh Pond Road
Elevation gain: 831 feet
Distance: 4.0 miles out and back
Hiking time: 2 to 3 hours
Difficulty: Moderate
Season: Late May to October
Trail surface: Woodland path
Land status: Appalachian Trail corridor and Nahmakanta Public Reserved Land
Nearest town: Brownville
Other users: Hunters in season

Water availability: Crescent Pond
Canine compatibility: Dogs must be under control at all times.
Fees and permits: Entrance fee paid at gate on Jo-Mary Road
Other maps: *DeLorme: Maine Atlas & Gazetteer*, map 50; USGS Rainbow Lake West
Trail contact: Nahmakanta Public Reserved Land, (207) 941-4412, www.maine.gov/nahmakanta; KI Jo-Mary Multiple-Use Forest, (207) 435-6213, www.northmainewoods.org

Finding the trailhead: From the bridge over the Pleasant River in Brownville on ME 11, drive north 15.7 miles. Turn left onto Jo-Mary Road at the Jo-Mary Campground sign. The gate where you pay the fee is 0.1 mile from ME 11. From the gate, drive 5.9 miles to a fork in the road. Bear right onto Wadleigh Pond Road. At 11.4 miles from the gate, you will cross a stream and the Appalachian Trail (AT). At 14.1 miles from the gate, you will pass another gate that is remotely controlled from the gate where you paid your fee. At 15.8 miles from the first gate, you pass the Turtle Ridge Trail. At 19.7 miles from the first gate, you come to a T-intersection. Turn right, staying on Wadleigh Pond Road. At 20.6 miles from the first gate, the road bends left and a smaller road goes straight; bear left, staying on Wadleigh Pond Road. At 20.6 miles from the first gate, you will pass a road on the right that leads to the south end of Nahmakanta Lake and beyond into the Debsconeag Wilderness. At 24.9 miles from the first gate, there will be a small, unmarked parking area on the left. Turn in here and park. The AT is 20 feet farther down the road. The hike follows the northbound AT on the west side of the road next to the parking area. GPS: N45 45.809' / W69 10.540'

The Hike

The Appalachian Trail climbs a small hill through a spruce forest. Nothing grows beneath the trees but moss and rocks. You descend gently to the shore of Crescent Pond. The trail loops around the pond, crossing multiple granite ledges with access to the picturesque pond. After you've walked about three-fourths of the way around, the trail heads west.

Upper Pollywog Falls

Turn left onto the blue-blazed Pollywog Trail. There's no sign at the intersection, but you can't miss the blazes. Follow this trail south, crossing Crescent Pond's narrow outlet stream. Across the stream go around a huge boulder, then slab around the hill you climbed at the beginning of the hike.

You'll reach an unmarked junction. Turn right, staying on the Pollywog Trail, and descend an old twitch trail. You'll be able to hear Lower Pollywog Falls. The trail levels out and crosses a ledge.

Turn right onto the Upper Falls Trail at the sign. This trail descends to the bouldery expanse at the waterfall. It's easiest to reach the falls by staying high and left on the rocks. You'll come out onto an open expanse of bedrock. Above you to the left, Pollywog Brook flows out of the pond. It drops through a rocky bed then leaps down a wide crack in the bedrock, falling 20 feet into a pool. This is one of the more picturesque waterfalls in Maine.

To visit the Lower Falls, which is about 0.2 mile downstream out of sight, return to the Pollywog Trail. Turn left and then almost immediately turn left again onto the Lower Falls Trail. This trail wanders downstream. The last 200 feet to the pool at the base of Lower Pollywog Falls is very steep.

Lower Pollywog Falls drops 20 feet over exposed bedrock that crosses the stream. The falls are far across the large pool against the cliff on the far side of the gorge. A huge slab of granite juts out of the hillside, hanging over the waterfall. If you don't mind swimming in water almost black from tannin, this is a good pool. Once you've enjoyed the waterfall, retrace your steps to the parking area.

Below Lower Pollywog Falls, the brook drops through a deep gorge. It's almost continuous whitewater to Rainbow Stream. The Appalachian Trail follows the brook, high on the ridge with some nice views of the gorge.

The Pollywog Trail continues south beyond the Upper Falls Trail. It follows the southeast shore of Pollywog Pond all the way to the short stream between this pond and Wadleigh Pond. The stream drops almost 20 feet in 100 yards. About half the drop is a waterfall into Pollywog Pond. Getting there would add about 4 miles to your hike.

Upper and Lower Pollywog Falls

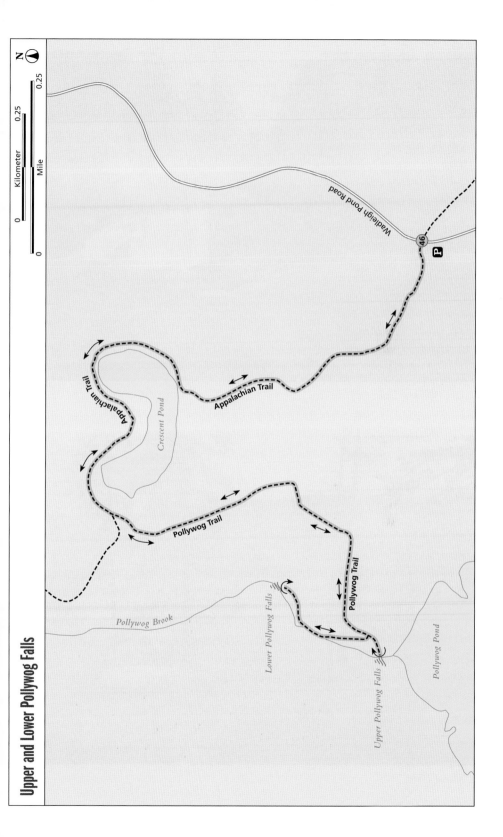

Lower Pollywog Falls

Crescent Pond

Miles and Directions

0.0 Begin at the northbound Appalachian Trail on the west side of Wadleigh Pond Road.

0.5 Cross over a small hill to Crescent Pond.

1.1 Loop around Crescent Pond. Turn left onto the unsigned, blue-blazed Pollywog Trail.

1.5 Bear right (downhill) at an unmarked intersection.

1.7 Turn right onto the Upper Falls Trail at the sign.

1.8 Reach Upper Pollywog Falls. To continue the hike, return to the Pollywog Trail.

1.9 Turn left back onto the Pollywog Trail and almost immediately turn left again onto the Lower Falls Trail at the sign.

2.1 Reach the base of Lower Pollywog Falls. To complete the hike, return to the Pollywog Trail.

2.3 Turn left back onto the Pollywog Trail. Retrace your steps to the trailhead.

4.0 Arrive back at the trailhead.

47 Debsconeag Falls

Between Fifth and Fourth Debsconeag Lakes, a stream drops through a narrow gorge. The largest waterfall is a slide where the stream follows a bedrock joint down the moss-covered stone, dropping 30 feet into a pool. This is a very remote and little-visited waterfall.

Start: Debsconeag Backcountry Parking Area
Elevation gain: 465 feet
Distance: 2.4 miles out and back
Hiking time: About 2 hours
Difficulty: Easy
Season: Late May to October
Trail surface: Woods road and woodland path
Land status: Nahmakanta Public Reserved Land
Nearest town: Millinocket and Brownville
Other users: Hunters in season

Water availability: Fourth Debsconeag Lake
Canine compatibility: Dogs must be under control at all times.
Fees and permits: Entrance fee paid at gate on Jo-Mary Road
Other maps: *DeLorme: Maine Atlas & Gazetteer*, maps 42 and 50; USGS Nahmakanta Stream and Rainbow Lake East
Trail contact: Nahmakanta Public Reserved Land, (207) 941-4412, www.maine.gov/nahmakanta

Finding the trailhead: From the bridge over the Pleasant River in Brownville, drive north on ME 11 15.6 miles. Turn left onto Jo-Mary Road; there is a large sign for Jo-Mary Campground at the intersection. Drive 0.1 mile to the gate; stop and pay the fee. Drive 6 miles to a fork in the road. Turn right, staying on Jo-Mary Road. Drive 8.2 miles to the Hedgehog gate. This gate is no longer staffed; it will be opened remotely by the person at the Jo-Mary gate. Drive 1.7 miles, where you will pass the trailhead parking for Tumbledown Dick Falls. Continue driving 4 miles to an intersection. Turn right, staying on Jo-Mary Road. Drive 0.9 mile to Nahmakanta Stream Road. Turn right and drive 1 mile. The road bears right at a fork. Drive another 2 miles, passing the side road to the boat launch at the foot of Nahmakanta Lake. At 0.1 mile beyond the side road, Nahmakanta Stream Road crosses the Appalachian Trail and then Nahmakanta Stream. Across the stream the road is much rougher, but still passable by most cars. From the bridge, drive 1 mile to the parking area on the left. The road continues down Fourth Debsconeag Lake; do not drive down the hill to the lake. The hike starts down the hill on the road. GPS: N45 44.723' / W69 05.478'

The Hike

The eight Debsconeag Lakes drain into the Penobscot River at Omaha Beach just below Debsconeag Falls. This hike isn't to that drop—there's no trail to it. To see it, you'll have to take a whitewater rafting trip on the West Branch. The hike is to the waterfall on the stream between Fifth and Fourth Debsconeag Lakes. This stream is an important transition in the chain of lakes. Those above it are small and shallow; those below are deep and much larger. The stream drops nearly 300 feet between the lakes.

Debsconeag Falls

The hike follows the road from the parking area down to Fourth Debsconeag Lake. This lake is the only one in the chain with a camp on it. Before reaching Chewonki's Debsconeag Lakes Wilderness Camps, you'll turn left onto the Debsconeag Backcountry Trail. The trail follows the stream through an open forest. You don't start climbing until you get to the waterfall.

Debsconeag Falls drops 30 feet down a face of smooth, mossy rock. The water hugs a joint in the rock where the cliff face meets the rock that blocks the stream's course. In spring the water erupts from the top and churns down the chute into a deep pool. By summer the stream's anger has subsided and the waterfall settles into a picturesque tumble.

Above the falls, the stream crashes through a boulder-strewn bed. It's so loud that one day I nearly walked into a young bull moose heading down the trail. The hike ends within view of Fifth Debsconeag Lake, where the trail forks.

There are two other waterfalls nearby you can add to this hike. They are both deeper into the Debsconeag Backcountry. At the fork in the trail, bear right. The trail skirts around the bottom of Fifth Debsconeag Lake, then climbs to Stink Pond. About a mile from the fork, you'll cross a small stream where it squeezes between two boulders. The waterfall here is most dramatic in the spring. Upstream the water slides down a steep dome of granite. Early in the season, this is a beautiful slide waterfall that

Debsconeag Falls

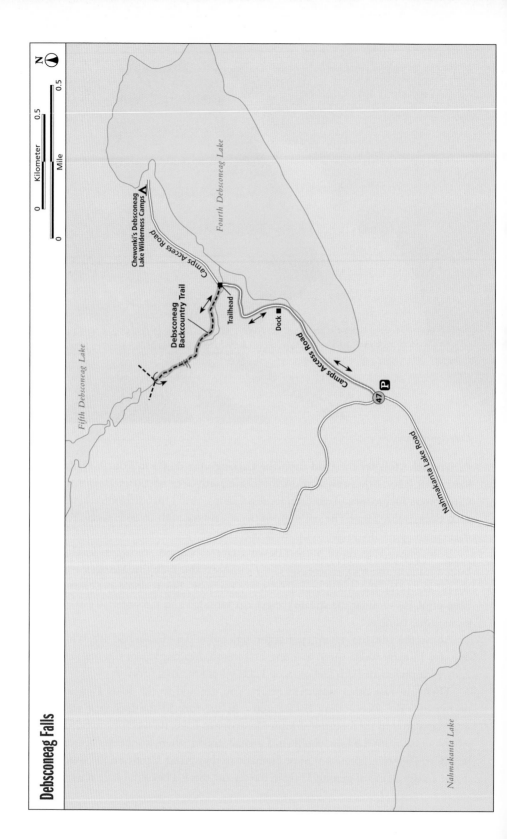

N

0   0.5   Kilometer   0.5
0   Mile

Fifth Debsconeag Lake

Chewonki's Debsconeag Lake Wilderness Camps

Debsconeag Backcountry Trail

Trailhead

Camps Access Road

Fourth Debsconeag Lake

Dock

Camps Access Road

P
47

Nahmakanta Lake Road

Nahmakanta Lake

Looking down Debsconeag Falls

drops more than 50 feet. The trail actually climbs the rock with the water much of the way. The swampy shore of Stink Pond is a good place to find carnivorous plants. The whole hike is moose country.

Miles and Directions

0.0 Start at the Debsconeag Backcountry Parking Area.

0.4 Hike downhill on the road to the dock on Fourth Debsconeag Lake.

0.7 Continue on the road around the north shore of the lake to the Debsconeag Backcountry Trailhead. Turn left onto the trail.

1.0 Reach the base of Debsconeag Falls.

1.2 Reach the top of the falls. To complete your hike, retrace your steps to the trailhead.

2.4 Arrive back at the trailhead.

48 Moxie Falls

Moxie Falls is one of the largest waterfalls in New England. None so powerful is as high in Maine. The easy walk to the viewing platforms around the falls passes through a hardwood forest that abounds in spring wildflowers. The black slate cliffs around Moxie Falls and its 80-foot main drop make it the most dramatic waterfall in Maine.

Start: Moxie Falls Trailhead
Elevation gain: 233 feet
Distance: 1.9 miles out and back
Hiking time: About 1 hour
Difficulty: Easy
Season: May and June for maximum water flow and wildflowers; July to October for average water flow
Trail surface: Graded woodland path and boardwalk

Land status: Private timberland and state preserve
Nearest town: The Forks
Other users: Hunters in season
Water availability: None
Canine compatibility: Dogs must be under control at all times.
Fees and permits: None
Other maps: *DeLorme: Maine Atlas & Gazetteer*, map 40; USGS The Forks
Trail contact: None

Finding the trailhead: From US 201 in The Forks, take Lake Moxie Road east. Drive 1.8 miles. The trailhead parking is on the left at a brown sign for Moxie Falls. The trailhead is on the north side of the parking area. GPS: N45 21.242' / W69 56.426'

The Hike

The Forks is in the heart of Maine's whitewater country. The Kennebec River rages through its gorge between Indian Pond and the town. In summer rafts and kayaks crowd the river on their wet, wild rides. The Dead River, which empties into the Kennebec River at The Forks, is just as popular. It drops from Flagstaff Lake through miles of churning whitewater to the Kennebec. Just outside of town, on Moxie Stream, is one of New England's largest waterfalls.

The hike to Moxie Falls passes through a hardwood forest that abounds with spring wildflowers. Don't rush to the waterfall; take your time to enjoy the woods along the way. The best time to enjoy both the woods and the waterfall is late May, when Moxie Stream is still high and the trees haven't fully leafed out yet. This season has the added advantage that you are likely to have the trail to yourself. Because Moxie Stream flows out of Moxie Pond, supplying it with a steady water flow, the falls remain strong all through the summer. You can hear the falls as soon as you get out of your car at the trailhead.

The trail first comes to the upper falls, a stair-step cascade that drops 30 feet across a series of ledges that span the stream. The maples hang dense out over the water, the

Moxie Falls

stream a narrow, churning corridor through the woods. Around a bend of calm water is the main falls. There is a railed deck right at the top of the falls. The stream leaps out and drops to a deep pool surrounded by black cliffs. The bedrock here is slate that has been upended, creating towering cliffs with smooth faces. Below the pool is another, smaller waterfall, easy to miss in the mist that hangs in the air.

From above the falls to the Kennebec River, Moxie Stream drops 300 feet in less than a mile. The main drop, right in the middle of this descent, is 80 feet. Not the highest waterfall in Maine, but none are as high with the water flow that Moxie Stream maintains. The falls are all the more dramatic because of the way the black

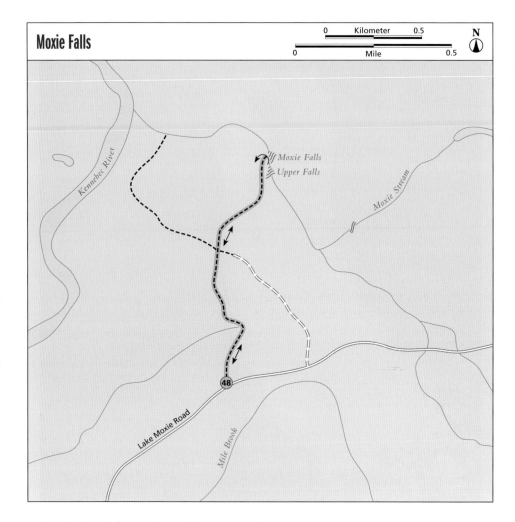

slate bedrock frames them. The slate bedding is stood on end, making sheer walls below the falls on both banks. The mist from the falls keeps the rock wet and inky black. The lush vegetation atop the cliffs leans out over the void, soaking up the sun and spray.

The trail continues around to two viewing platforms atop the cliffs with views across the pool of Moxie Falls. Many people try to make their way down to the stream from here, but there is no trail and no safe way down to Moxie Stream. The hillside is too steep and covered with loose rocks. The trail continues on, along the nearly vertical hillside as far as the confluence of Moxie Stream with the Kennebec River. Far below, Moxie Stream churns over jumbled rocks. Not part of the hike, the trail beyond the falls is worth exploring for at least a short distance.

Moxie Stream above the falls is quite steep with many ledges.

Miles and Directions

0.0   Begin from the trailhead on the north side of the parking area.

0.5   The trail crosses an ATV trail; on the other side of the trail is a state sign for Moxie Falls.

0.8   The trail reaches a wooden deck with views upstream on Moxie Stream of the upper falls.

0.9   The trail reaches a deck at the top of Moxie Falls with views of the falls and the slate gorge downstream.

0.95 The official trail ends at two decks atop cliffs with views of Moxie Falls. A rough trail continues along the nearly vertical hillside all the way to the confluence of Moxie Stream and the Kennebec River. There is no safe way to reach the stream below the falls. To complete the hike, return the way you came.

1.9   Arrive back at the trailhead.

49 Houston Brook Falls

An easy descent through towering pines brings you to the base of Houston Brook Falls. The waterfall is a 40-foot horsetail down a rough rock face. The trail climbs to the top of the main falls, where you can see several smaller waterfalls upstream. There's a nice pool at the base of Houston Brook Falls.

Start: Houston Brook Falls Trailhead
Elevation gain: 119 feet
Distance: 0.6 mile out and back
Hiking time: About 1 hour
Difficulty: Easy, with steep scramble to top of waterfall
Season: May to October
Trail surface: Woodland path
Land status: Private timberland

Nearest town: Bingham
Other users: None
Water availability: None
Canine compatibility: Dogs must be under control at all times.
Fees and permits: None
Other maps: *DeLorme: Maine Atlas & Gazetteer*, map 30; USGS Bingham
Trail contact: None

Finding the trailhead: From the junction of US 201 and ME 16 in Bingham, follow ME 16 west. Drive 0.2 mile, crossing the Kennebec River and coming to a T-intersection. Turn right onto Ridge Road. Drive 3.4 miles. Park on the right in front of the Pleasant Ridge transfer station. The trailhead is at the west end of the parking area. GPS: N45 04.158' / W69 56.198'

The Hike

The upper Kennebec River valley is an area of complex geology. There's lots of evidence of the way glaciers rearranged the landscape as well as evidence of violent upheavals hundreds of millions of years ago. Between Skowhegan and Jackman there are a dozen types of bedrock varying in age from 450 to 250 million years old.

Houston Brook flows from an area of low, wooded mountains to Wyman Lake just above the dam. It cuts through slate where the bedding has been turned nearly vertical. This gives Houston Brook Falls a ragged appearance. The stream bounces down the rock face off numerous fins of black bedrock.

To get there, park in front of the local transfer station and look for the trailhead sign. The trail descends through towering pines. The hillside is all straight trunks, roots, and rusty needles. The trail comes out near the base of the falls.

There's a pool for swimming, but mostly it's a jumble of bedrock and boulders. To your right, you can see where Houston Brook empties into Wyman Lake. To your left, Houston Brook Falls crashes 40 feet down the vertical slate bedding in a couple of horsetails. In spring the rock face is one churning mass of whitewater. This is one of Maine's most photogenic waterfalls.

Houston Brook Falls

Looking down Houston Brook Falls

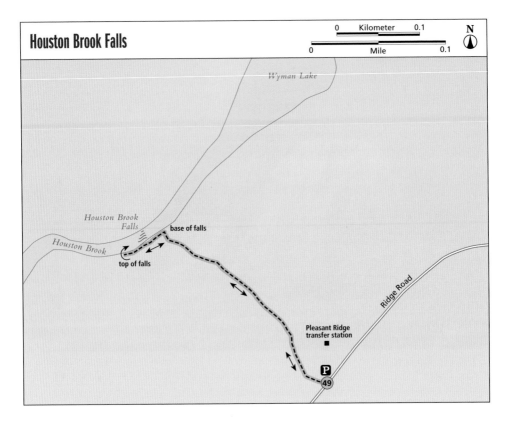

A rough trail climbs the steep hill next to the waterfall. Atop the falls, you get a nice view of the falls itself and several smaller waterfalls just upstream.

Miles and Directions

0.0 Start from the Houston Brook Falls Trailhead.

0.2 Descend gently through a pine forest to the base of Houston Brook Falls.

0.3 Climb steeply to the top of the waterfall. To complete the hike, retrace your steps to the trailhead.

0.6 Arrive back at the trailhead.

50 Grand Falls Dead River

Grand Falls is one of the largest remaining natural waterfalls in New England. The Dead River plunges 40 feet, creating a horseshoe falls more than 100 feet wide. The trail leads to the top of a nearby rock formation with a fine view.

Start: Maine Huts and Trails trailhead at north-west end of parking area
Elevation gain: 67 feet
Distance: 1.0 mile out and back
Hiking time: About 1 hour
Difficulty: Easy, with steep stone stairs near waterfall
Season: May to October
Trail surface: Woodland path and multiuse trail
Land status: Maine Huts and Trails

Nearest town: The Forks
Other users: Whitewater rafters and hunters in season
Water availability: None
Canine compatibility: Dogs must be under control at all times.
Fees and permits: None
Other maps: DeLorme: Maine Atlas & Gazetteer, maps 40 and 29; USGS Basin Pond
Trail contact: None

Finding the trailhead: From the bridge over the Kennebec River in The Forks, follow US 201 north. Drive 2.9 miles. Turn left onto Lower Enchanted Road (there's a street sign). Drive 4.8 miles. Bear left, staying on Lower Enchanted Road. Drive 9.1 miles to the bus parking area. Bear right. Drive 0.3 mile downhill to the parking area at the end of the road along the Dead River. The trailhead is at the northwest end of the parking area along the road. GPS: N45 18.058' / W70 13.315'

The Hike

The hardest part about getting to Grand Falls is the 15-mile drive down a sometimes rough logging road. The remoteness of the trailhead keeps this waterfall wild and uncrowded. Maine Huts and Trails has a hut nearby and built a trail to the falls. You start where Spencer Stream flows into the Dead River. Whitewater rafters use this spot as a put-in for their Dead River trips. As a result, there's a large parking area and porta-potties.

Before you complain about the long, bumpy drive to the trailhead, remember that in late fall 1775 Benedict Arnold led 1,100 men up the mostly unexplored Kennebec River to attack Quebec. They portaged around Grand Falls Dead River using the ponds to the west still known as the Carry Ponds. The expedition bogged down in the swampy region upstream (what is now Flagstaff Lake), and less than half the men reached the St. Lawrence River. Their surprise attack failed.

The hike begins by crossing Spencer Stream on a snowmobile bridge. Across the stream, you follow a multiuse trail through the riverside forest. You can see Grand Falls across a large, wide bend in the river.

The steps up to the overlook

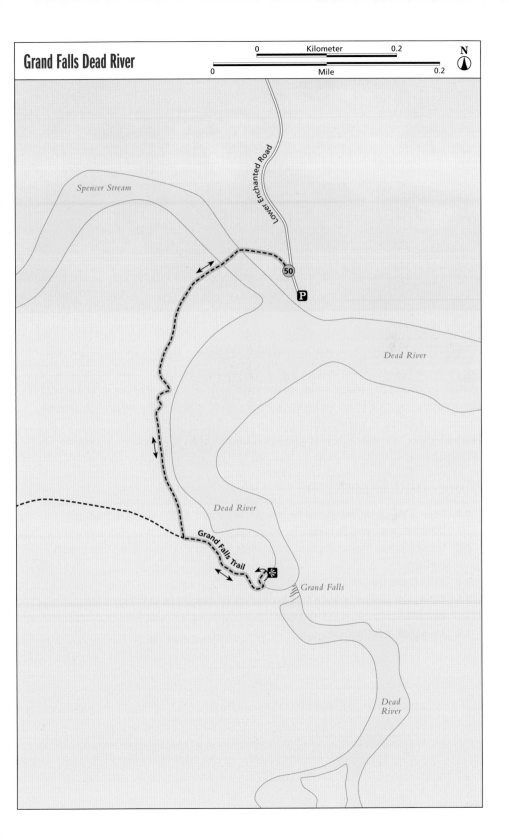

Grand Falls Dead River

Spencer Stream

Lower Enchanted Road

50

P

Dead River

Dead River

Grand Falls Trail

Grand Falls

Dead River

N

0   Kilometer   0.2

0   Mile   0.2

Grand Falls

The marked trail leaves the multiuse trail, crosses a marsh, and climbs a towering pine-covered rock formation. The overlook puts you above the waterfall near its base. In spring the entire width of the river roars over the 40-foot drop. Later in the summer, there's a bulge of bedrock on the near side that the water falls around. Because the Dead is a good-sized river regulated by a dam upstream (that creates Flagstaff Lake), the falls is scenic year-round. In fact, it's a common destination for snowmobilers.

Miles and Directions

0.0 Begin at the signed trailhead on the river side of the road. In 300 feet, cross Spencer Stream on a snowmobile bridge.

0.2 Follow the Dead River upstream on the multiuse trail. You get views of Grand Falls through the trees.

0.3 Turn left onto the Grand Falls Trail.

0.5 Climb to an overlook of Grand Falls. To complete the hike, retrace your steps to the trailhead.

1.0 Arrive back at the trailhead.

51 Cold Stream Falls

Cold Stream Falls has a lot to offer: It's very remote, has a good-sized pool for swimming at its base, and drops 20 feet through an angled eruption of bedrock. The trail along the stream to the falls is relatively flat, passing through a mostly hardwood forest. Upstream from the falls is a high, vertical cliff on the far bank.

Start: Cold Stream Trailhead at north end of parking area
Elevation gain: 312 feet
Distance: 2.4 miles out and back
Hiking time: About 2 hours
Difficulty: Moderate. The hike is easy, but the trail in the first half mile can be swampy and difficult to follow.
Season: Late May to October
Trail surface: Woodland path

Land status: Plum Creek timberland
Nearest town: Jackman and The Forks
Other users: Hunters in season and anglers
Water availability: None
Canine compatibility: Dogs must be under control at all times.
Fees and permits: None
Other maps: DeLorme: Maine Atlas & Gazetteer, map 40; USGS Johnson Mountain
Trail contact: None

Finding the trailhead: From the US 201 bridge over the Kennebec River in The Forks, follow US 201 north. Drive 7.7 miles. Turn right onto Capitol Road (at the street sign). Drive 1 mile. Cross Cold Stream and turn left onto Mountain Brook Road. Drive 0.8 mile. Bear left, staying on Mountain Brook Road. Drive 0.4 mile. The unmarked but obvious parking area is on the left. The trailhead is at the north end of the parking area. GPS: N45 27.109' / W70 02.477'

The Hike

Cold Stream flows out of a group of small ponds nestled into low, hardwood-covered hills east of Parlin Pond. The stream maintains good flow through the summer. The trail to the waterfall is used mostly by trout fishermen. The stream below the falls—with its cold water, shaded course, and stony bed—is great trout habitat.

Two trails leave the parking area. The obvious one descends north directly to the stream. This route is often wet and swampy, and the trail can be hard to follow. Your best bet is to stay right on slightly higher ground and watch for flagging on the trees. Eventually, the trail reaches Cold Stream. The rest of the way to the waterfall, the trail is wide and easy to follow.

The other trail from the parking area (less obvious and to the right of the main one) stays high and dry. Its disadvantage is that it takes much longer to reach the stream and is overgrown with brambles in the summer. The distance on each trail is the same.

The walk along Cold Stream is pleasant. The hardwoods shade the trail, and dappled light dances on the water rushing over rounded rocks. In spring the forest floor is carpeted with wildflowers. The stream valley is wide and shallow, but as you approach

Cold Stream Falls

Looking down Cold Stream Falls

Cold Stream Falls

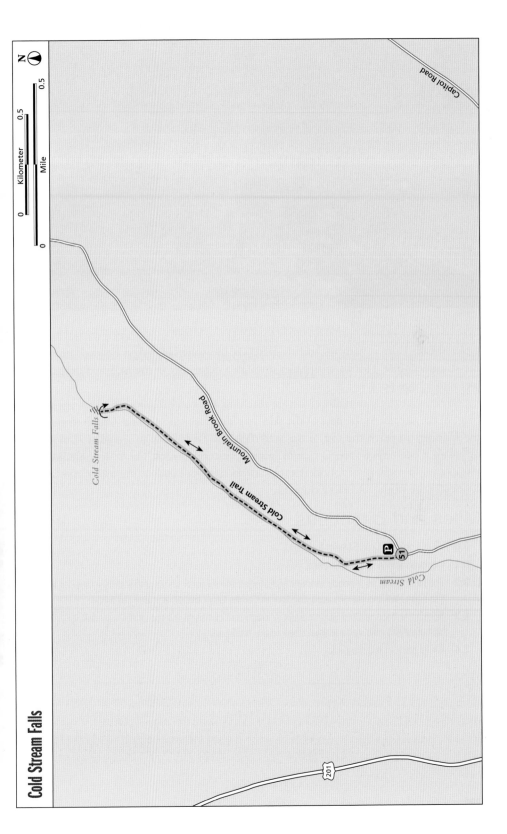

Cold Stream Falls

Cold Stream Falls

Mountain Brook Road

Cold Stream Trail

Cold Stream

201

51

P

N

Kilometer
0   0.5   0.5

Mile
0   0.5

Capitol Road

The trail along Cold Stream

Cold Stream Falls, it narrows and steepens. At the waterfall, naked bedrock crosses the stream's course. The water tumbles through a deformity in the rock and drops 20 feet into a large pool.

You can see the waterfall well before reaching it as you hike around a wide, gentle bend in the stream. At the base of the falls, boulders litter the ground. Climb through the boulders to reach the top of the waterfall. The far bank is an irregular cliff; just upstream it becomes a vertical face of smooth, featureless rock. The near bank, inexplicably, is a stone wall of rounded, mossy rocks. The trail ends at the top of the falls. Evidently, the trout stay below the falls.

Miles and Directions

0.0 Start from the Cold Stream Trailhead.

0.1 Descend gently to Cold Stream.

0.2 Follow flagging on a poorly marked trail around the swampy shore of the stream, staying to the right. Past the marshy area, the trail becomes very obvious and easy to follow.

1.2 Reach the base of Cold Stream Falls. A rough trail climbs to the top of the waterfall. To complete the hike, retrace your steps to the trailhead.

2.4 Arrive back at the trailhead.

52 Parlin Falls

Upper Parlin Falls is a pretty chute where Parlin Stream slides down a granite joint, dropping 20 feet in less than 100 yards. Below this waterfall the stream enters a deep gorge, where it drops nearly 200 feet in a few tenths of a mile. There are numerous waterfalls within the gorge but no way to get to them. A rough trail follows the gorge and leads to Lower Parlin Falls, where the stream exits the gorge in a giant 40-foot horsetail waterfall.

Start: Intersection of Parlin Falls Road and Smith Pond Road
Elevation gain: 410 feet
Distance: 1.4 miles out and back
Hiking time: About 2 hours
Difficulty: Strenuous. The trail to Lower Parlin Falls is poorly marked and maintained, requiring some bushwhacking.
Season: Late May to October
Trail surface: Woodland path

Land status: Plum Creek timberland
Nearest town: Jackman
Other users: Hunters in season
Water availability: None
Canine compatibility: Dogs must be under control at all times.
Fees and permits: None
Other maps: *DeLorme: Maine Atlas & Gazetteer*, map 40; USGS Long Pond
Trail contact: None

Finding the trailhead: From the US 201 bridge over the Kennebec River in The Forks, follow US 201 north. Drive 13.6 miles. Pass the rest area on the shore of Parlin Pond. Drive 2.6 miles. Turn right onto Parlin Mountain Road. Drive 0.4 mile. Turn left onto unmarked Smith Pond Road. Drive 1.3 miles. Pass a road on the right, then park on the left at an intersection with unmarked Parlin Falls Road that's on the left. Do not drive up Parlin Falls Road; the road is impassible except for very high clearance vehicles. Walk the 0.2 mile to the trailhead. Parking GPS: N45 32.757' / W70 04.631'

The Hike

From the parking area at the end of Parlin Falls Road, a short trail leads downhill—steeply in places—to Upper Parlin Falls. This waterfall represents a transition. Upstream, Parlin Stream flows out of Parlin Pond and winds through marshy, low country. At Upper Parlin Falls it begins its descent through a granite gorge.

The stream slides down a joint in the granite to a pool and disappears around a bend. To see where the stream goes, you need to climb the trail back toward the trailhead. Just before the trail reaches the parking area, turn left on an unmarked but obvious trail. This trail follows the stream high above the rim of the deep gorge. In places you have views through the trees of the stream far below. In a few tenths of a mile, the stream drops almost 200 feet. There are numerous waterfalls, pools, and slides; Big Parlin Falls is largest of these. The stream drops at least 50 feet in a dramatic slide that you can only get a distant look at.

Upper Parlin Falls

Lower Parlin Falls

Parlin Falls

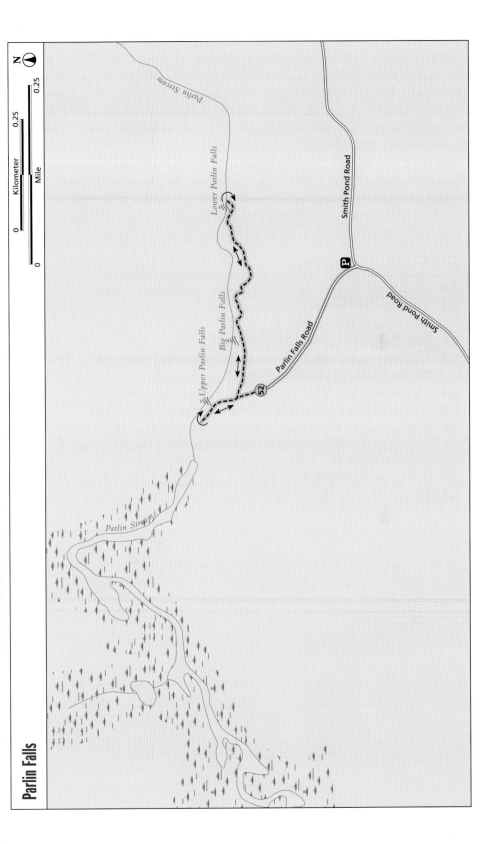

N

Kilometer
0   0.25   0.25

Mile
0   0.25

Parlin Stream

Lower Parlin Falls

Big Parlin Falls

Upper Parlin Falls

52

Parlin Falls Road

Smith Pond Road

Smith Pond Road

P

Parlin Stream

Where the trail begins to descend, it becomes less distinct. Try to follow its path and descend slowly. You'll see and hear Lower Parlin Falls through the trees below you. When you're past it, descend down to the stream. You'll come out downstream of the large pool at the base of the waterfall. Lower Parlin Falls is a dramatic 40-foot horsetail. In spring, on the east side of the rock face, the stream rages down a plunge beside the wide, gentle horsetail.

Parlin Falls are among the most compelling in Maine. Unfortunately, to see them all requires some work and bushwhacking. If you take the time to reach Lower Parlin Falls, you won't be disappointed. Even a short hike to Upper Parlin Falls will be rewarding. It's a picturesque slide with lots of bedrock to explore, offering various views of the waterfall.

Miles and Directions

0.0   Start at the parking area at the intersection of Parlin Falls Road and Smith Pond Road.

0.2   At the end of Parlin Falls Road, bear right into a parking area. The Parlin Falls Trailhead is at the far end of the gravel area.

0.3   Descend steadily to the base of Upper Parlin Falls.

0.4   Scramble on exposed bedrock to the top of Upper Parlin Falls. To continue the hike, follow the Parlin Falls Trail back toward the trailhead.

0.5   Two hundred feet short of the trailhead, turn left on a rough but obvious trail.

0.6   Hike atop the steep gorge that Parlin Stream flows through. Pass Big Parlin Falls.

0.8   As the gorge widens, the trail begins to descend and eventually peters out. Continue descending to the base of Lower Parlin Falls. To complete the hike, retrace your steps to the Parlin Falls Trail.

1.1   Turn left onto the Parlin Falls Trail.

1.4   Arrive back at your vehicle.

53 Mattawamkeag River

The Mattawamkeag River flows through a black slate gorge with vertical bedding that juts 40 feet into the air. The river winds between humps of worn slate that look like lava, flowing over small falls and through deep pools. Less than 2 miles downstream, the river drops 6 feet over slate ledges at Gordon Falls, then races through a series of rapids ending at Lower Gordon Falls.

Start: Upper Gordon Falls Trailhead
Elevation gain: 297 feet
Distance: 1.2 miles in 2 out and backs
Hiking time: About 2 hours
Difficulty: Moderate due to off-trail scrambling
Season: Late May to October
Trail surface: Woodland path and slate bedrock
Land status: Private timberlands
Nearest town: Mattawamkeag

Other users: Hunters in season
Water availability: None
Canine compatibility: Dogs must be under control at all times.
Fees and permits: None
Other maps: *DeLorme: Maine Atlas & Gazetteer*, map 44; USGS Mattawamkeag
Trail contact: Mattawamkeag Wilderness Park, (207) 290-0205, www.mwpark.com

Finding the trailhead: From exit 244 off I-95, follow ME 157 east. Drive 11 miles. Turn right onto US 2. Drive 0.4 mile. Cross the Mattawamkeag River and turn left onto Dept Road at the Mattawamkeag Wilderness Park sign. Drive 3.4 miles (the road turns to gravel as you leave Mattawamkeag village). Cross the bridge over Big Gordon Brook. Bear left. Drive 1.6 miles. Pass the unmarked Lower Gordon Falls Trailhead parking. Drive 0.1 mile. Park on the wide right shoulder across the road from the unmarked Upper Gordon Falls Trailhead. GPS: N45 30.259' / W68 17.829'. After hiking Upper Gordon Falls, continue driving on Mattawamkeag Wilderness Park Road for 1.4 miles. Turn left into the Slewgundy Heaters parking area at the sign. GPS: N45 30.931' / W68 17.038'

The Hike

The Mattawamkeag River drains a large portion of southern and eastern Aroostook County. It's one of the Penobscot River's largest tributaries. The stretch of river between Kingman and Mattawamkeag is wild; in fact, the Mattawamkeag River is the longest unregulated river in Maine. Just upstream from the hike is Mattawamkeag Wilderness Park, which maintains a hiking trail that hugs the south bank of the river from the campground to beyond Gordon Falls. This hike makes use of it and short trails that connect the River Trail to Mattawamkeag Wilderness Park Road.

At Gordon Falls the river makes a wide, slow turn then enters what looks like a lava field. The bedrock is slate, with the bedding turned on end. It's been weathered very irregularly. The river flows through crumbling rock, creating numerous pools

Slewgundy Heaters

and channels. Because so much of the headwaters of the Mattawamkeag is marsh, the river maintains good flow throughout the summer.

The water is deeply stained from tannins. It often looks as black as the rock it flows over and around. The bedrock is sharp in places and rarely flat. It's not the most inviting landscape for swimming, but it's dramatic to look at. In early summer, after the river's flow has abated somewhat, wild columbine blooms in the cracks and crannies in the rock, adding a splash of color.

Slewgundy Heaters, a mile upstream from Gordon Falls, is a slate gorge. The river drops down a small waterfall then races between black cliffs 40 feet high. Rough humps of slate and irregular towers of bedrock line the river within and below the gorge. The word *slewgundy* is a different spelling of *slugundy*, which means "small waterfall" or "rapids." There are certainly plenty of both in this section of the Mattawamkeag River.

The River Trail passes atop the gorge; a chain-link fence protects visitors from falling. Access to the gorge is gained upstream from the fence, where you can climb down the steep slope and clamber around on the mounds of black rock. The bedding here is less vertical, so the rock is often smooth. In the eddies where the current is weak, you can swim in water that is dark with tannin and very deep.

Downstream from the trailhead, you can climb down to the river at the base of the gorge and walk along the shore upstream. This gives you dramatic views of the rock along the shore and a real sense of the depth of the gorge.

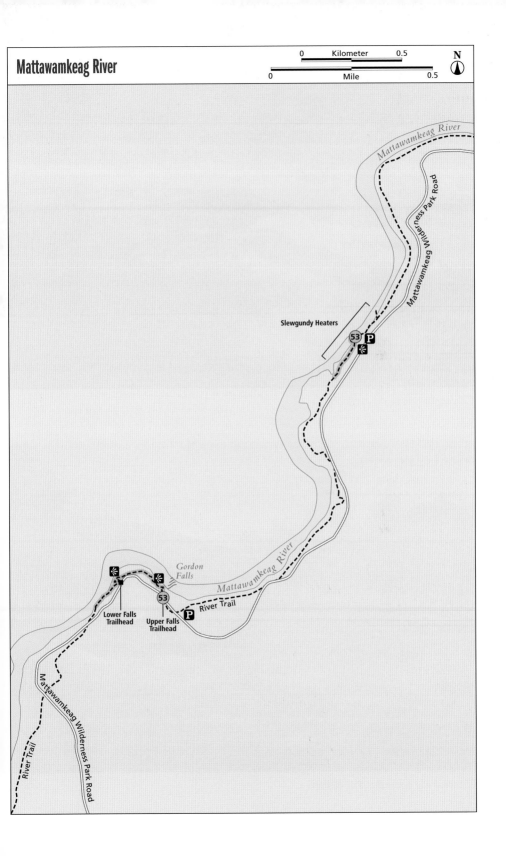

Mattawamkeag River

Slewgundy Heaters

53 P

Mattawamkeag River

Mattawamkeag Wilderness Park Road

Gordon Falls

Mattawamkeag River

River Trail

53 P

Lower Falls
Trailhead

Upper Falls
Trailhead

River Trail

Mattawamkeag Wilderness Park Road

River Trail

0 Kilometer 0.5

0 Mile 0.5

N

Gordon Falls from the overlook

Gordon Falls across the slate bedrock

Miles and Directions

0.0 Start from the Upper Gordon Falls Trailhead.

0.1 Hike straight toward the river. Reach an overlook of Gordon Falls. Retrace your steps 200 feet, then turn right (downstream) onto the River Trail.

0.3 When you reach the trail that leads to the Lower Gordon Falls Trailhead, turn right. Pass the downstream River Trail. Reach an overlook of Lower Gordon Falls. Retrace your steps to the downstream River Trail. Turn right onto the River Trail.

0.4 Leave the River Trail and drop out onto rocks at the base of Lower Gordon Falls. Return to the River Trail and follow it back upstream to the Upper Gordon Falls Trailhead.

0.7 Arrive back at the Upper Gordon Falls Trailhead. To continue the hike, drive east (upstream) on Mattawamkeag Wilderness Park Road 1.4 miles to the Slewgundy Heaters Trailhead.

0.7 From the overlook platform at the Slewgundy Heaters Trailhead, follow the River Trail upstream. In 350 feet, follow the unmarked trail left. Descend steeply to the river. After exploring the exposed bedrock along the shore, return to the Slewgundy Heaters Trailhead to continue the hike.

1.0 Cross over the overlook platform and follow the River Trail downstream.

1.1 Where the fence ends at the base of the Heaters, make your way down to the riverside. After exploring this area, complete the hike by returning to the Slewgundy Heaters Trailhead.

1.2 Arrive back at the Slewgundy Heaters Trailhead.

54 Orin Falls

Orin Falls is a beautiful stretch of Wassataquoik Stream in the Katahdin Woods and Waters National Monument. The river drops over low ledges and slides through clear pools amid piles of granite boulders. Upstream, North Turner Mountain quietly watches over the noisy stream.

Start: Orin Falls Trailhead
Elevation gain: 421 feet
Distance: 6.2 miles out and back
Hiking time: About 4 hours
Difficulty: Moderate due to distance
Season: Late May to October
Trail surface: Old woods road and woodland path
Land status: Katahdin Woods and Waters National Monument
Nearest town: Medway

Other users: None
Water availability: Wassataquoik Stream
Canine compatibility: Dogs must be under control at all times.
Fees and permits: None
Other maps: *DeLorme: Maine Atlas & Gazetteer*, map 51; USGS Whetstone Mountain, Deasey Mountain, and Katahdin Lake
Trail contact: Katahdin Woods and Waters National Monument, (207) 456-6001, www .nps.gov/kaww

Finding the trailhead: From exit 244 off I-95, follow ME 157 west. Drive 1 mile. Turn right onto ME 11 north. Drive 9 miles. Pass the rest area at Grindstone Falls. Continue north on ME 11 for 11 miles. Where ME 11 makes a hard right, turn left onto Swift Brook Road. Drive 5.2 miles. Bear left, staying on Swift Brook Road. Drive 1.8 miles. Cross the East Branch Penobscot River just below Whetstone Falls. Drive 5 miles, passing several side roads. Reach Loop Road and turn right. Drive 1.3 miles. Turn right at the sign for Orin Falls. Drive 2.5 miles. Park at where the road is blocked. The trail is a continuation of the road. GPS: N45 55.353' / W68 42.324'

The Hike

Remember that in northern Maine, "falls" means "rapids." There's no big waterfall at Orin Falls. Instead, Wassataquoik Stream drops through a boulder field. The stream slides over ledges and eddies into deep, clear pools. It's a beautiful stretch of river, with great swimming holes.

To get there, you mostly follow an old woods road. You hike through an old borrow pit and up onto an esker. The trail follows the esker upstream near (but not within sight of) Wassataquoik Stream. The esker peters out and you drop down to Katahdin Brook. This stream drains out of Katahdin Lake and shouldn't be confused with Katahdin Stream, which drains the mountain's southern flank.

For a mile and a half, you're hiking on the International Appalachian Trail (IAT). The trail starts in the monument near the Bernard Mountain Trailhead and wanders north and east to Forillon National Park in Quebec at the eastern tip of Gaspe

Orin Falls

North Turner Mountain visible over Orin Falls

Grindstone Falls on the East Branch

Peninsula. The trail then jumps to Newfoundland. After crossing that island, it jumps to Iceland, then Scotland. This may seem like a crazy idea, but geologically these lands are all related. Between about 400 and 250 million years ago, they were all part of the same supercontinent.

About a mile after you leave the IAT, you cross the Monument Line. This is a survey line drawn in 1825. When Maine became a state in 1820, its boundaries were still in dispute. A joint British/Maine surveying team first surveyed the eastern boundary (the one straight line on Maine's borders). From the bottom of that survey line, they began surveying west across the state to determine the western boundary. Late in 1825, the team crossed the path you're hiking. They made it to the top of Hamlin Peak before abandoning the project for the year—there was no way to survey down the cliff into Northwest Basin. The Monument Line was used to lay out the rectangular grid of townships in northern Maine. As you hike across the line, you pass from T3 R8 into T4 R8.

A short distance farther, you turn right and head straight for Wassataquoik Stream at Orin Falls. The falls is a series of small drops and pools that descends about 60 feet in a few tenths of a mile. Far upstream, North Turner Mountain quietly watches over the tumbling river. This is one of Maine's best swimming holes.

Orin Falls

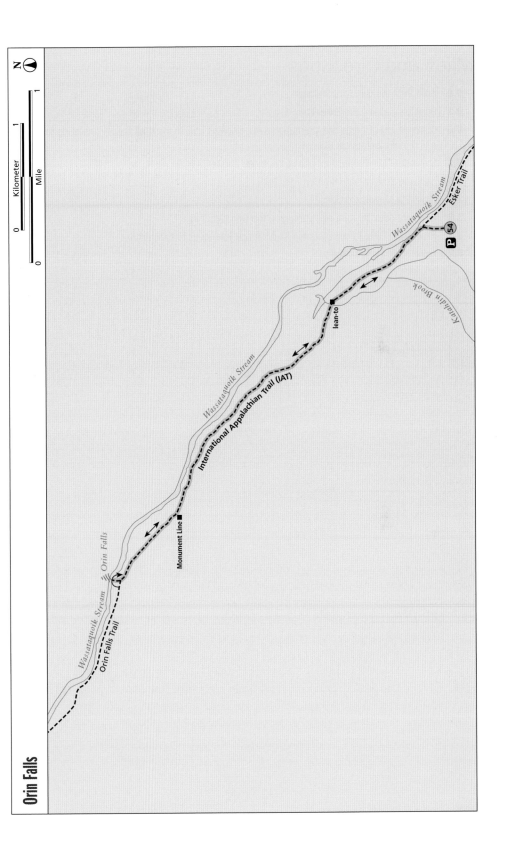

Miles and Directions

0.0 Start from the Orin Falls Trailhead.

0.2 Bear left, passing the Esker Trail.

0.5 Continue straight onto the International Appalachian Trail. To the right, the IAT descends to a ford of Wassataquoik Stream.

0.9 Cross Katahdin Brook, then pass a campsite and lean-to.

1.5 Continue straight onto the Orin Falls Trail.

2.4 Cross the Monument Line.

3.0 Turn right onto the footpath, staying on the Orin Falls Trail.

3.1 Reach Orin Falls. To complete the hike, retrace your steps to the trailhead.

6.2 Arrive back at the trailhead.

55 Blueberry Ledges

Blueberry Ledges is a huge expanse of semi-open granite bedrock that Katahdin Stream slides down. On and around the ledges grow birch trees and, of course, blueberries. It is one of the more extraordinary sights in Baxter State Park. Below the ledges proper are two good-sized waterfalls. The hike reaches the ledges from the south, beginning at Abol Beach. This route follows Abol Stream, with fine views of Katahdin, before turning north toward Blueberry Ledges.

Start: Abol Stream Trailhead at end of Abol Beach Road
Elevation gain: 740 feet
Distance: 6.5-mile reverse lollipop
Hiking time: 3 to 4 hours
Difficulty: Moderate
Season: May to October
Trail surface: Woodland path
Land status: Baxter State Park and Appalachian Trail corridor
Nearest town: Millinocket. There is a store and restaurant at Abol Bridge, 0.5 mile off the hike.

Other users: Hunters in season
Water availability: None
Canine compatibility: Dogs are not allowed in Baxter State Park.
Fees and permits: None for Maine residents; auto entrance fee for nonresidents
Other maps: *DeLorme: Maine Atlas & Gazetteer*, map 50; USGS Abol Pond
Trail contact: Baxter State Park, (207) 723-5140, https://baxterstatepark.org

Finding the trailhead: From exit 244 off I-95, follow ME 157 west through Medway and East Millinocket to Millinocket. Where ME 157 ends, turn right onto Katahdin Avenue. Drive 0.2 mile. Turn left onto Bates Street at the Baxter State Park sign. As you leave Millinocket, Bates Street becomes Baxter Road. Follow Baxter Road to the park's south entrance. It's 35.8 miles from I-95 to the Togue Pond Gate. From the Togue Pond Gate, drive 3 miles on Park Tote Road. Turn left onto Abol Beach Road. Drive 0.5 mile to the end of the road and the trailhead. GPS: N45 50.410' / W68 56.347'

The Hike

The Blueberry Ledges Trail runs 4.4 miles from the Tote Road just east of Katahdin Stream Campground to the Appalachian Trail (AT) near Abol Bridge. Along its course, the trail descends about 500 feet. The ledges are 1.7 miles north of the AT and 3 miles south of the Tote Road. This hike gets to Blueberry Ledges from the south, using the Abol Stream Trail that begins at the Abol Beach picnic area in Baxter State Park.

Blueberry Ledges is a huge, semi-open expanse of bare granite that Katahdin Stream slides down. There are numerous slides, sluices, and waterfalls—and, of course, lots of blueberries growing where they can on the broken bedrock around and

Blueberry Ledges

beneath small birch trees. It's one of the more extraordinary sights in Baxter. You could spend hours exploring the ledges and falls and not see it all.

To get there, follow the Abol Stream Trail west from Abol Beach. The trail crosses a sandy esker then parallels Abol Stream. The stream moves languidly through low, marshy country. To the north the land rises, forested from this wetland to Katahdin. The mountain is visible along much of the trail. The second half of this trail is outside the park and is used occasionally by ATVs and snowmobiles.

The trail ends at the AT at a spot about a half mile from Abol Bridge. Follow the AT north back into the park. From the bridge over Abol Stream, you have your last view of Katahdin. The trail loops around the deadwater at the mouth of Abol Stream. Across the swampy pool is a commercial campground on the spot where Henry David Thoreau camped in 1846.

At the large AT kiosk, bear right onto the Abol Pond Trail. From here, you hike north over sandy soil through a birch forest. The trail climbs very gently.

A mile north of the AT, the trail crosses a granite ledge. You can hear Katahdin Stream to your left. Two unmarked, but obvious, side trails descend to the stream. Each trail visits a good-sized waterfall. This is the base of Blueberry Ledges.

The trail crosses more open granite before reaching the main area of Blueberry Ledges. The trail bears right and climbs away from the ledges, but you need to follow

Blueberry Ledges

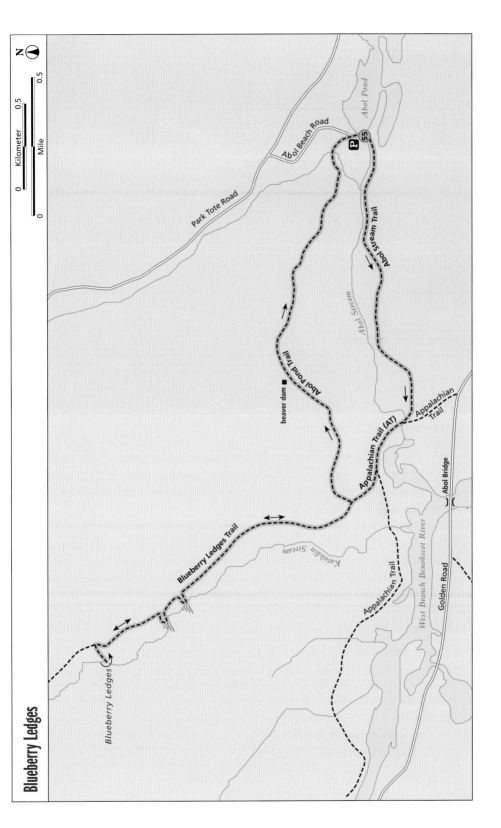

The first waterfall on Katahdin Stream you'll reach

the open granite left down to Katahdin Stream. Take time to explore the area, looking for hidden sluices and waterfalls. If you visit in late summer, snack on the abundant blueberries. But remember, where the stream slides down the bare rock can be slippery, and footing can be uneven. Take care.

On the return hike, follow the Abol Pond Trail. This trail crosses semi-open sandy areas and passes an extremely long beaver dam before descending to an interesting "bridge" over Abol Stream.

This hike is about the same distance as hiking directly to Blueberry Ledges from the north, but infinitely more varied and interesting.

Miles and Directions

0.0 Start from the Abol Stream Trailhead at the end of Abol Beach Road.

1.2 The trail follows Abol Stream with views of Katahdin and the marshy stream. The trail ends at the Appalachian Trail. Turn right, heading northbound. ***Option:*** From this junction it is 0.5 mile southbound on the AT to Abol Bridge, where there is a store and restaurant.

1.5 The trail crosses Abol Stream and arrives at a junction where there is a large information kiosk. Bear right onto the Abol Pond Trail.

1.7 Go straight onto the Blueberry Ledges Trail.

2.5 Where the trail crosses a granite ledge and you can hear Katahdin Stream, an unmarked side trail on the left leads 300 feet to a waterfall at the base of Blueberry Ledges. After exploring around the falls, return to the Blueberry Ledges Trail.

2.6 Just past the first side trail, turn left onto another unmarked side trail.

2.7 The side trail crosses open ledges. At a stone fire ring, turn left and descend to Katahdin Stream, where there is a huge logjam. A waterfall is visible just upstream. After exploring this waterfall, return to the Blueberry Ledges Trail.

3.2 The trail emerges onto the open ledges. Turn left off the trail and follow the granite bedrock to Katahdin Stream. To complete the hike, return on the Blueberry Ledges Trail the way you came.

4.8 Arrive back at the Abol Pond Trail. Turn left.

5.4 The trail passes along the base of a very long beaver dam.

6.3 The trail crosses Abol Stream.

6.4 The Abol Pond Trail ends at Abol Beach Road. Turn right and follow the road.

6.5 Arrive back at the trailhead.

56 Katahdin Stream Falls

Katahdin Stream drops 80 feet in two connected plunges amid blocks of orange granite. Below the falls, the stream tumbles through a narrow canyon and under the trail. Most hikers are so focused on beginning their climb of Mount Katahdin that they barely notice one of Maine's most scenic waterfalls.

Start: Hunt Trailhead in Katahdin Stream Campground
Elevation gain: 539 feet
Distance: 2.4 miles out and back
Hiking time: About 2 hours
Difficulty: Easy
Season: Late May, when the trail opens, to October, when the trail closes
Trail surface: Woodland path
Land status: Baxter State Park
Nearest town: Millinocket
Other users: None
Water availability: Katahdin Stream

Canine compatibility: Dogs are not allowed in Baxter State Park.
Fees and permits: None for Maine residents; auto entrance fee for nonresidents. You need to make a reservation for a parking spot at the trailhead to ensure access. Reservations can be made online or by phone up to four months in advance.
Other maps: *DeLorme: Maine Atlas & Gazetteer*, map 50; USGS Mount Katahdin
Trail contact: Baxter State Park, (207) 723-5140, https://baxterstatepark.org

Finding the trailhead: From exit 244 off I-95, follow ME 157 west through Medway and East Millinocket to Millinocket. Where ME 157 ends, turn right onto Katahdin Avenue. Drive 0.2 mile. Turn left onto Bates Street at the Baxter State Park sign. As you leave Millinocket, Bates Street becomes Baxter Road. Follow Baxter Road to the park's south entrance. It's 35.8 miles from I-95 to the Togue Pond Gate. From the Togue Pond Gate, drive 7.9 miles on Park Tote Road. The day-use parking area is on the right in Katahdin Stream Campground. The trailhead is at the back of the campground. GPS: N45 53.247' / W68 59.977'

The Hike

The Hunt Trail leaves Katahdin Stream Campground and ends on Baxter Peak on Mount Katahdin, the highest point in Maine. It's the last 5 miles of the Appalachian Trail, and it's taken thru-hikers almost 2,200 miles to get here. This is the largest single climb on the entire AT.

Don't worry, the climbing doesn't start until after Katahdin Stream Falls. The trail climbs gently, often within hearing of Katahdin Stream. Just after you pass the trail up the Owl, the Hunt Trail crosses Katahdin Stream. This section was rerouted in the summer of 2019 when the bridge collapsed. Upstream you can see where the stream exits a deep granite canyon choked with boulders. You can hear Katahdin Stream Falls, but can't see it yet.

Katahdin Stream Falls ▶

Katahdin Stream Falls

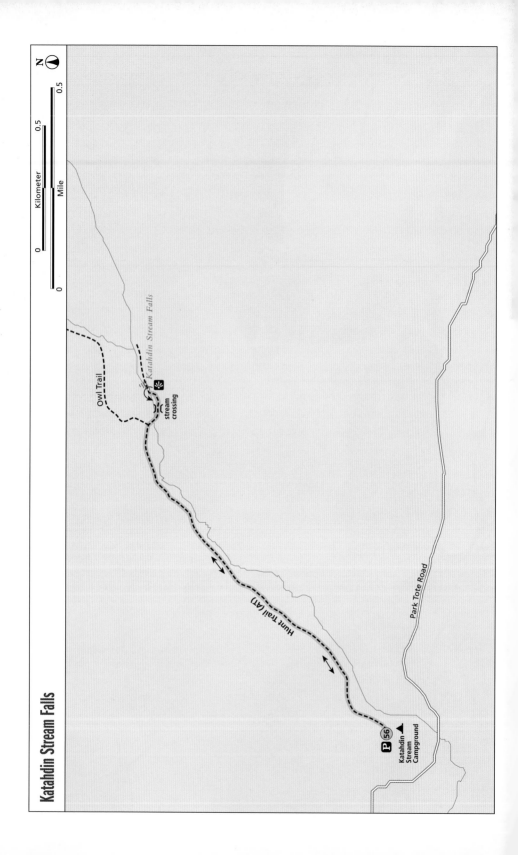

Katahdin Stream Falls

The trail turns left and climbs granite slabs beside the stream. At the waterfall, a very short, marked side trail leads to an overlook. In front of you, the base of the falls is about 40 feet straight down. Katahdin Stream plunges 30 feet down square-sided granite blocks, then does it again and again. The total drop is 80 feet. The waterfall loses some of its oomph as summer progresses, but is still extremely photogenic even at low flow.

Katahdin Stream Falls is one of the highest in Maine, but farther upstream, far from any trail, is Maine's highest waterfall. The Owl and Katahdin are separated by a steep ravine more than 1,500 feet deep. Katahdin Stream flows out of Witherle Ravine on Mount Katahdin and down through the ravine to Katahdin Stream Falls. Another stream drains the west side of the Saddle, joining Katahdin Stream in the ravine. This stream is essentially one giant waterfall. Near the bottom is a single plunge of nearly 800 feet known as Katahdin Falls, by far the highest waterfall in Maine. You can see Katahdin Falls from the summit of the Owl. But from that height, it's a tiny white line on the side of the mountain.

Miles and Directions

0.0 Start from the Hunt Trailhead at the back of the Katahdin Stream Campground.

1.1 Pass the Owl Trail.

1.2 The Hunt Trail crosses Katahdin Stream at the base of Katahdin Stream Falls. Across the stream, the trail climbs to an overlook near the top of the falls. To complete the hike, retrace your steps to the trailhead.

2.4 Arrive back at the trailhead.

57 Little Abol Falls

Little Abol Falls is an easy walk from Abol Campground. The trail climbs very little along its route through a hardwood forest. The falls are on one of the branches of Abol Stream. Above the falls the stream tumbles through mossy boulders over smooth orange granite. The falls drop 15 feet into a shallow pool of similar granite littered with rounded stones. It's a picturesque falls and good place to cool off on a hot day.

Start: Ranger station across Park Tote Road from day-use parking area
Elevation gain: 341 feet
Distance: 1.8 miles out and back
Hiking time: About 1 hour
Difficulty: Easy
Season: May to October
Trail surface: Woodland path
Land status: Baxter State Park
Nearest town: Millinocket

Other users: None
Water availability: None
Canine compatibility: Dogs are not allowed in Baxter State Park.
Fees and permits: None for Maine residents; auto entrance fee for nonresidents
Other maps: *DeLorme: Maine Atlas & Gazetteer*, map 50; USGS Mount Katahdin
Trail contact: Baxter State Park, (207) 723-5140, https://baxterstatepark.org

Finding the trailhead: From exit 244 off I-95, follow ME 157 west through Medway and East Millinocket to Millinocket. Where ME 157 ends, turn right onto Katahdin Avenue. Drive 0.2 mile. Turn left onto Bates Street at the Baxter State Park sign. As you leave Millinocket, Bates Street becomes Baxter Road. Follow Baxter Road to the park's south entrance. It's 35.8 miles from I-95 to the Togue Pond Gate. From the Togue Pond Gate, drive 5.6 miles on Park Tote Road. The day-use parking area is across the road from Abol Campground. The hike starts at the ranger station. GPS: N45 52.417' / W68 57.837'

The Hike

The several branches of Abol Stream drain the south face of Katahdin. The stream's name is shortened from the Penobscot word *Abalajakomejus*, which roughly translates as "treeless expanse"—probably a reference to the slide the Abol Trail originally followed. The slide is high on the face of Katahdin between the branches of the stream.

The branches of the stream come together in a marshy area south and east of Stump Pond. The stream then flows south toward the west end of Abol Pond. The stream turns west, joined by Abol Pond's outflow. It meanders through marshy lowlands from there to the West Branch at Abol Bridge.

Little Abol Falls is on the east branch of Abol Stream. There is no Big Abol Falls, but there is an Abol Falls on the West Branch just downstream from Abol Bridge. The "little" in the falls' name is a reference to the size of the stream, not the waterfall.

The hike to the falls follows an old woods road through hardwood forest. There is very little elevation gain. The trail ends at the top of the falls. The stream tumbles

Little Abol Falls

Small flume downstream from Little Abol Falls

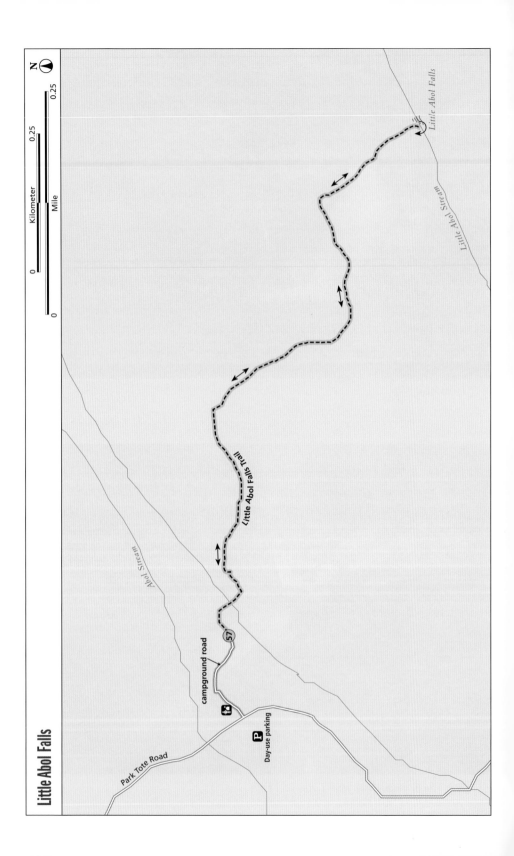

Little Abol Falls

Little Abol Falls

Little Abol Stream

Little Abol Falls Trail

57

campground road

Park Tote Road

Day-use parking

Abol Stream

N

Kilometer
0   0.25   0.25

Mile
0   0.25

down through the woods, dropping down small granite ledges. Rounded, mossy boulders line the stream. The water rushes across smooth orange granite that shines through the shallow stream.

The stream pinches between rough boulders and drops about 15 feet into a pool. Like above the falls, the floor of the pool is smooth granite covered with rounded cobbles. On the far side of the stream, jagged layers of bedrock poke out of the hillside—a fine place to cool off on a hot summer day. Take time to explore the stream below the falls. Not only is there a great pool, but farther downstream there's an interesting flume.

Miles and Directions

0.0 Start at the ranger station across Park Tote Road from the day-use parking area.

0.1 Walk through the campground, staying to the right. The marked trailhead is between sites 8 and 10. In 100 feet the wide trail fords a rushing stream.

0.9 The trail climbs gently to Little Abol Falls. To complete the hike, return the way you came.

1.8 Arrive back at the trailhead.

58 Big and Little Niagara Falls via Lily Pad Pond

To reach Niagara Falls, you hike to Beaver Brook, then paddle down the stream and across Lily Pad Pond to another trail. From the pond you have spectacular views of the mountains from Moose Mountain to Katahdin. The Windy Pitch Pond Trail begins on the south shore of Lily Pad Pond, then crosses a small hill to reach Little and Big Niagara Falls. The views of the waterfalls are better from the west bank than from the Appalachian Trail on the east bank. Beyond the falls, the trail crosses a mossy forest to Windy Pitch Pond.

Start: Sentinel Link Trailhead at southeast end of day-use parking area
Elevation gain: 474 feet
Distance: 6.2 miles out and back
Hiking time: 1 to 2 hours
Difficulty: Strenuous due to distance
Season: May to October
Trail surface: Woodland path and flat-water canoeing
Land status: Baxter State Park
Nearest town: Millinocket

Other users: None
Water availability: None
Canine compatibility: Dogs are not allowed in Baxter State Park.
Fees and permits: None for Maine residents; auto entrance fee for nonresidents
Other maps: DeLorme: Maine Atlas & Gazetteer, map 50; USGS Doubletop Mountain
Trail contact: Baxter State Park, (207) 723-5140, https://baxterstatepark.org

Finding the trailhead: From exit 244 off I-95, follow ME 157 west through Medway and East Millinocket to Millinocket. Where ME 157 ends, turn right onto Katahdin Avenue. Drive 0.2 mile. Turn left onto Bates Street at the Baxter State Park sign. As you leave Millinocket, Bates Street becomes Baxter Road. Follow Baxter Road to the park's south entrance. It's 35.8 miles from I-95 to the Togue Pond Gate. From the Togue Pond Gate, drive 10.4 miles. Turn left onto Kidney Pond Road. Drive 1.2 miles to the day-use parking area at the end of the road. The trailhead is at the southeast end of the parking area. GPS: N45 53.621' / W69 02.931'

The Hike

Lily Pad Pond is little more than a wide spot in Beaver Brook just before it empties into Nesowadnehunk Stream. The pond is ringed by marsh and densely packed laurel and cranberry bushes, with the occasional spruce or larch standing like sentries. Alders grow as close as they dare, creeping in from along Nesowadnehunk Stream. It's a pretty spot where you might see moose or ducks. To the west rises the rounded hump of Sentinel Mountain, its crown showing bald spots here and there. To the north—from the west all the way around to the east—is a line of great mountains: Moose and Doubletop, then the Nesowadnehunk Valley; Western Peak and Mount

Little Niagara Falls in May

O-J-I ,with Mount Coe peeking out from behind and the long ridge of Barren Mountain; the huge mass of Katahdin from the Northwest Plateau to the Knife Edge. A magnificent view.

To get there, you follow the Sentinel Link Trail along the south shore of Kidney Pond. Take the side trail to Colt Point, which sits in the bend of the kidney. From its rocky shore, you have fine views of the entire pond and the mountains beyond. You can rent a canoe at Kidney Pond Campground and paddle down the pond to Lily Pad Landing, saving almost a mile of walking.

The Lily Pad Pond Trail is less mossy than many of the other trails that lead south from Kidney Pond, but it's a pleasant walk. The trail ends with a boardwalk through an alder break to Beaver Brook. The brook flows from the Beaver Ponds just outside the park southwest of Celia and Jackson Ponds. Upstream from the trail's end, the brook tumbles out of the woods into a wet meadow. Early in the summer, you can paddle its sinuous course to the woods. Downstream, Beaver Brook widens, hemmed in by dense bushes. Pitcher plants, sundews, cotton grass, and all manner of bog plants grow among the bushes on the dense mat of moss.

Paddle downstream and into Lily Pad Pond. The view of the mountains opens up as you put distance between yourself and land dry enough to support forest. To the west you can see Moose and Doubletop Mountains. Across the Nesowadnehunk Valley from them, you can see West Peak and Mount O-J-I. To the north are Barren Mountain and Katahdin. It's a unique and spectacular view.

To continue the hike, paddle to the east end of the pond, where it narrows to a rock-filled stream. The takeout is a flat, open area just beyond where the outlet stream disappears into rock-choked alders.

The view west across Lily Pad Pond

Big Niagara Falls in August

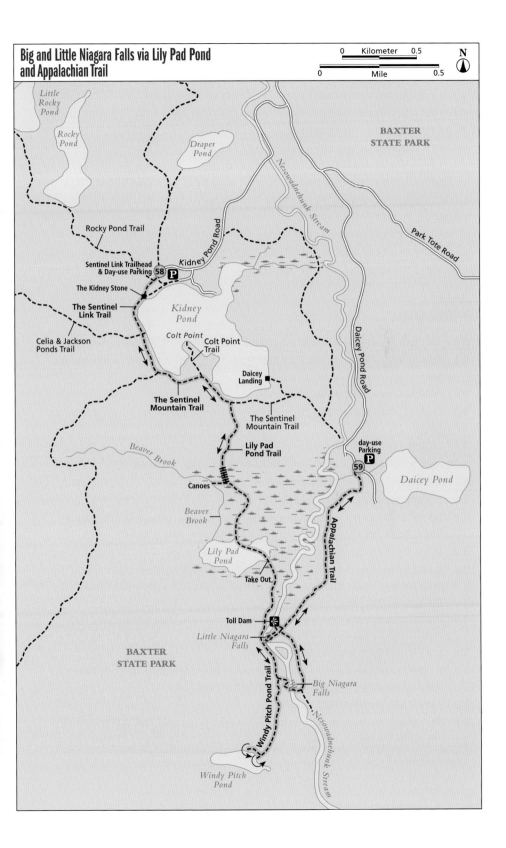

Big and Little Niagara Falls via Lily Pad Pond and Appalachian Trail

0   Kilometer   0.5

0   Mile   0.5

N

Little Rocky Pond

Rocky Pond

Draper Pond

BAXTER STATE PARK

Nesowadnehunk Stream

Park Tote Road

Rocky Pond Trail

Kidney Pond Road

Sentinel Link Trailhead & Day-use Parking **58** P

The Kidney Stone

The Sentinel Link Trail

Kidney Pond

Daicey Pond Road

Celia & Jackson Ponds Trail

Colt Point   Colt Point Trail

Daicey Landing

The Sentinel Mountain Trail

The Sentinel Mountain Trail

day-use Parking **59** P

Daicey Pond

Beaver Brook

Lily Pad Pond Trail

Canoes

Beaver Brook

Appalachian Trail

Lily Pad Pond

Take Out

Toll Dam

Little Niagara Falls

Windy Pitch Pond Trail

Big Niagara Falls

Nesowadnehunk Stream

BAXTER STATE PARK

Windy Pitch Pond

The Windy Pitch Pond Trail enters the woods and climbs a small, rocky hill. You can hear the falls on Nesowadnehunk Stream. You drop down off the hill to Little Niagara Falls. Short, unmarked side trails lead to both the top and base of the falls. The view of the falls from its base is far superior to the view you get from the Appalachian Trail on the other side of the stream.

A short distance farther, you come to a short side trail that leads to the top of Big Niagara Falls. An unmarked but well-worn trail continues down to the base of the falls. Again, the view from this vantage is better than from the other side of the stream.

The Windy Pitch Pond Trail continues another half mile to its namesake pond. This small pond is surrounded by dense forest. Exposed rock is visible on the steep slopes south and west of the pond. There is a rental canoe on the north shore where the trail ends.

This is very nearly a perfect hike, with beautiful woods, pretty ponds, waterfalls, spectacular views, wildlife, and solitude. It is a hike to take your time with. Make it last the entire day and really explore.

Miles and Directions

0.0 Start from the Sentinel Link Trailhead at the southeast end of the day-use parking area.

0.1 Pass the Rocky Ponds Trail and the Kidney Stone—a large erratic boulder to the left of the trail.

0.3 Pass the Celia & Jackson Ponds Trail.

0.5 Continue straight ahead along the south shore of Kidney Pond onto the Sentinel Mountain Trail.

0.7 Turn left onto the Colt Point Trail.

0.9 Arrive at Colt Point. To continue the hike, return to the Sentinel Mountain Trail.

1.1 Turn left onto the Sentinel Mountain Trail.

1.3 Turn right onto the Lily Pad Pond Trail.

1.6 The trail emerges from the woods and crosses a marshy area on bog boards, ending at Beaver Brook. Unlock your canoe and paddle downstream, east to the left.

2.0 Beaver Brook opens into Lily Pad Pond.

2.2 Cross Lily Pad Pond to the southeast. The landing is beyond the rocks at the mouth of the outlet stream. Be sure to pull your canoe all the way out of the water before leaving it. The Windy Pitch Pond Trail is to the south.

2.5 The trail crosses a small hill and reaches Little Niagara Falls. There are unmarked side trails to both the top and base of the falls.

2.8 Turn left onto the side trail to Big Niagara Falls.

3.0 The trail reaches the top of the falls and continues down the rocky slope to the base of the falls. To continue the hike, return to the Windy Pitch Pond Trail.

3.2 Turn left onto the Windy Pitch Pond Trail.

3.5 The trail ends on the north shore of Windy Pitch Pond at the rental canoe. To complete the hike, return the way you came.

6.2 Arrive back at the trailhead.

59 Big and Little Niagara Falls via Appalachian Trail

Big and Little Niagara Falls on Nesowadnehunk Stream are two of Baxter State Park's wilder falls. They are also among the most accessible. The short hike along the south-bound Appalachian Trail is an easy walk on a section of wide, flat trail through an evergreen forest full of rocks and moss. The hike first visits the Toll Dam, a remnant of Nesowadnehunk Stream's history of log drives. Below the dam are the two falls and the rapids above and below them. At each falls are large areas of granite that you can climb on and explore, offering different views of each falls.

See map on p. 239.
Start: Day-use parking area where Appalachian Trail crosses Daicey Pond Road
Elevation gain: 118 feet
Distance: 2.8 miles out and back
Hiking time: 2 to 3 hours
Difficulty: Easy
Season: June to September
Trail surface: Woodland path
Land status: Baxter State Park
Nearest town: Millinocket
Other users: None

Water availability: Nesowadnehunk Stream at Toll Dam
Canine compatibility: Dogs are not permitted in Baxter State Park.
Fees and permits: None for Maine residents; auto entrance fee for nonresidents
Other maps: DeLorme: Maine Atlas & Gazetteer, map 50; USGS Doubletop Mountain and Rainbow Lake East
Trail contact: Baxter State Park, (207) 723-5140, https://baxterstatepark.org

Finding the trailhead: From exit 244 off I-95, follow ME 157 west through Medway and East Millinocket to Millinocket. Where ME 157 ends, turn right onto Katahdin Avenue. Drive 0.2 mile. Turn left onto Bates Street at the Baxter State Park sign. As you leave Millinocket, Bates Street becomes Baxter Road. Follow Baxter Road to the park's south entrance. It's 35.8 miles from I-95 to the Togue Pond Gate. From the south entrance of Baxter State Park at Togue Pond Gate, drive 10.1 miles on Park Tote Road. Turn left onto Daicey Pond Road at the sign for Daicey Pond. Drive 1.5 miles; the day-use parking area is on the right where the Appalachian Trail crosses the road. The hike follows the southbound AT. GPS: N45 52.940' / W69 01.909'

The Hike

Nesowadnehunk Stream runs for 17 miles from Little Nesowadnehunk Lake just west of Baxter State Park south to the Penobscot River. The first 5 miles from the lake to Nesowadnehunk Field drop very little. Between Nesowadnehunk Field and Kidney Pond Road, the stream is much wilder, dropping in a series of falls and rapids, including Ledge Falls along the Tote Road. Between Kidney Pond and Daicey Pond, Nesowadnehunk Stream is relatively flat again, winding among ponds and marshy

Little Niagara Falls

areas choked with alder. Below Daicey Pond, the stream begins a wild descent to the Penobscot River. The two largest waterfalls in this section of Nesowadnehunk Stream are Little and Big Niagara Falls.

Beginning in the mid–1800s, Nesowadnehunk Stream was the waterway used to float logs from what is now western Baxter State Park to the Penobscot River—and on to Bangor or Old Town to be milled. Nesowadnehunk Field was created as a farm to raise grain and other food for the animals used in the logging operations as well as the loggers themselves. Along the Tote Road between Kidney Pond and Ledge Falls there is a memorial cross to the unknown river driver—a testament to the dangers and wildness of Nesowadnehunk Stream.

The hike that follows the Appalachian Trail (AT) to the falls first passes the old Toll Dam, originally built in 1879. Most of the dam washed away in 1932, but part of it still clings to the far shore of the stream. This dam was used to regulate the water flow down Nesowadnehunk Stream during the log drives. From the site of the Toll Dam, you can look upstream and see Mount O-J-I framed by the stream.

A short distance farther southbound on the AT, you come to a side trail to Little Niagara Falls. The trail leads out onto a flat expanse of granite that Nesowadnehunk Stream veers around before plunging into a deep pool. Rumor has it that this pool offers some of the region's best wild trout fishing. You can climb around on the rocks here and get several different perspectives on Little Niagara Falls. When the stream is running low, a large sandy beach along the pool is exposed that is a good swimming spot.

Less than a mile downstream is Big Niagara Falls. The falls are somewhat higher and more of a plunge than Little Niagara Falls. Rather than a pool below the falls, there is a jumble of huge boulders—many with trees growing on top—that Nesowadnehunk Stream makes its way around. Looking downstream from Big Niagara Falls gives you a good idea of what Nesowadnehunk Stream looks like the rest of the way to the Penobscot River.

You can lengthen the hike as much as you want by following the AT as it descends beside the stream past several named and unnamed falls and rapids, including Rocky Rips, Windy Pitch, and Nesowadnehunk Slide, the last within sight of the Penobscot River. Hiking all the way to Pine Point where Nesowadnehunk Stream empties into the West Branch Penobscot River adds almost 4.5 miles to your hike. Or you can enjoy the easy hike back to the trailhead through the evergreen forest full of rocks and moss.

Big Niagara Falls

Windy Pitch

Miles and Directions

0.0 Start from the southbound Appalachian Trail at the south end of the parking area.

0.1 Arrive at the junction with the Daicey Pond Trail. Turn right and continue on the southbound AT.

0.8 A marked side trail leads 200 feet to the Toll Dam site on Nesowadnehunk Stream.

0.9 A marked side trail leads 300 feet to the top of Little Niagara Falls.

1.4 A marked side trail leads 500 feet to the top of Big Niagara Falls. To complete the hike, return the way you came. ***Option:*** You can continue hiking southbound on the AT, passing Rocky Rips, Windy Pitch, and Nesowadnehunk Slide. Out and back these add 4.4 miles.

2.8 Arrive back at the trailhead.

60 Wassataquoik Stream

This hike visits two waterfalls on Wassataquoik Stream. First, at Ledge Falls, the stream flows over a series of wide granite ledges. There are several pools and plenty of smooth rock to sun on. Second, Grand Falls is a deep granite gorge filled with jumbles of boulders. The stream drops 100 feet through this chaos of granite. A fine pool is accessible at the base of the falls.

Start: Roaring Brook Trailhead
Elevation gain: 799 feet
Distance: 16.2 miles out and back
Hiking time: 2 days; camp at one of the Wassataquoik Stream lean-tos or nearby Russell Pond campground.
Difficulty: Strenuous due to distance
Season: June to October
Trail surface: Woodland path
Land status: Baxter State Park
Nearest town: Millinocket
Other users: None

Water availability: Roaring Brook near trailhead and Wassataquoik Stream
Canine compatibility: Dogs are not allowed in Baxter State Park.
Fees and permits: None for Maine residents; auto entrance fee for nonresidents. You need to make a camping reservation. Reservations can be made online or by phone up to four months in advance.
Other maps: *DeLorme: Maine Atlas & Gazetteer*, map 51; USGS Mount Katahdin
Trail contact: Baxter State Park, (207) 723-5140, https://baxterstatepark.org

Finding the trailhead: From exit 244 off I-95, follow ME 157 west through Medway and East Millinocket to Millinocket. Where ME 157 ends, turn right onto Katahdin Avenue. Drive 0.2 mile. Turn left onto Bates Street at the Baxter State Park sign. As you leave Millinocket, Bates Street becomes Baxter Road. Follow Baxter Road to the park's south entrance. It's 35.8 miles from I-95 to the Togue Pond Gate. From the Togue Pond Gate, turn right onto Roaring Brook Road. Drive 8 miles to the end of the road. Hiker parking is in the lot to the left. The hike begins at the ranger station—where you need to sign in before hiking—at the north end of the parking area. GPS: N45 55.180' / W68 51.444'

The Hike

Wassataquoik Stream rises in the Klondike, the high swampy plateau between Katahdin and the Katahdinaughuoh Mountains. It flows northeast between towering mountains into a wide, flat valley. Ponds and bogs interrupt the valley's forest, and numerous streams drain the surrounding mountains. The most important of these streams, Turner Brook, flows from Wassataquoik Lake through a series of ponds and deadwaters to Wassataquoik Stream southeast of Russell Pond. It's very moosey country.

The mountains around the valley—North Turner, Russell, Mullen, Wassataquoik, South Pogy, North Pogy, South Traveler, and Sable Mountains—are all untrailed. The Pogy Mountains are the most remote place east of the Mississippi River.

Ironically, this part of Baxter State Park may have been the most intensively used and altered by logging. In 1858 the Wassataquoik Valley was called New England's last wilderness. Selective logging had been going on for years, mostly for white pine. Adventurers and climbers began using the logging roads to access the region and climb Katahdin from the north.

Things changed on October 16, 1883, when the Tracy-Love logging operation began. The date is certain because it's etched onto the side of Inscription Rock, a huge boulder sitting in Wassataquoik Stream above Grand Falls. The loggers felled trees, built numerous dams, and built an extensive logging camp just east of today's park boundary.

A major forest fire in 1903 destroyed the logging camp and stopped work for a time. Eventually, the camp was rebuilt as New City farther upstream. More roads were pushed up the valleys of Wassataquoik Stream and its tributaries. Many of the road-beds are today's trails. Dams were built to allow logs to be run down the steep, rocky streams. An even more extensive fire in 1915 brought logging in the Wassataquoik Valley to an end.

Russell Pond is the epicenter of the valley today. There is a campground with lean-tos, tent sites, and a bunkhouse. Trails ray out in every directions.

There are three basic ways to hike in to Russell Pond. First, you can hike in from the north on the Pogy Notch Trail. It's 8.7 miles from Lower South Branch Pond to Russell Pond. The hiking is relatively easy and there are no challenging stream fords.

Second, you can hike in from the west on the Wassataquoik Lake Trail. It's 16.7 miles from Nesowadnehunk Field to Russell Pond. This is the longest route and the only one that involves climbing. Sections are very wet, overgrown, or obscured by blowdowns. Its advantages are that it passes through very remote, little-visited country and passes Wassataquoik Lake and Green Falls, the most remote waterfall in the East.

Third, you can hike in from the south on the Russell Pond Trail. It's 7.2 miles from the Roaring Brook Trailhead to Russell Pond. This is the shortest and most-used route. Its disadvantages are that it's not very interesting and involves a sometimes dangerous ford of Wassataquoik Stream. The route followed by this hike is a modification of the Russell Pond Trail route, adjusted to deal with both of its downsides and head more directly to the waterfalls.

The Russell Pond Trail heads north from Roaring Brook. There is little elevation change on the entire first day. Be sure to stop at Whidden Ponds. There is a fine view of Katahdin across the pond. This pond is the source of the South Branch of Was-sataquoik Stream.

The trail roughly follows the stream, usually on a sidehill above it. Where the trail comes within sight of the stream, bear right onto the Wassataquoik Stream Trail. The stream will be your constant companion until you reach the main stem of Wassata-quoik Stream. You get occasional views of the surrounding mountains—here a view of the graveled face of North Turner Mountain, there the hump of Caverly Lookout.

Grand Falls

By the time the stream widens before joining with Wassataquoik Stream, you'll have glimpsed all the surrounding mountains.

Just before the ford of Wassataquoik Stream, a side trail leads to two lean-tos on the shore of a wide spot in the stream, perfect for swimming. The ford of Wassataquoik Stream is at a wide, shallow spot above a large pool. The streambed is rounded wash stones that offer easy footing. Across the stream, turn right and head toward the waterfalls. In just over a half mile, you reach Ledge Falls. The stream slides down a long series of granite ledges. There are several nice pools in the clear water, and you have a great view of the Traveler over the falls.

The Grand Falls Trail continues downstream. As the trail passes between Bell Pond and Wassataquoik Stream, it becomes wet and overgrown. With care you can make it through without getting your feet wet. Look for beaver activity.

Just west of a three-way junction, the trail crosses Bell Pond's outlet, where it empties into Wassataquoik Stream. Inscription Rock is the huge boulder sitting on the edge of the stream. The inscription is mostly worn off, visible now as a stain on the face of the boulder. In 1883 the Tracy and Love logging operation began here and the date and company name were etched into the rock.

The trail reaches a junction. All three trails are called the Grand Falls Trail. Go straight, following the shore of Wassataquoik Stream. It's a short walk to Grand Falls, a quarter-mile section of steep water that pours through a narrow granite gorge, dropping 100 feet. The stream drops in a series of small falls and fights through boulder

Ledge Falls

fields. The trail skirts the top of cliffs overlooking this maelstrom. The sheer scale of this waterfall is hard to comprehend; photos tend to make it look much smaller than it actually is.

It's possible, with great care, to climb down into the gorge near the end of the trail to a good swimming hole. On your return hike, take time to visit Bell Pond. Turn right at the three-way intersection. It's about a half mile to the north shore of the pond. Along the way, you'll cross an interesting bog and cross some ledges.

Miles and Directions

Day 1

- **0.0** Start from the Roaring Brook Trailhead at the north end of the parking area.
- **0.1** In 350 feet, pass the ranger station then the Chimney Pond Trail. Go straight onto the Russell Pond Trail, crossing the bridge over Roaring Brook. Pass the Roaring Brook Nature Trail and then the Sandy Stream Pond Trail.
- **1.2** Pass the north end of the Sandy Stream Pond Trail.
- **1.4** A short bog boardwalk leads to the shore of Whidden Pond.
- **2.7** The trail passes a very large boulder.
- **3.3** The trail approaches the South Branch of Wassataquoik Stream. Bear right onto the Wassataquoik Stream Trail.
- **5.7** The trail crosses numerous small brooks. Turn right onto the short side trail to the Wassataquoik Stream lean-tos.

Day Two follows map (p. 250)

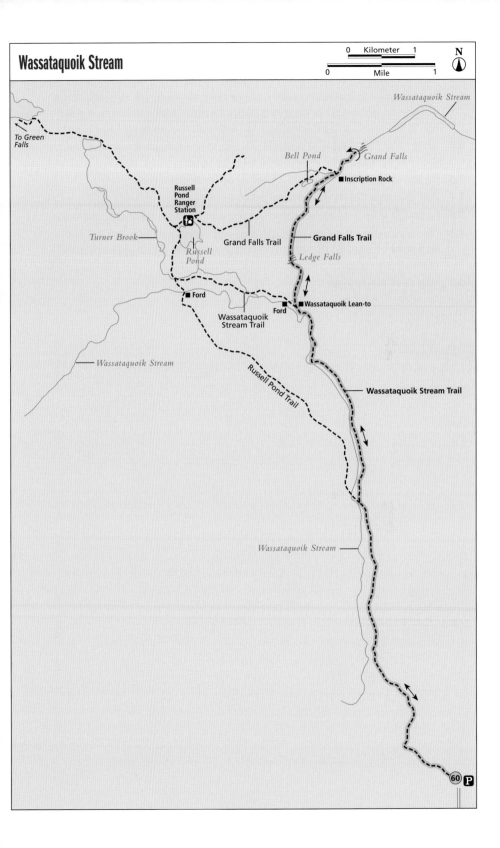

Wassataquoik Stream

0 Kilometer 1
0 Mile 1

N

Wassataquoik Stream

To Green
Falls

Bell Pond Grand Falls

■ Inscription Rock

Russell
Pond
Ranger
Station

Grand Falls Trail **Grand Falls Trail**

Turner Brook

*Russell
Pond*

Ledge Falls

■ Ford

■ Ford ■ Wassataquoik Lean-to

Wassataquoik
Stream Trail

Wassataquoik Stream

Russell Pond Trail

Wassataquoik Stream Trail

Wassataquoik Stream

60 P

Day Two

5.8 Cross to the island along the shore of Wassataquoik Stream to the ford.

5.9 Ford the stream. In summer the water is usually about knee-deep with moderate current. In spring this crossing can be dangerous. Across the stream reenter the woods and turn right at the junction onto the Grand Falls Trail. To the left, it's 1.9 miles to Russell Pond.

6.6 Reach Ledge Falls. There is no viewpoint or access to Wassataquoik Stream. You need to force your way through the underbrush to reach the ledges.

7.5 The trail crosses an overgrown and flooded section south of Bell Pond.

7.7 The trail crosses Bell Pond's outlet and passes Inscription Rock.

7.8 Go straight at the three-way intersection, staying along the shore of Wassataquoik Stream.

8.1 The trail follows the top of the gorge, with numerous overlooks at Grand Falls. The trail ends at the base of the falls atop a cliff. To complete the hike, retrace your steps to the trailhead.

16.2 Arrive back at the trailhead.

61 South Branch Falls

An easy hike leads to the falls, less a waterfall than a quarter-mile race. The water churns through and around rifts in the slate bedrock. The trail crosses the rock, with fine views and a few swimming opportunities.

Start: South Branch Falls Trailhead at back of parking area
Elevation gain: 216 feet
Distance: 1.0 mile out and back
Hiking time: About 1 hour
Difficulty: Easy
Season: May to October
Trail surface: Woodland path
Land status: Baxter State Park
Nearest town: Patten

Other users: None
Water availability: None
Canine compatibility: Dogs are not allowed in Baxter State Park.
Fees and permits: None for Maine residents; auto entrance fee for nonresidents
Other maps: *DeLorme: Maine Atlas & Gazetteer*, map 51; USGS Wassataquoik Lake
Trail contact: Baxter State Park, (207) 723-5140, https://baxterstatepark.org

Finding the trailhead: From exit 624 off I-95, turn west following the signs to Baxter State Park. Drive 0.3 mile. Bear right onto ME 11 north. Drive 9.8 miles into Patten. Turn left onto ME 159 at the sign for Baxter State Park. Drive 26.4 miles to the Matagamon Gate in Baxter State Park. From the Matagamon Gate, drive 7 miles on Park Tote Road. Turn left onto South Branch Road. Drive 1.3 miles. The trailhead parking is on the left. The trailhead is at the back of the parking area. GPS: N46 07.211' / W68 54.367'

The Hike

South Branch Falls is less a waterfall than a quarter-mile race. The stream churns along the edge of a huge hump of bedrock. It slides through narrow V-shaped joints in the slate, drops into deep swirling pools, and crosses ledges, erratically following the route of least resistance.

The hike to the falls is short and flat. Just before the falls, there's a steep descent to the bedrock hump. The trail crosses the bedrock from where the water pools up before racing through the falls to where it relaxes into a wide, calm pool where strings of bubbles eddy into the distance.

The pool below the falls and the larger pools within the falls offer hot hikers a cool summer respite. After a bracing swim, you can dry and warm yourself on the rough, bare rock. It's understandable that you might be tempted to jump into the water from one of the cliffs. Don't be—most of the race is too narrow and swift for safe swimming.

While you're relaxing on the rocks, be sure to take in the surrounding forest. In spring the hardwoods are various fresh greens, tinted with red or yellow. In fall the

A hiker looking at the pool below South Branch Falls

Cliff at the head of South Branch Falls

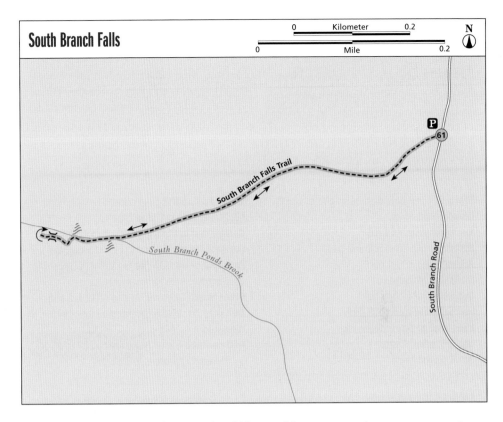

South Branch Falls

woods explode with color. Varied wildflowers bloom across the seasons, attracting pollinators and songbirds. And always, the water rushes noisily through the falls.

Miles and Directions

0.0   Start from the trailhead at the back of the parking area.

0.4   The trail descends to a large dome of rock. Follow the blazes over the rock, stopping to explore the stream below.

0.5   The trail descends off the bedrock dome and ends on a finger of rock that juts out into South Branch Ponds Brook below the falls. To complete the hike, return the way you came.

1.0   Arrive back at the trailhead.

62 Howe Brook Falls

The Howe Brook Trail follows Howe Brook from near where it flows into Lower South Branch Pond upstream past lower falls and on to upper falls. The lower falls is a long series of drops, pools, and sluices over and around exposed bedrock. The falls offers several large swimming holes and sunny flat rocks to dry out on. The upper falls is a single drop off a cliff that arcs across the valley. The section of the brook just below the upper falls is much like the lower falls, except even more vertical.

Start: Day-use parking area at end of South Branch Pond Road
Elevation gain: 964 feet
Distance: 6.2 miles out and back
Hiking time: 3 to 4 hours
Difficulty: Moderate
Season: June to October
Trail surface: Woodland path
Land status: Baxter State Park
Nearest town: Patten
Other users: None

Water availability: Lower South Branch Pond near trailhead and Howe Brook
Canine compatibility: Dogs are not allowed in Baxter State Park.
Fees and permits: None for Maine residents; auto entrance fee for nonresidents
Other maps: *DeLorme: Maine Atlas & Gazetteer*, map 51; USGS Traveler Mountain and Wassatoquoik Lake
Trail contact: Baxter State Park, (207) 723-5140, https://baxterstatepark.org

Finding the trailhead: From exit 624 off I-95, turn west following the signs to Baxter State Park. Drive 0.3 mile. Bear right onto ME 11 north. Drive 9.8 miles into Patten. Turn left onto ME 159 at the sign for Baxter State Park. Drive 26.4 miles to the Matagamon Gate in Baxter State Park. Drive 7 miles on Park Tote Road. Turn left onto South Branch Pond Road at the sign for South Branch Pond. Drive 1.9 miles to the end of the road where the day-use parking is. Begin the hike by walking into the campground past the ranger station. GPS: N46 06.518' / W68 54.050'

The Hike

The landscape of Baxter State Park is one shaped by water. Most famously, the glaciers of the last ice age scraped the mountains down to bedrock and left the nearly vertical-sided bowls of the basins of Katahdin. But, in fact, as the earth warmed and the ice retreated, water continued shaping the land. You can see this being played out along the hike to Howe Brook Falls.

The first you see of Howe Brook, near where it flows into Lower South Branch Pond, is a wide bed of football-sized rocks, all worn round over time as the flowing water jostled them against one another. Most of the summer, the stream almost disappears beneath the rocks, making for easy, dry crossing. In the spring, overflowing with snowmelt, Howe Brook rages between its banks. Even after a hard summer rain, the water rises over the rocks, making a crossing a cold, wet prospect. The sound of the

Hiker braving the very cold water at Upper Howe Brook Falls

stream rushing over the rocks fills the whole valley between the Traveler and South Branch Mountain.

The lower falls is not one waterfall but several hundred yards of drops, pools, and sluices. The water backs up behind exposed masses of bedrock and either slides in thin sheets over the rock or finds a weakness in the rock and creates a crack that the water widens year by year. The pools collect rounded rocks visible through the crystal-clear water. In places the stream has undercut overhanging rock faces, creating shaded pools overhung by cedars. Mostly the lower falls is a sunny place with expanses of bare bedrock, which is kept smooth and clear by annual scourings of spring runoff. During the summer they make for a great place to sit and sun after a dip in one of the cool pools.

The trail beyond the lower falls is washed out in several places, forcing you to either step from stone to stone in the streambed or struggle on the steep slopes above Howe Brook on the rerouted trail. These washouts occur on the outside of bends in the stream, where the water beats on the stream bank, trying to go straight rather than bend with the streambed. Over time the stream gets wider and rockier. The hardwood trees of the surrounding forest hold the bank in place with their roots. Roots and rocks stick out of the undercut banks, as the smaller, lighter soil and rocks fall away.

Lower Howe Brook Falls

The upper falls is a single drop off a 20-foot cliff that arcs from bank to bank. You can see the bedding in the rock and its uneven weathering—very different from the smooth, hard rock at the lower falls. Just downstream from the upper falls the bedrock is more like that around the lower falls. If you explore downstream, you'll see where the stream flows through a series of cracks in the bedrock. Some are very narrow still; others have widened to where you would not call them cracks any longer.

High above Howe Brook, unseen through the hardwood forest, rise the several peaks of the Traveler. The mountain makes a half circle around Howe Brook's valley. The bare summits of the mountain are rhyolite in various stages of weathering.

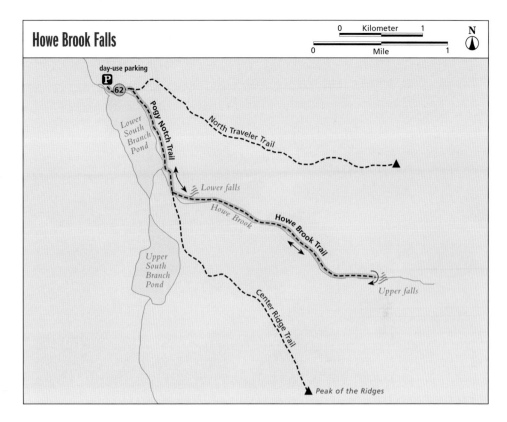

0   Kilometer   1

0   Mile   1

N

day-use parking

Lower South Branch Pond

Pogy Notch Trail

North Traveler Trail

Lower falls

Howe Brook

Howe Brook Trail

Upper South Branch Pond

Upper falls

Center Ridge Trail

Peak of the Ridges

The hard, volcanic rhyolite originated in the same volcanic activity as the smooth bedrock of the lower falls. Glaciers scoured out the valley Howe Brook flows down to Lower South Branch Pond, and now the stream continues to eat into the bedrock. Year by year this alters the course of the stream, carrying more and more of the mountain down to the pond. In our lifetimes, these changes are small and seen only in the rearranging of rock in the streambed and the undercutting of the stream's banks.

Miles and Directions

0.0 Start by walking past the ranger station and through the campground.

0.2 Turn right onto the Pogy Notch Trail. Remember to sign in at the trailhead.

0.3 Pass the North Traveler Mountain Trail.

0.9 The trail circles around Lower South Branch Pond to a small beach where canoeists leave their boats to continue on foot.

1.0 Turn right onto the Howe Brook Trail.

1.2 The trail follows the stream to the beginning of the lower falls. The lower falls is a series of drops, pools, and sluices that continue for more than 0.1 mile.

Two hikers contemplating the churning water within Lower Howe Brook Falls

3.1 The trail follows Howe Brook, turning away from the stream to make the last climb to the upper falls, where the trail ends. Be sure to explore Howe Brook downstream from the falls, where it drops through a series of sluices. To complete the hike, return the way you came to the trailhead.

6.2 Arrive back at the trailhead.

63 Grand Pitch Webster Stream

Grand Pitch is a long way from anywhere. The waterfall is one of the highest Grand Pitches in Maine and is powerful. The stream above and below the falls is scenic and worth exploring. On the hike to the falls, you pass through some of Maine's richest logging history.

Start: Freezeout Trailhead at back of Trout Brook Farm campground
Elevation gain: 671 feet
Distance: 12.8 miles out and back
Hiking time: About 8 hours
Difficulty: Strenuous. The hiking is easy, but it's very long.
Season: Late May to October
Trail surface: Woodland path
Land status: Baxter State Park
Nearest town: Patten
Other users: None

Water availability: Trout Brook near trailhead and Webster Stream
Canine compatibility: Dogs are not allowed in Baxter State Park.
Fees and permits: None for Maine residents; auto entrance fee for nonresidents
Other maps: *DeLorme: Maine Atlas & Gazetteer*, maps 50 and 56; USGS Trout Brook Mountain and Frost Pond
Trail contact: Baxter State Park, (207) 723-5140, https://baxterstatepark.org

Finding the trailhead: From exit 624 off I-95, turn west following the signs to Baxter State Park. Drive 0.3 mile. Bear right onto ME 11 north. Drive 9.8 miles into Patten. Turn left onto ME 159 at the sign for Baxter State Park. Drive 26.4 miles to the Matagamon Gate in Baxter State Park. Drive 1.6 miles on Park Tote Road. Turn right into Trout Brook Farm. Drive 0.3 mile through the campground to the end of the road. The trailhead is at the north end of the parking area. GPS: N46 10.034' / W68 51.106'

The Hike

The hike begins with a crossing of Trout Brook on a high wooden bridge. Downstream the brook disappears into a large marshy area before draining into Grand Lake Matagamon. Notice on the south shore the slate that angles down into the water. You'll see this later at the confluence of Webster Stream and Little East Branch Penobscot River and again around Grand Pitch. People think granite when they think Baxter State Park, but the park's geology is more complex. Here in the far north of the park, the bedrock is slate, just as it is farther south in the Central Highlands.

You hike past the walk-in campsites, then enter real wilderness. It wasn't always. Trout Brook Farm was a booming town built around a sawmill. This area wasn't added to Baxter State Park until 1960. The Freezeout Trail was a road then.

The trail wanders northwest, alternating between open wet areas and hardwood forest, offering good opportunities for wildflowers and wildlife viewing. As you near Grand Lake Matagamon, the trail climbs a small hill, crossing over an open ledge. The

Grand Pitch

trail descends and crosses a beaver-flooded valley. Across another small hill, a side trail leads 100 feet to the shore of Grand Lake Matagamon across a giant sawdust pile. A hundred years ago, this was the site of a sawmill.

For the next 2.5 miles, the trail mostly stays within sight of the lake, but rarely comes close to it. One exception is where you hike through the Northwest Cove campsite.

The trail makes a sharp left where a side trail leads straight ahead to the Little East Branch Lean-to. This is worth exploring. The lean-to is near the confluence of Webster Stream and the East Branch Penobscot River. The two then flow together around some islands and into the lake.

The Freezeout Trail follows Webster Stream upstream. There are a couple of very short side trails to interesting features on the river. Bear right on the Grand Pitch Trail at the small, inconspicuous sign. The trail passes Grand Pitch then turns away from the stream and ends at the Freezeout Trail.

Grand Pitch earned its name. The stream drops 30 feet in a double plunge (it's a single plunge near the far bank). Even in summer, the water roars over the falls, shaking the ground beneath your feet.

The Freezeout Trail continues upstream all the way to Webster Lake. Above Grand Pitch, there's a smaller waterfall in 0.1 mile. Past that the trail leaves the stream and crosses an area of huge black slabs of slate. It comes back to the stream at a black sand

The sawdust pile on the shore of Grand Lake Matagamon

Along Webster Stream below Grand Pitch

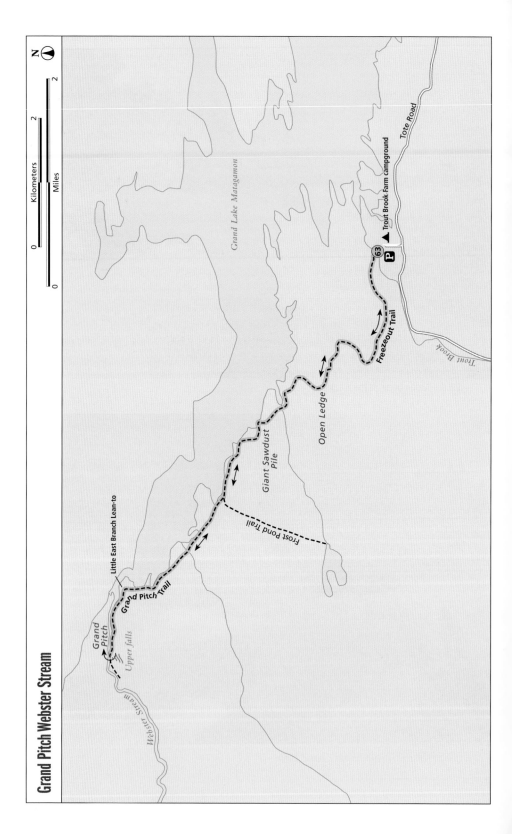

Grand Pitch Webster Stream

N

Kilometers
0   2   2

Miles
0   2

Grand Pitch

Upper falls

Webster Stream

Little East Branch Lean-to

Grand Pitch Trail

Frost Pond Trail

Giant Sawdust Pile

Open Ledge

Freezeout Trail

Grand Lake Matagamon

63
P
Trout Brook Farm campground

Tote Road

Trout Brook

beach in an eddy above another small waterfall. The beach is a little less than a mile from Grand Pitch.

This hike is too long to do in one day and have time to explore Webster Stream. Consider making it an overnight trip staying at the Little East Branch Lean-to.

Miles and Directions

0.0 Start from the Freezeout Trailhead. Cross Trout Brook and hike past walk-in campsites.

2.3 After crossing several marshy areas, the trail climbs gently to an open ledge.

3.2 Descend from the hill. A short side trail leads out to Grand Lake Matagamon across a giant pile of sawdust.

4.1 Pass the Frost Pond Trail.

5.6 Turn left, staying on the Freezeout Trail. Straight ahead is the Little East Branch Lean-to.

6.1 Follow Webster Stream upstream. Bear right at a small sign for Grand Pitch.

6.3 Reach the base of Grand Pitch. To continue the hike, follow the Grand Pitch Trail west.

6.5 Arrive back at the Freezeout Trail. Turn left and follow the trail all the way back to the trailhead. *Option:* You can turn right on the Freezeout Trail and hike 0.1 mile to a smaller waterfall on Webster Stream. Beyond that waterfall, the Freezeout Trail passes through an area of huge slate slabs, eventually reaching a black sand beach above another small waterfall. This adds about 1.5 miles to your hike.

12.8 Arrive back at the trailhead.

64 Sawtelle Falls

An easy walk through the woods, past one of the largest white pines you'll ever see, leads to the top of Sawtelle Falls. The stream plunges 20 feet down a seam in the bedrock, then makes a sharp left and flows beneath a 40-foot cliff.

Start: Sawtelle Trailhead, 100 feet north of bridge over Sawtelle Brook
Elevation gain: 51 feet
Distance: 1.0 mile out and back
Hiking time: About 1 hour
Difficulty: Easy
Season: Late May to October
Trail surface: Woodland path
Land status: Private timberland

Nearest town: Patten
Other users: Hunters in season
Water availability: None
Canine compatibility: Dogs must be under control at all times.
Fees and permits: None
Other maps: *DeLorme: Maine Atlas & Gazetteer,* map 51; USGS Hay Lake
Trail contact: None

Finding the trailhead: From exit 264 off I-95, turn west. Drive 0.3 mile. Bear right onto ME 11. Drive 9.8 miles into Patten. Turn left onto ME 159 at the sign for Baxter State Park. Drive 15.9 miles. Cross the Seboeis River. Drive 0.7 mile. Turn right onto Scraggly Lake Road (there's a street sign). Drive 1.5 miles. Cross Sawtelle Brook on the troll bridge. After crossing the bridge, park on the shoulder on the right. The unmarked but obvious trailhead is 100 feet past the bridge. GPS: N46 09.383' / W68 39.488'

The Hike

On the easy walk to Sawtelle Falls, you pass a huge white pine. The basal circumference is at least 18 feet. It towers over the trees around it, somehow missed by generations of loggers—kinda like Sawtelle Falls. This one is a gem that no one knows about.

Sawtelle Brook flows out of a swampy deadwater that keeps water levels high through the summer. The stream rushes under the troll bridge (local camp owners have decorated and signed the bridge) near the trailhead and through the spruce. It reaches a narrow gorge of black slate, worms into a crack in the rock, and leaps almost 20 feet down into a deep pool. Sawtelle Brook then takes a hard left and rushes through the gorge and on toward the Seboeis River.

It's an underrated waterfall. The only challenge is finding a spot to get a good photo of it. The trail reaches the top of the falls, with a good view down at it (a pretty unphotogenic perspective). Rough trails wander across the top of the gorge. There's a fairly easy climb down into the gorge, but not a clean look at the whole waterfall. The trail's on the wrong side of the gorge.

Rather than worry about the photo, carefully observe the colors: Inky black slate beds turned nearly on end. Root beer water loaded with tannin churned into a foam.

Sawtelle Falls

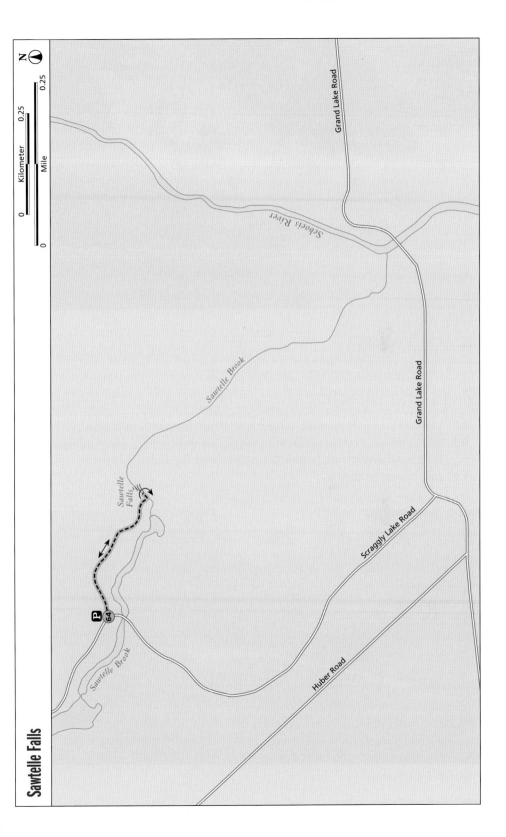

Sawtelle Brook

Sawtelle Falls

Sawtelle Brook

64

Seboeis River

Grand Lake Road

Grand Lake Road

Scraggly Lake Road

Huber Road

N

0   0.25   Kilometer   0.25
0   Mile

Sawtelle Falls

Dark green spruce and pale green aspens crowding the stream. Rusty needles cushioning the trail.

Miles and Directions

0.0 Start from the Sawtelle Trailhead, 100 feet north of the bridge over Sawtelle Brook.

0.5 The trail follows an old logging road to a small meadow, then continues through the woods to the top of Sawtelle Falls. To complete the hike, retrace your steps to the trailhead.

1.0 Arrive back at the trailhead.

The gorge below Sawtelle Falls

65 Shin Falls

The hike to the falls is short and easy. The descent to the base of the falls can be challenging, but the view is worth the work. Shin Brook drops 40 feet down a nearly vertical face of slate. The pool below the falls is a fine swimming hole.

Start: Trailhead west of parking area where road turns right
Elevation gain: 184 feet
Distance: 0.9 mile out and back
Hiking time: About 1 hour
Difficulty: Easy
Season: June to October
Trail surface: Woodland path
Land status: Private woodlands

Nearest town: Shin Pond Village
Other users: Hunters in season
Water availability: Shin Brook below falls
Canine compatibility: Dogs must be under control at all times.
Fees and permits: None
Other maps: *DeLorme: Maine Atlas & Gazetteer*, map 51; USGS Hay Brook Mountain
Trail contact: None

Finding the trailhead: From I-95 exit 264, drive north on ME 158 10 miles to Patten. Turn left on ME 159 (Shin Pond Road) at the sign for the north entrance to Baxter State Park. Drive 14.7 miles west, passing Shin Pond. (At Shin Pond the state route ends and the road name changes to Grand Lake Road, although there are no signs.) Turn left onto a gravel logging road; there is a small wooden sign on a tree pointing to Shin Brook Falls. The turn is 0.9 mile east of where Grand Lake Road crosses the Seboeis River. Drive 0.3 mile south on the logging road. Park on the left where the road makes a sharp right turn. The trailhead is just west of the parking area on the south side of the road. There is a sign on a tree next to the trail. GPS: N46 08.532' / W68 36.956'

The Hike

Sometimes in Maine you can find the most extraordinary things where you least expect. Shin Falls is like that. Shin Brook is a short stream that runs from Shin Pond around Sugarloaf Mountain to the Seboeis River, a total distance of 5 miles. The falls is about halfway between Shin Pond and the Seboeis River. The stream bends around some slate bedrock, dropping twice over ledges that block the stream. Each drop is about 8 feet. The stream then plunges 40 feet over a cleft in the slate. Huge, broken boulders lie in the falls and at its base. Mist hangs in the air above the pool beneath the falls and along the rock face next to the drop. It is one of Maine's most scenic waterfalls.

The hike is relatively flat, through a mixed forest that has some wet spots—a good hike for a variety of spring wildflowers. The trail to the bottom of the falls is more like a scramble down a slide than a hike. But the view from the base of the falls is worth the effort. The pool at the bottom of the falls is ideal for swimming on a warm day. Because the stream flows roughly west at the falls, the falls and the pool tend to be

Shin Falls

in full sun during the summer. The dark slate rock warms up in the sun. After a swim in the cool stream, the warmth of the rocks is especially welcome. All this light and contrast also makes for great photographs.

The main trail leads out to the rocks at the top of the falls. You can stand on the edge of the stream right where it plunges off the drop. The trail loops upstream past the two smaller drops. The stream appears dark and calm in the pool below the falls, then it wiggles out and winds away toward the Seboeis River. A few miles downstream, Shin Brook empties into the Seboeis River just below that river's Grand Pitch (hike 66).

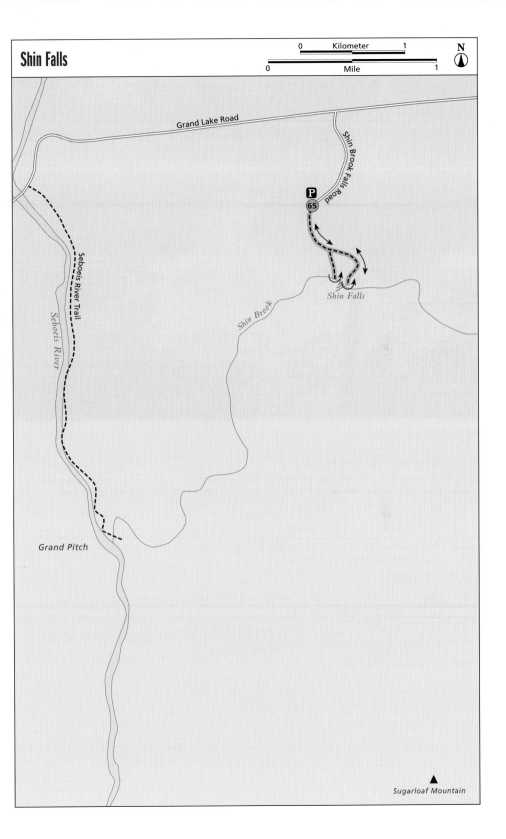

Shin Falls

Grand Lake Road

Shin Brook Falls Road

P
65

Shin Falls

Shin Brook

Seboeis River Trail

Seboeis River

Grand Pitch

Sugarloaf Mountain

0   Kilometer   1

0   Mile   1

N

Looking down Shin Falls

Miles and Directions

0.0 Start from the trailhead west of the parking area. There is sign on a tree next to the trail.

0.1 The trail comes to a fork. Turn left.

0.2 Turn right onto a trail that is marked with faded red flagging.

0.3 The trail descends steeply down to Shin Brook at the pool below the falls. To continue the hike, climb back up to the main trail.

0.4 Turn right onto the main trail.

0.5 Turn right onto a side trail marked with blue flagging. The main trail becomes too wet to continue past the blue-flagged trail.

0.6 The trail comes to the top of the main falls and loops around upstream past the two upper falls. To compete the hike, return the way you came.

0.9 Arrive back at the trailhead.

66 Grand Pitch Seboeis River

Grand Pitch isn't a single waterfall but a tightly packed series of ledges. The river drops a total of 20 feet across 3-foot ledges. Beside the river a crumbling lump of rhyolite gives you a bird's-eye view of the falls. Below the falls where Shin Brook flows into the Seboeis River is a flat patio of bedrock shaded by evergreens.

Start: Seboeis River Trailhead
Elevation gain: 167 feet
Distance: 2.2 miles out and back
Hiking time: About 2 hours
Difficulty: Moderate due to rough trail
Season: May to October
Trail surface: Woodland path
Land status: Private land
Nearest town: Shin Pond Village

Other users: Hunters in season
Water availability: Seboeis River
Canine compatibility: Dogs must be under control at all times.
Fees and permits: None
Other maps: *DeLorme: Maine Atlas & Gazetteer,* map 51; USGS Bowlin Brook
Trail contact: None

Finding the trailhead: From I-95 exit 264, drive north on ME 158 10 miles to Patten. Turn left on ME 159 (Shin Pond Road) at the sign for the north entrance to Baxter State Park. Drive 15.6 miles west, passing Shin Pond. (At Shin Pond the state route ends and the road name changes to Grand Lake Road, although there are no signs.) Just before the road crosses the Seboeis River, turn right into the parking area. There's a large wooden sign at the trailhead on the south side of the road. GPS: N46 08.601' / W68 37.975'

The Hike

From the parking area, you can see the confluence of Sawtelle Brook and the Seboeis River. Less than a mile upstream on the brook is Sawtelle Falls (hike 64). Upstream on the river is a narrow, mile-long gorge of nearly continuous whitewater. There are no trails to the gorge, and it's not recommended for canoes. Evidently, the gorge is so narrow and steep that there's no place to portage around the steep sections.

Below the parking area, the Seboeis River calmly winds through wild country to the East Branch Penobscot River. In 20 miles, there's only one portage—unlike the East Branch, which has four. It's a great place to begin your backcountry canoeing career.

That one portage is around Grand Pitch. It's an easy mile hike along the riffled river to the falls. The trail mostly follows the route of an abandoned woods road through low, swampy ground punctuated by ledges.

Grand Pitch is a tightly packed series of irregular ledges between domes of rhyolite. The river drops about 20 feet in this short stretch. You can easily climb the dome of rock and get a nice bird's-eye view of Grand Pitch.

Grand Pitch

Grand Pitch

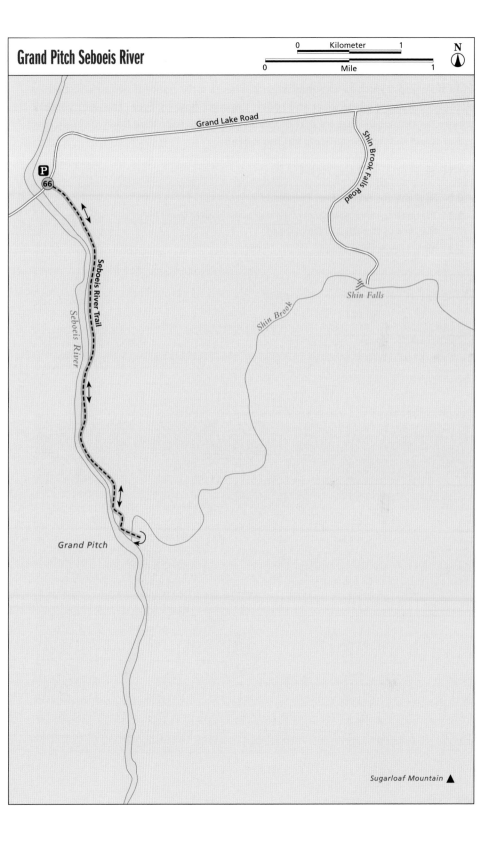

Grand Pitch Seboeis River

Grand Lake Road

Shin Brook Falls Road

Shin Falls

Shin Brook

Seboeis River Trail

Seboeis River

P
66

Grand Pitch

Sugarloaf Mountain ▲

0 Kilometer 1

0 Mile 1

N

The trail drops down from the dome to the confluence of the Seboeis River and Shin Brook. Shin Falls (hike 65) is about a mile up the brook, but there's no trail from here and it's not an easy bushwhack. There's a flat patio of bedrock shaded by evergreens—a nice place to sit and watch the river flow by. From this spot you can see the last of the falls that are part of Grand Pitch. The river then flows around a low gravel island before disappearing around a bend.

Miles and Directions

0.0 Start from the Seboeis River Trailhead.

1.1 The trail follows the east shore of the river to the base of Grand Pitch. To complete the hike, retrace your steps to the trailhead.

2.2 Arrive back at the trailhead.

67 East Branch Penobscot River

This hike along the East Branch visits four waterfalls. All are unique. Stair Falls is a series of steps the river descends. Haskell Rock Pitch is geologically unusual and offers fine views of nearby mountains. Pond Pitch is a fine 10-foot drop. Grand Pitch is an unusual 30-foot horseshoe waterfall. The hike offers good opportunities to see wildlife.

Start: Grand Pitch Trailhead on International Appalachian Trail
Elevation gain: 865 feet
Distance: 9.0 miles out and back
Hiking time: 5 to 6 hours
Difficulty: Strenuous due to distance
Season: Late May to October
Trail surface: Woods road converted to hiking trail
Land status: Katahdin Woods and Waters National Monument
Nearest town: Shin Pond Village (nearest gas is in Patten)

Other users: None
Water availability: East Branch
Canine compatibility: Dogs must be under control at all times.
Fees and permits: None
Other maps: *DeLorme: Maine Atlas & Gazetteer*, map 51; USGS The Traveler and Bowlin Brook
Trail contact: Katahdin Woods and Waters National Monument, (207) 456-6001, www .nps.gov/kaww

Finding the trailhead: From exit 264 on I-95, follow ME 158 west toward ME 11. Drive 0.5 mile. Bear right onto ME 11. Drive 9.6 miles into Patten. Turn left onto ME 159 west at the sign for Baxter State Park. Drive 24.6 miles. Cross the East Branch Penobscot River. Drive 0.2 mile. Turn left onto Messer Pond Road at the sign for Katahdin Woods and Waters National Monument. Drive 0.6 mile. Enter the monument. Continue driving 3.6 miles, passing Old River Road and Oxbow Road. Park on the right at the sign for hiking parking. The trail is the gravel road on the left next to the trailhead sign. GPS: N46 04.799' / W68 47.696'

The Hike

In Maine, when people refer to the East Branch or West Branch, it's known that they're talking about the Penobscot River. The East Branch rises in a chain of small ponds northeast of Chamberlain Lake in the Allagash country. It flows into Grand Lake Matagamon with Webster Stream. Grand Lake Matagamon is naturally two lakes connected by a thoroughfare, but the dam raised the lake level and created one very large lake. The East Branch that most people know begins at the dam. It flows from there south to the confluence with the West Branch in Medway (visible from the bridge on I-95).

The East Branch isn't Maine's longest river, but it is one of the wildest. The dam at Grand Lake Matagamon is the only one on the river, which has eight major falls or pitches. It's one of the premier paddling experiences in the United States. Much of the river's course is now in Katahdin Woods and Waters National Monument. The International Appalachian Trail (IAT) hugs the west bank from Wassataquoik Stream to Matagamon. This gives hikers access to several of the falls on the river.

In northern Maine, a "falls" is a rapid in the stream that is runable by canoe. A "pitch" is a waterfall that must be portaged around. Most rivers in northern Maine have a "grand pitch." Generally, this is a waterfall worth hiking to. These terms date back to the days when there were no roads in the Maine woods and loggers got around by boat and floated their logs downstream to mills.

The hike mostly follows the IAT, which uses abandoned logging roads. This makes for easy walking and good wildlife viewing. In several places you have views of the mountains to the west in Baxter State Park. You follow an old road from the trailhead toward the East Branch. A side trail leads a half mile to Stair Falls. Here the East Branch rushes over a series of five ledges that cross the river. Each ledge is only a few feet high. Upstream from Stair Falls the river meanders through low, swampy country. Below, the river is more direct and rocky.

Stair Falls

Pond Pitch

The next waterfall downstream is Haskell Rock Pitch. The river backs up behind the natural dam of the ledges that cross the river, creating a lakelike deadwater. Most waterfalls along the East Branch have a deadwater above them. You can see the deadwater from either Haskell Hut or the Haskell Pitch campsite.

Haskell Rock is a large, roundish boulder on a pedestal in the middle of the river. Upstream, a small waterfall lets the river rush out of Haskell Deadwater. Downstream, the river crashes through a narrow canyon. Haskell Rock is named for a nineteenth-century logging baron. The rock is composed of conglomerate (as is the exposed bedrock along the shore). It looks like someone roughly cemented stones and gravel together. You can use the carry trail to explore the area around Haskell Rock Pitch.

Another mile downstream, you reach Pond Pitch. Again, use the carry trail to visit the top and base of the waterfall. The East Branch drops 10 feet over an irregular ledge that spans the river. This waterfall is named for Little Messer Pond, which is about a half mile west of the river. There's a trail from the IAT that leads to it.

A half mile farther downstream, you leave the IAT and follow the Grand Pitch Carry Trail along the river. As the name suggests, Grand Pitch is the largest waterfall on the East Branch. It's a 30-foot horseshoe drop. An unmarked side trail leads out to the top of the waterfall. Getting a head-on view of the waterfall is more challenging. The carry trail follows atop the gorge downstream to a gravel beach. The beach is around a bend from Grand Pitch and the woods atop the gorge are so dense that you barely get a look at the waterfall. To really see it, you have to bushwhack to the edge of the gorge and find a place where you can descend the 30 feet to the river. It's a bit of work, but well worth it. Grand Pitch thunders between irregularly rising rock walls.

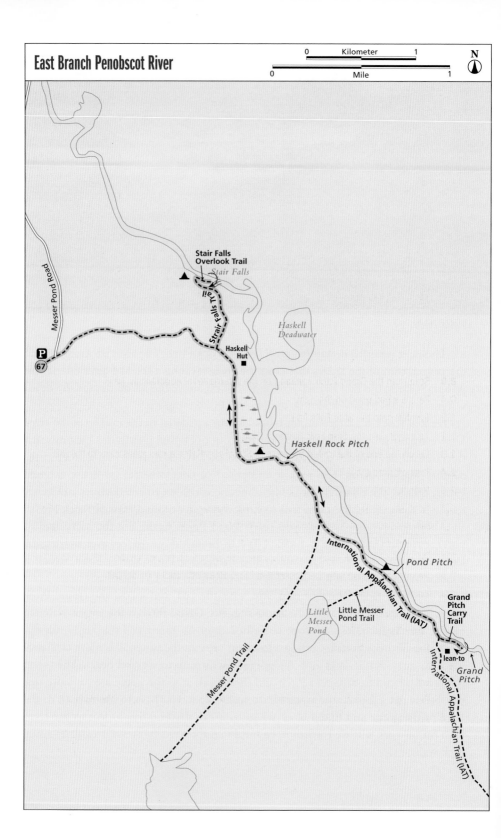

East Branch Penobscot River

0   Kilometer   1
0   Mile   1

N

Messer Pond Road

**Stair Falls
Overlook Trail**

Stair Falls

Stair Falls Trail

*Haskell
Deadwater*

**Haskell
Hut**

P
67

Haskell Rock Pitch

Pond Pitch

International Appalachian Trail (IAT)

**Grand
Pitch
Carry
Trail**

*Little
Messer
Pond*

**Little Messer
Pond Trail**

lean-to

*Grand
Pitch*

International Appalachian Trail (IAT)

Messer Pond Trail

Grand Pitch

Miles and Directions

0.0 Start from the Grand Pitch Trailhead on the International Appalachian Trail.

0.4 Pass a small pond on the right.

1.2 Turn left onto the Stair Falls Trail.

1.7 Turn right onto the Stair Falls Overlook Trail.

1.8 Reach the end of the trail at the base of Stair Falls. Retrace your steps back to the IAT.

2.4 Turn left onto the IAT.

2.6 Pass the trail to Haskell Hut.

3.2 Pass the trail to Haskell Rock Pitch campsite. *Option:* You can turn left on the campsite trail and follow it 350 feet past the campsite to Haskell Deadwater. Then follow the carry trail 0.2 mile along the river to Haskell Rock Pitch and rejoin the IAT.

3.4 Reach Haskell Rock Pitch. To continue the hike, bear right, staying on the IAT.

3.8 Reach the junction with the Messer Pond Trail. Bear left, staying on the IAT.

4.3 Bear left onto the Pond Pitch Carry Trail.

4.4 Reach the end of the trail at the base of Pond Pitch. Retrace your steps back to the IAT.

4.5 Turn left onto the IAT.

4.9 Bear left onto the Grand Pitch Carry Trail.

5.1 Turn left onto an unmarked but obvious trail and walk 100 feet to Grand Pitch. Retrace your steps back to the IAT.

5.3 Bear right back onto the IAT. To complete the hike, follow the IAT back to the trailhead.

9.0 Arrive back at the trailhead.

About the Author

Greg Westrich has lived in Maine since 1996. He's working diligently on red-lining the state. Before settling in Maine, he spent his adult life wandering around the country having adventures and looking for a home. Greg has visited every state but Hawaii and almost every Canadian province. Don't ask him about hiking unless you have a couple of hours to spare.

Angel Falls

Hiking Waterfalls Maine is Greg's fourth full-color guide published by Falcon, the others being *Hiking Maine, Hiking Maine's Baxter State Park*, and *Hiking New Hampshire*. Falcon has also published three of his pocket hiking guides, *Best Easy Day Hikes Camden, Best Easy Day Hikes Greenville*, and *Best Easy Day Hikes Portland, Maine*. He's also the author of numerous articles and stories.

Greg's day job is teaching writing and literature at Husson University in Bangor and at Eastern Maine Community College. He lives in the woods north of Bangor with his wife, Ann, and their two children who love basketball more than hiking. He's okay with that. The family has two cats, a dog, an aquarium, ten chickens, and a lot of deer that eat the hostas and Ann's vegetable garden.

Greg created and runs the Maine's Wicked Wild 25 hiking list and Facebook page. He wants everyone to find their wicked wild hiking self.

You can follow Greg's adventures on Facebook or his website, gregwestrich.com. There are videos of many of the hikes in this guide on his Facebook page.